The Urban Dialogue

An analysis of the use of space in the Roman city of Empúries, Spain

Alan Kaiser

BAR International Series 901
2000

Published in 2016 by
BAR Publishing, Oxford

BAR International Series 901

The Urban Dialogue

ISBN 978 1 84171 097 6

BAR Publishing is the trading name of British Archaeological Reports (Oxford) Ltd.
British Archaeological Reports was first incorporated in 1974 to publish the BAR
Series, International and British. In 1992 Hadrian Books Ltd became part of the BAR
group. This volume was originally published by Archaeopress in conjunction with
British Archaeological Reports (Oxford) Ltd / Hadrian Books Ltd, the Series principal
publisher, in 2000. This present volume is published by BAR Publishing, 2016.

Printed in England

BAR
PUBLISHING

BAR titles are available from:

BAR Publishing
122 Banbury Rd, Oxford, OX2 7BP, UK
EMAIL   info@barpublishing.com
PHONE   +44 (0)1865 310431
FAX   +44 (0)1865 316916
www.barpublishing.com

Table of Contents

List of Tables

List of Figures

FOREWORD

This project represents a modified version of my doctoral dissertation completed in 1999. Since then, additional data have been collected and added to the text.

I have many people to thank for their assistance and support. Murray McClellan, James Wiseman, and Ricardo Elia all patiently read early versions of this work and offered invaluable comments and suggestions. Kenneth Kvamme also helped with the statistical analyses described in this work and generously shared the results of his magnetometry prospection at Empúries with me. Nonetheless, all errors in the work must be seen as mine alone. I also owe Boston University a debt of thanks for providing me with funding to work at Empúries. The staff at the Conjunt Monumental de Empúries deserves a hardy thanks for their support and good humor during my visits there. In particular I am indebted to former site director Jordi Pardo i Rodríguez, who first invited me to the site, and subsequent directors M. Aurora Martín i Ortega and Xavier Aquilué i Abadías, who allowed me to stay. Finally, I would like to thank Christine Lovasz for her unwavering support.

INTRODUCTION

Were there ever so many cities, inland and maritime? Were they ever so thoroughly modernized? Could a person in the past travel thus, counting up cities by the number of days on the road, sometimes even going past two or three of them...?

...You may contrast the tribe of the past with the city there today. Indeed, it may be said that they were virtually kings of wilderness and fortresses, while you alone govern cities.

Aelius Aristides, *To Rome* 93 (trans. Lewis and Reinhold 1955, 137)

Ancient Roman culture was a city-based culture. Wherever they went, the Romans utilized existing cities and towns or founded new ones to act as the basic administrative and cultural building blocks of their empire (Garnsey and Saller 1987, 26). Archaeologists and antiquarians have long recognized the importance of the city to the Romans and so have often based their investigations in Roman urban centers. These cities and towns provided the architecture and works of art that scholars eagerly sought. Two of the earliest archaeological sites to be discovered and excavated, sites which helped to shape the discipline of archaeology itself since the mid-18th century, were the Roman towns of Pompeii and Herculaneum. Historians have also recognized the importance of Roman cities because of their prominence in ancient texts. From a very early date, historians have mined these texts in order to gain a picture of daily city life (Laurence 1997).

It comes as a surprise, then, that after more than two hundred years of study our understanding of Roman urbanism is so limited. There are few archaeological and historical subjects that we can so fully describe without being explained (Mattingly 1997, 210-218). The excellent preservation of Roman urban sites in North Africa and Campania, combined with the fact that most of the ancient authors lived in cities has allowed archaeologists, art historians, and historians to thoroughly investigate the details of urban life. Archaeologists and art historians have described types of statuary, wall-painting styles, and public monuments, placing this material in chronological order, thus making it possible to trace stylistic changes and influences. Historians delight in relating the features of urban life, emphasizing the details that were important to ancient writers, including visits to baths, descriptions of public monuments, or the daily routine of a client.

Yet, until recently, few scholars have attempted to understand the Roman city as a social phenomenon. Those who have gone beyond mere description have focused on specific details about the city. For instance, some scholars have discussed the role of the Roman city in the structure of the ancient economy (see Section 2.2), while others have searched for the origins of the orthogonal form common to many Roman cities (see Section 2.3). While such approaches may lead to explanations of specific aspects of the Roman city, they do not constitute theories

of Roman urbanism; instead they are theories of the origins of capitalism or the diffusion of Greek techniques of town planning. Few scholars have focused on the Roman city itself as a unit worthy of study (see Section 2.4).

The present study attempts to rectify this situation by examining the Spanish site of Empúries as a manifestation of a Roman city, not as an example of larger economic or historical issues. Through an intensive study of the arrangement of space in Empúries, I have tried to gain an understanding of the meaning of that city to its residents and visitors. Classifying all excavated buildings in the city according to their use, I have searched for commonalities in the location of buildings with similar functions throughout the city. After identifying these commonalities, I have related them to social norms with the intention of determining how specific groups located certain activities in the city.

Crucial to both the methodology and the interpretations offered here is a combination of the archaeological and textual evidence for Roman urban activity. This is, indeed, the great strength of classical archaeology. At their best, classical archaeologists pose questions and suggest interpretations that would not be possible if they had either the archaeological or the textual evidence alone. The present study draws on both written sources and the archaeological record to argue that the Romans purposely arranged urban space to reflect and reproduce their social system, a conclusion for which both sources of evidence were necessary.

In many ways the approach described in this work has been inspired by, and represents a challenge to, the work of one of the few scholars who focused directly on the Roman city itself, Richard Raper (1977 and 1979). Raper wanted to go beyond the details of daily life and seek the meaning of the use of space to the inhabitants of Pompeii. He did this by analyzing a map of the site in which all architectural spaces were divided into one of 12 categories of land use. Using methodologies developed by geographers, Raper looked for patterning in the location of specific uses of space. He came to the conclusion that some areas were reserved for certain public uses, notably the forum. He also found that shops were usually located along major thoroughfares. Other than this, however,

Raper concluded that there was no patterning or meaning in the use of space at Pompeii. He found houses of the wealthy beside those of the poor, while shops and workshops were liberally sprinkled about the city with no apparent rhyme or reason to their distribution. Raper's thesis that there is no patterning to the use of space in Roman cities has been widely accepted by scholars studying Pompeii and Roman urbanism in general to the point where the Raper thesis has recently been referred to as the "current paradigm" (Robinson 1997, 136).

While Raper's study was innovative and important, his conclusion is contra-intuitive. Few, if any societies, were more hierarchical than Roman society. Everyone had a place in the social order, a place that they often indicated by the use of a variety of forms of material culture including clothing, food and drink, inscriptions on public monuments, etc. It cannot be disputed that the Romans gave social meaning to the use of the space, at least on the small scale. According to custom and law, certain areas of seating in theaters and amphitheaters were reserved for groups according to their status. These customs and laws were continually subverted and challenged as people of lower status tried to sit in areas reserved for those with higher status (Juv. i.147; Mart. ii.29; id. v.8; id. v.14; id. v.23; id. v.27; id. vi.9; Suet. *Aug.* xiv; id *Iul.* xxxix.2). In a society where the location of one's seat in the theater or amphitheater was charged with social meaning, it is difficult to believe that the location of buildings and activities within a city could be devoid of meaning.

To challenge Raper's conclusion, I decided it was necessary to do a similar type of analysis at another Roman city. Turning away from the Roman towns of Pompeii and Herculaneum, the traditional basis for descriptions and models of Roman urbanism allowed me to gain a fresh perspective. One site that is admirably suited for a study of Roman urbanism is the Spanish archaeological site of Empúries (fig. 1). "Empúries" is the Catalan spelling for the name of the site, it is also known by the Castillian Spanish name of "Ampurias." Three successive directors of the archaeological site of Empúries, Jordi Pardo i Rodríguez, M. Aurora Martín i Ortega, and Xavier Aquilué i Abadías, all generously gave me unrestricted access to the site during the summers of 1995, 1996, and 1998. This allowed me to thoroughly study every wall, plaza, and street, comparing the physical remains to published plans and interpretations.

Located on the Spanish Mediterranean coast a little more than 100 km north of Barcelona and less than 50 km south of the French border, Empúries was the subject of nearly continuous archaeological excavations since 1908, when the Barcelona-based Junta de Museus acquired the property. Excavations have continued almost without interruption to the present. These excavations were of the highest quality when judged by the archaeological standards of their day and the excavation records provide much important and useful contextual information. As a result, the site provides a good source of data for the investigation of Roman urbanism.

Phocean Greek traders founded the original colony (Palaiapolis) in the sixth century B.C. on a small island in the Mediterranean. Within a generation the settlement spread to the mainland (Neapolis). The Greek city was an important base for Roman military activity during the Second Punic War and the Roman *castrum*, or military fort, built immediately to the west of the Greek settlement, quickly grew into a Roman city. By the beginning of the first century A.D., the Greeks and Romans combined their neighboring cities, destroying the walls that separated them. The joining of the two cities ushered in a brief period of prosperity. The decline of the city followed as residents began to abandon the site. Although some parts of the site continued in use without interruption until the present day, much of the site was abandoned after A.D. 100, never to be reoccupied. Given this cessation of activity, and the absence of a successor city built on top of the previous settlement, most of Empúries was preserved in its first-century form (Sanmartí and Nolla 1993, 7-11).

Over the last 90 years, archaeologists have excavated approximately five percent of the Palaiapolis, nearly one-hundred percent of the Republican and Imperial levels in Neapolis, and about ten percent of the Roman city, providing a remarkably large sample of excavated structures and material.

The purpose of the present study is to examine the use of space at Empúries in order to identify clues to the social system that created the final urban form of the first-century city. This study will demonstrate how one can interpret the arrangement of space within a city in order to determine what social norms were at work to produce the form of that city. The technique Raper used at Pompeii will be shown to be inappropriate for discerning patterns in the use of urban space. This study will suggest some alternative techniques that identify more subtle patterns of the use of space at Empúries. Key to undertaking this analysis has been the synthesis of enormous amounts of excavation data, a process greatly simplified by the use of one of the computer programs written for the express purpose of analyzing spatial data known under the general label of Geographic Information Systems, or GIS. GIS is a tool that has been under-utilized in ancient urban studies. Two pioneering studies in the use of GIS in urban studies, Robinson at Pompeii and Romano at Corinth, are still in the preliminary stages but have great potential (Robinson 1997; Romano 1999; 1996; Romano and Tolba 1995, 163-174; Romano and Schoenbrun 1993, 177-190). One other completed study, Smith's investigation of viewshed in ancient Athens using GIS, has not been followed up by other investigators (1995).

The particular program used in this study, Idrisi 2.0 for Windows, has a useful feature that allows one to link digitized maps to a database. I linked digitized plans of Empúries with a database I created from published accounts of excavations at the site. The database records the find spot of numerous artifacts excavated between 1848 and the mid-1990s. Using the digitized plans and the linked database I was able to test the interpretations of archaeologists for the type and period of use of specific buildings at Empúries and determine if the data agreed with their interpretations. As the published plans also contained some mistakes, I examined every excavated wall at the site, correcting mistakes in publications and recording additional unpublished data about specific rooms. In this way, I feel confident that the interpretations of function that I propose for every building at Empúries have a strong basis in the artifactual and architectural data.

GIS did not simply allow for more efficient organization of the data, however, it also allowed for advanced statistical analyses to be performed on the data. A simple operation, such as having the computer display structures with different uses in different colors, allowed for the exploration of the data and for the discovery of patterns. In addition, the sophisticated statistical tests available in Idrisi allowed for the testing of the strength of those patterns. These tests made it possible to go beyond simple visual impressions and to obtain a statistical confirmation for the patterns observed.

Once the patterns in the use of urban space were described, it was possible to identify the group of residents of the city that would have had an influence on where specific activities were located. By establishing who in the city would have been responsible for the placement of structures with specific uses, it became possible to speculate on what may have motivated their decisions. Textual evidence was integral to these interpretations.

This study should prove useful to archaeologists interested in issues of ancient urbanism both for the site it describes and for the techniques it utilizes. Empúries is a significant archaeological site that is not as well known outside of Spain as it deserves to be. Evidence from the site can offer much to debates on Greek colonization, ethnicity Roman cities, and ideology in monumental architecture. The present work is the most extensive to date in English describing the site.

More importantly, though, this study outlines non-destructive ways of gaining new information about archaeological sites. In these days when there is discussion about the appropriateness of any excavation, as excavation destroys non-renewable cultural resources, such studies are needed. It is important to develop techniques that allow us to gain information without excavating. There is an enormous potential for integrating old excavation data with standing architecture at sites to allow us to make new statements about sites excavated long ago. Much of this potential has originated with technical and methodological developments in the application of statistical and GIS techniques to archaeological data (cf. Cahill 1991; Allison 1997; Nevett 1999). No doubt similar studies will be appearing in the future.

In the following chapters, I undertake an analysis of a Roman city in a manner that has not been previously attempted. Chapter 2 is an exploration of some of the various theoretical approaches to the study of Roman urbanism. Chapter 3 gives a history of the site of Empúries, tracing its growth from a Greek colony to an important Roman city, followed by its decline and use as a small Late Antique and later medieval fortified village. It also describes a history of the rediscovery and excavation of the site up to the present. This description places the excavations in their cultural and historical contexts in order to better explain the types of work were carried out at the site and the quality of the data produced by different excavators. Chapter 4 is a presentation of the data. It is a description of every type of structure at Empúries, including the period of use, the function of the structures, and, when possible, a description of how that function changed over time. Chapter 5 presents an analysis of the data. It includes a description of patterns in the use of space in first-century Empúries and an explanation of the techniques employed to identify these patterns. In addition, Chapter 5 includes an interpretation of what these patterns may have meant to the ancient inhabitants of the city, and, finally, a brief description of how the use of space differed during the Republican and Late Antique periods. Chapter 6 is a summary of the study and places the results in the broader context of Roman urban society.

THEORIES OF ROMAN URBANISM

Do theories of the ancient city matter?
C. R. Whittaker 1995

2.1 Introduction

Whittaker asks this question as the title to a recent article reviewing theoretical approaches to the Roman city over the last 25 years. He believes it is necessary to ask if theory matters because "...familiarity with the debate leads to boredom, as though it did not matter any longer" (Whittaker 1995, 22). The debate to which he is referring is the argument over the utility of the Weber-Finley model of the consumer city. At the end of his article, Whittaker concludes that theory does, in fact, matter to the study of the ancient city. He gives a luke-warm endorsement of the consumer city model simply because he perceives it to be the only theoretical approach left that has not been discredited.

This rather depressing assessment of the state of theory in the study of the ancient city in general and, more specifically of the Roman city, neglects varied and dynamic theoretical approaches archaeologists and historians are currently developing and applying. Whittaker consciously limits his investigation to recent studies of the economy of ancient cities for the simple reason that most debate on the Roman city has been dominated by elaborations of, or attacks on, the consumer city model. In applying these economic blinders, however, Whittaker chooses to ignore other promising approaches archaeologists and historians have developed to search for meaning in the ancient city. This chapter reviews the consumer city model and analyzes how it has come to dominate theoretical discussions of the Roman city among both historians and archaeologists. It then explores archaeological alternatives to the consumer city approach. Starting with theories about the origins of the orthogonal layout and definitions of the Roman city, the chapter goes on to describe more recent attempts to move beyond the constituent components of the city in order to find a deeper meaning, one that had significance to Roman urbanites themselves. The chapter concludes by outlining how I will approach Roman urbanism in the following chapters and the assumptions I will be making.

2.2 The Consumer City

The first scholar to apply economic theory to the ancient city was M. Weber who wrote a series of articles published in *Archiv für Sozialwissenshaft und Sozialpolitic* and *Handwörterbuch der Staatwissenshaften* between 1909 and 1921 . Weber applied W. Sombart's concept of a pre-capitalistic early medieval city to the ancient world (Finley 1982, 17). Based on his reading of the ancient sources, Weber determined that cities paid for their maintenance through legal claims, that is to say, through rents and taxes on the agricultural producers in the countryside. He claimed that the cities were not required to return anything to the countryside (1958, 153; 1988, 2-4). Weber argued that the Roman patricians dominated urban life because the wealth they collected from rents allowed them the time to attend political meetings. These revenues also allowed the patricians to pay for expensive military equipment that helped them defend the city from external threats (1958, 121). Weber viewed the ancient city as something distinct from the modern city. He asserted that there was a fundamental break between antiquity and the present, and that a new form of city was created during the medieval period (Weber 1988, 45-46). Weber believed the ancient city had a more primitive economy than the medieval or modern city.

M. Rostovtzeff challenged Weber's primitivist view of the Roman city. Using both historical and archaeological evidence, Rostovtzeff challenged Weber's conclusion that the land-owning elite dominated Roman cities. Instead, he suggested the urban *bourgeoisie*, a middle class falling between the old noble families who had dominated Roman politics and the proletariat and slaves who worked on the land and in the workshops, came to have the major voice in urban politics (Rostovtzeff 1926, 17). According to Rostovtzeff, the *bourgeoisie* wanted to live comfortably in urban centers and so helped build, maintain, and adorn cities with all of the amenities known to the Romans, including fresh water, an adequate food supply, paved streets, public education, etc. (Rostovtzeff 1926, 133-139). They paid for these amenities through the proceeds gained from the capitalistic exploitation of agricultural land and investments in industry and commerce (Rostovtzeff 1926, 18). Rostovtzeff envisioned a lively local and regional trade in cheap, mass-produced goods produced in small industrial workshops as well as in basic food stuffs from which the *bourgeoisie* investors benefited (Rostovtzeff 1926, 66-67; 90; 167-168). In short, Rostovtzeff saw the ancient city as parallel with the modern city, not fundamentally different from it as Weber argued.

The radically different interpretations of the economic basis of the Roman city that Weber and Rostovtzeff advocated arose to a large degree from the type of evidence they were considering. The authors of the ancient texts, Weber's main sources, idealized those who were self-sufficient and made their livelihood from their own land. Those who sold their labor or goods in order to earn their bread were considered to have a lower status (Finley 1973, 41-61). Archaeological evidence, integral to Rostovtzeff's work (Rostovtzeff 1926, xiv), is replete with evidence for industry and commerce, since production and distribution of goods leaves many obvious physical remains. The seeming ubiquity of commercial and industrial establishments at Pompeii was strong evidence for Rostovtzeff that the elite did not scoff at participation in such activities (Rostovtzeff 1926, 72). It is probably for this reason that the modernist reasoning of Rostovtzeff held much more appeal for archaeologists interested in theoretical issues than the primitivist arguments of Weber. During the mid-twentieth century, modernist concepts frequently appeared in the interpretations of archaeologists, often taken for granted with little explicit theoretical discussion (Finley 1988, 20). The most substantive support for, and elaboration of, Rostovtzeff's views of an urban *bourgeoisie* came from the archaeologists working at Pompeii. Maiuri argued that after the earthquake of A.D. 62, the elite left the ruined Pompeii and a powerful middle class began its rebuilding (Maiuri 1951, 47). Day argued for a large commercial wine industry based in and around the city (Day 1932). Moeller interpreted evidence for the activities of the fullers as proof they were a class of entrepreneurs who influenced the politics in Pompeii for the benefit of their industry, arguing that the so-called Eumachia building on the forum of the city was their guild-hall (Moeller 1976).

Despite the enthusiasm among archaeologists for Rostovtzeff's model of the Roman city, in the end it was the successors of Weber who successfully discredited Rostovtzeff and his followers. Jones questioned the scale of industrial and commercial activity in the Roman city, citing the high cost of land transportation and the poverty of peasant and urban populations (Jones 1974, 37-38). Jongman forcefully challenged Day's evidence and argued that the villas around Pompeii produced cereals for subsistence, not wine to sell (Jongman 1988, 202). Jongman also led a devastating attack on Moeller's vision of Pompeii's fullers by pointing out the small scale of the industry and the lack of evidence for Moeller's claim that the Eumachia served as the fullers' guild hall (Jongman 1988, 183-185). By emphasizing the great diversity of craft production in the city, Jongman was able to argue that Pompeii and its hinterland were self-sufficient, thus arguing that Pompeii was in fact a consumer city of the type described by Weber (Jongman 1988, 186).

Weber's model of the consumer city underwent a remarkable revival thanks to the work of the ancient historians Jones and Finley. Both scholars shifted the focus of the debate away from economic explanations of behavior, which inspired much of the modernists' work, towards social explanations of behavior. Jones and Finley argued that actions in ancient societies had social motivations, not economic ones. There was a high-status way to earn a living in antiquity, usually by supplying most of one's needs directly from the produce of one's own land, and a low-status way, through wage labor. Jones and Finley pointed out that ancient commerce was constrained by technology. Bad roads, simple carts, and primitive sailing technology made the movement of goods on a large scale difficult or impossible. Thus, ancient cities had to have been self-sufficient. They relied on the territory around the city to supply all of their needs because they had to. Town and country were tied together as wealthy landowners chose to live in the city and bring the produce of their estates to the urban center for consumption. The wealth taken from the city's territory was returned to some extent in the form of goods and services, but trade beyond the city and its territory was minimal (Jones 1974; Finley 1973, 131-139).

The Weber-Finley consumer city came to be the "new orthodoxy" and has dominated debate among archaeologists and ancient historians for the last twenty-five years (Hopkins 1983, ix-xv). Supporters of the consumer city model have sought to elaborate it and test its implications. Hopkins

produced seven correlates to the Weber-Finley model that could be converted into archaeologically testable hypotheses (Hopkins 1983). Greene outlined the types of archaeological evidence and techniques available for studying the ancient economy, consciously rooting his discussion in the Weber-Finley model (Greene 1986). Parkins elaborated the role of the elite in the consumer city, justifying their occasional participation in the market as necessary to meet such temporary demands placed on their resources as the quest for political office and the necessity of providing dowries for their daughters (Parkins 1997). Detractors have sought either to modify the consumer city model or to challenge it entirely. Osborne argued, contrary to Weber and Finley, that written and archaeological evidence suggested ancient urban elites were as eager for economic profit as anyone (Osborne 1991). It should be noted that Osborne was countered by Whittaker who challenged Osborne's reading of Finley, arguing that he overlooked Finley's distinction between profit from property investment and profit from capital investment (Whittaker 1995, 11-12). Burnham and Wacher challenged the applicability of Finley's ideas to evidence from Roman Britain given the indications of trade in manufactured goods on a scale much larger than Finley's theory would have allowed (Burnham and Wacher 1990, 43). Engels rejected the Weber-Finley model completely, citing the example of Roman Corinth. He argued that the countryside around Corinth was incapable of supporting the urban population and that additional income had to be generated to pay for basic foodstuffs. Engels hypothesized that this income came from port and religious services provided by the city, thus producing what he called a "service economy" in the city, rather than a consumer economy (Engels 1990). The concept of the service city is controversial in classical archaeology and the writings of Engels have been quite rightly attacked for serious methodological problems (Saller 1991; Laurence 1994b, 9-10; Whittaker 1995, 12-14).

With the ascension of the Weber-Finley model, however, the ancient city became lost. Finley had transformed the debate, shifting the attention of scholars away from the city itself and towards the broader issue of the ancient economy. His emphasis on the dominant role of agriculture in the ancient economy, coupled with the rapid destruction of rural archaeological sites during the economic growth of post-World War II Europe, encouraged archaeologists to focus their attention on the countryside. The development of surface survey as a valuable tool in Mediterranean archaeology caused many archaeologists to address economic questions on the regional, rather than on the local, level (Alcock, Cherry, and Davis 1994, 137-138; Barker 1995, 6-16). In survey, cities became only one component of an entire landscape. Finley's revival of the consumer city model led to the marginalization of Roman cities in discussions of the Roman economy, an ironic shift from the period when Weber first proposed the consumer city model making cities the focus of economic debate.

2.3 Origin and Definition of Roman Urbanism

Archaeologists interested in other aspects of Roman urbanism had their own theoretical debates. These centered on the origins and definition of Roman urbanism. This was a uniquely archaeological problem, one that could not be answered through the consultation of ancient texts and so was of little concern to ancient historians. The debate over the origins of the grid layout began in the second half of the nineteenth century with the discovery of the orthogonal layout of the Etruscan city of Marzabotto (Castagnoli 1971, 2). The Etruscans were believed to have been immigrants from somewhere in the eastern Mediterranean and the towns with the earliest known orthogonal layouts existed in the Near East. The obvious question became whether they had brought this technique with them when they emigrated, whether they had learned it from the Greeks after the Greeks had begun building colonies with gridded street plans in southern Italy, or whether they had developed it independently. The first of these arguments was discredited when the supposed Near Eastern origin of the Etruscans was rejected (Spivey 1997, 11-24). Of the other two options, excavations had settled the question by the 1970s. Etruscan and Italian Greek cities with orthogonal layouts appeared close in time, but the Greek sites have been shown to be earlier and thus probably provided the inspiration for the Etruscans. The Romans learned the technique both from the Etruscans and the Greeks (Ward-Perkins 1974, 25; Owens 1991, 96). The intensity of the debate, however, led scholars to take local contributions to the form of a city as a serious possibility. Thus it became valid to argue either for the diffusion of the Roman urban form from the Italian peninsula to the provinces or the evolution of the urban form locally in the provinces.

With the question of the origins of the orthogonal system answered, another fundamental theoretical debate began, how was one to define a Roman city? This was an issue of great importance among British archaeologists in particular because Romano-British cities were so different in appearance from their Italian counterparts, raising the interesting issue of the degree to which these differences arose from a synthesis of local ideals of urbanism with Roman ideals. Prior to the 1970s, the definition of a Roman city seemed self-evident based on its form. Roman cities had an orthogonal plan, a forum adorned with a *capitolium*, or temple dedicated to Jupiter, Juno and Minerva, a *curia* or council house, and a basilica. In addition, Roman cities had a city wall, temples, homes, shops, a theater, an amphitheater, aqueducts and fountains, and finally triumphal arches, statues, and other objects of decoration (Grimal 1983; Sorrell 1976, 15-18). Roman cities throughout the empire were assumed to take Rome itself as the aesthetic model for the form of decoration in their cities (Grimal 1983, 4-5).

The problem with this definition of a city was that while it worked well for Roman Italy, it was not as useful for understanding urbanization in the western provinces. Few sites in Roman Britain had all of the characteristics mentioned above, yet many sites certainly functioned as cities (Wacher 1997, 24-25). In addition, Roman Britain had a much smaller population density than Italy and few, if any, towns could be claimed to have populations over 10,000, a common minimum insisted upon for a site to be considered a city (Todd 1993, 6). The figure of 10,000 inhabitants was first suggested by the ancient Greek city-planner Hippodamus (Arist., *Pol.* ii.5.2). It is unclear from Aristotle's text whether Hippodamus meant 10,000 citizens or 10,000 residents, an extremely important difference, as not all residents of the city were citizens (i.e. women, children, slaves, etc.).

A new definition of a city had to be devised to fit the provincial situation. In forming this new definition, British archaeologists argued for a fundamental theoretical shift in focus from the form of a city to its function (Burnham 1979, 257). From this point of view, a Roman city could be defined as a center of administration, trade, amusement, and protection. These functions were indicated by, but not limited to, the structures listed above, the administrative function by the forum and its associated structures, trade by shops and markets, amusement by theaters and amphitheaters, and protection by city walls (Wacher 1997, 36). The important difference between this new definition and the previous is that structures other than those traditionally identified with Roman cities could fulfill the roles necessary for the site to be considered a city. Thus the absence of a curia at a site did not necessarily denote the absence of a city council. The city council could have met in a basilica, temple, or theater, locations recorded as meeting places of city councils and even the Roman senate in ancient literature. Although it differed from its Italian counterparts, British archaeologists claimed, one could still speak of Romano-British urbanism.

2.4 The Search for Meaning

For some scholars, the theoretical debates outlined above were seen as sterile, because they overlooked the humanistic element of the Roman city. Rather than see the city as the mere location for certain types of social and economic activities, these scholars sought the meaning of the Roman city to its ancient inhabitants. The structuralist belief that architectural and urban forms could be "read" in order to decipher the social systems and beliefs that had created them heavily influenced theoretical approaches to the ancient city beginning with the work of Rykwert. A structuralist historian, Rykwert concluded that ancient cities in general, and Roman cities in particular, helped connect the ancients to the universe as they perceived it. The ceremonies of foundation recreated the formation of the universe, the streets were aligned to the cosmos with the *cardo*, or north-south oriented street, being the axis of the universe and the *decumanus*, or east-west oriented street, being the path along which the sun traveled (Rykwert 1964, 41-45). Rykwert was resurrecting the idea first articulated one-hundred years earlier that the ancient city had to be seen as a religious construct. One of the earliest theoreticians on matters of ancient urbanism was the historian Fustel de Coulanges. He concluded in *La Cité Antique*, published in 1864, that all aspects of city life, from the founding of the city to daily activities, were dictated by respect for the sanctity of the city as a place of common worship (Fustel de Coulanges 1956, 11 and 127).

Another scholar who sought the meaning of the Roman city to its ancient inhabitants was the architectural historian W. L. MacDonald. MacDonald argued that all Roman cities had a similar form that made it possible for a Roman arriving in a new city for the first time to find his or her way by following the clues familiar from other cities. Dubbing this scheme "urban armatures," he argued that all the main public structures in a Roman city were linked together by streets and squares, with junctions and entrances carefully marked by familiar architectural components that were similar throughout the empire (MacDonald 1986a and 1986b). Urban armatures, according to MacDonald, were one way that residents and visitors to the ancient city understood the city itself.

MacDonald's work made little impact on Roman urban studies. No other scholar has followed up his work, elaborating the idea of urban armatures or seeking them at sites not mentioned by MacDonald. Archaeologists have ignored his approach; MacDonald is rarely cited in works about specific sites or in synthetic works about Roman cities.

The historian Fear used a synthesis of the textual and archaeological evidence to search for the meaning of urban centers to the inhabitants of Roman Spain. He came to the conclusion that cities were established for reasons of immediate administrative need and for the personal glory of the founder, whose name would be immortalized in the name of the city. Building on definitions of Romano-British urbanism mentioned above, Fear argued that the outward appearance of the city mattered little as long as the functional administrative needs were met (Fear 1996).

Recently some archaeologists have begun to interpret the form and placement of public monuments, as well as the resulting changes to the urban structure, as ideological statements. Examining the evidence from Athens and Thasos in Greece, P. Gros argued the construction of new buildings with strong imperial associations during the Augustan era helped transform the urban centers and reorient the city planning as a whole (Gros 1990). Following Gros' lead, Keay argued that the urban structure of Tarraco (Tarragona) was transformed in the Augustan era by ideology. Tarraco was dramatically altered in the early imperial period by several massive construction projects. Keay argues these projects were sponsored by local elites in order to identify themselves with the Roman state. This was just one way local elites could seek political advancement. By ascribing to imperial ideology, local elites were also masking the difference in the balance of power between themselves and other non-elite families in the region, just as Augustus used ideology to mask his new unequal relationship with the Roman senate (Keay 1997).

2.5 The Raper Thesis and Beyond

Other archaeologists interested in finding meaning in Roman cities have been heavily influenced by the work of R. Raper (1977 and 1979). Dissatisfied with studies of Pompeii that concentrated only on the artifacts discovered in the city, he sought to reveal the "thought behind the town plan" (Raper 1977, 190). Raper insisted on studying Pompeii through the function of all buildings across the site, not in the traditional manner of examining the architectural form of individual monuments. The technique Raper used to analyze the use of space at Pompeii is described and critiqued in detail in

chapter 5 (section 5.3). In brief, what he did was cover a plan of Pompeii with a gird of squares each equivalent to 100 m on a side on the ground. He then tabulated the amount of building space within each grid devoted to different uses such as religion, commerce, residence, etc. The amount of space devoted to each use turned out to be nearly identical. He concluded that there was hardly any spatial patterning at Pompeii and that its plan revealed little about the ancient perceptions of the city. The few patterns he detected were the clustering of public buildings around central places such as the forum and the positioning of shops along important streets. While Raper's technique gained little following, his conclusion that there was little or no patterning to the use of Roman urban space has become accepted for Pompeii and other Roman urban sites (La Torre 1988; Jongman 1988, 270; Perring 1991, 273-293; Wallace-Hadrill 1991, 259; 1994, 135-136; and 1995, 43).

The reaction to Raper's methodology and conclusions has experienced an interesting evolution. His conclusions were first tested. W. Bates used a similar methodology at a different site, Silchester, to see if she could obtain similar results (Bates 1983, 134-143), while G. La Torre used a different methodology at the same site, Pompeii, to see if he could obtain similar results (La Torre 1988, 75-102). Although Bate's results challenged Raper's, La Torre's agreed that the use of space was without pattern at Pompeii. This confirmation allowed the Raper thesis to be generally accepted for Pompeii (Wallace-Hadrill 1991, 259 and 1995, 43; Jongman 1988, 270).

Following their acceptance for Pompeii, Raper's ideas were projected on to other Roman urban sites. Wallace-Hadrill suggested the random use of space was valid for the Roman city of Volubilis as well as Roman cities in general (1994, 135-136). D. Perring applied the idea to his examination of Romano-British urbanism (1991, 273-293). Most recently, E. J. Owens and J. C. Anderson have repeated Raper's claim that there was no real pattern to the arrangement of blocks containing domestic structures in Roman cities. Both authors, however, fail to cite Raper's study. Instead, Owens cites Wallace Hadrill (1991) and Anderson does not cite anyone, a sure sign that Raper's ideas have become generally accepted (Owens 1996, 20; Anderson 1997, 331). The Raper thesis has been justifiably referred to recently as the "current paradigm" (Robinson 1997, 136).

Despite its wide spread acceptance there still seems to be some underlying discontent with the Raper thesis. While stating explicitly that they ascribe to it, some scholars studying urban space at Pompeii have noted exceptions to the idea that the use of space lacks arrangement, pointing out patterns in the distribution of structures as varied as brothels and elite houses (Wallace-Hadrill 1995; Jongman 1988, 270). Curiously, in the most important recent work on urban space at Pompeii, R. Laurence fails to mention the Raper thesis at all (1994b). D. Robinson has interpreted this lacuna as tacit support for Raper's conclusions (Robinson 1997), although I would argue the opposite as Laurence's entire book is concerned with discovering patterns in the urban structure of Pompeii. Nonetheless, Laurence's failure to explicitly address Raper's conclusions has left the Raper thesis intact. Besides Bates (1983) only one other scholar has explicitly challenged the Raper thesis. Robinson argued that the placement of elite villas at Pompeii really does have meaning. He found villas to be separated from one another, perhaps to allow the clients to live near their patrons (Robinson 1997).

2.6 Approach to Roman Urbanism in the Present Work

The present work also challenges the Raper thesis. Currently, scholars of Roman urban space generally accept the conclusions of Raper that, with a few obvious exceptions, there was little spatial patterning in the Roman city and that similar uses of space were randomly scattered about the city. The technical aspects of Raper's analysis will be examined in detail in chapter 5 (section 5.3), where it will be shown to be incapable of identifying the patterns he sought. Therefore a new suite of techniques for identifying patterns in the use of space in the Roman urban environment is suggested. These techniques are applied to the study of Empúries and reveal that the use of space in the Roman city was highly structured.

The analytical techniques described in chapter 5 draw heavily on structuralist theory and practice. Structuralist spatial theory is based on two assumptions, that space is an element of daily life that is continuous and structured, and that different levels of access give social power to built space (Hillier and J. Hanson 1984). The power of built space is gained by including people in, and excluding them from, specific spaces. In this theoretical approach, there are two types of people, the "inhabitants" of the built space, those who control its form and, to some extent, the activities that take place inside that space, and the "visitors," those who do not hold such power over activities within the space. Wide streets, broad plazas, clustered shops, and visible monuments are all designed by the inhabitants of the city to help include visitors, making it easier for them to navigate the city, mingle with its residents and other visitors, and share in the city's unifying symbols. Narrow streets with many twists, long building façades with few doors, buildings that are difficult to find, all tend to exclude visitors, making the city difficult to navigate, isolating inhabitants from visitors. Structuralist scholars assume that the architects, builders, and urban planners locate and create structures with the goals of inclusion or exclusion in mind. They argue that the organization of space can be viewed as the "grammar" or "syntax" of a culture. It represents social norms, opening the spaces deemed appropriate for general public interaction and closing those where visitors are not welcomed. If one can find a way to decipher the patterns of inclusion and exclusion, they maintain, one can begin to understand the corresponding social norms (Hillier and J. Hanson 1984, 5-25; Markus 1993, 12-25; Gilchrist 1994, 151-160; Ferguson 1996, 4-24).

It is this last step, finding ways to decipher the patterns of inclusion and exclusion that explains the appeal structuralist theory has had for many archaeologists. Architectural and urban space is quantifiable. One can count a wide variety of architectural or urban elements in order to describe the arrangement of space, including the number of doorways which give access to a space, the number of streets that lead

to a plaza, the total area from which a certain monument can be seen. These counts can be compared as simple percentages or can be tested for significance with great statistical sophistication.

The scholars who have done the most to apply structuralist theory to the development of techniques for analyzing space are the sociologists Hillier and Hanson, who have developed a number of robust statistical techniques that allow for the description of space (Hillier and Hanson 1984). These statistics are quite useful and are used extensively in this study. Their techniques have become quite popular among archaeologists (Foster 1989, 40-50; Chapman 1991; Fairclough 1992; Morris 1994; Gilchrist 1994; Laurence 1994b; Locock 1994; Ferguson 1996; Smith 1999; Nevett 1999).

Unfortunately, Hillier and Hanson make one fundamental error, for which they have been taken to task by several authors. They assume that the statistics generated from their techniques represent explanations, and that their explanations are valid across cultures and time. For instance, they assume that their statistic of depth, representing the number of spaces one needs to cross in order to reach a space of interest, directly represents power (Hillier and Hanson 1984, 154-155). The customer or visitor to a modern American bank is given little power by being restricted to space with a shallow depth, the lobby, which is usually directly accessible from the street and thus has a depth of only one. Conversely, the power of the bank president, an inhabitant of the space, is manifested in the great depth of his or her office from the street, requiring one to pass through a number of spaces in order to reach it (Markus 1993, 24). While the equation of depth and power may be a valid explanation for differential depths in a modern American context, it does not necessarily hold for other cultures where the use of space is regulated in other symbolic ways (Upton 1992; Pearson and Richards 1994, 30).

In the fifth chapter of *The Social Logic of Space* Hillier and Hanson use their descriptive statistics to outline and explain the social relations represented by such culturally and temporally diverse structures as a modern Bedouin tent, a medieval European infirmary, and a nineteenth-century Ashanti shrine. Their explanation rings hollow however, as they fail to consider the contribution of aspects of these cultures to the final production of spatial arrangements, not mentioning, for instance, Bedouin sex-roles, Medieval notions of contagion, nor Ashanti attitudes towards their deities. Hillier and Hanson's statistics need to be seen merely as descriptions of space while the interpretations of those statistics need to be placed in the appropriate cultural context. For this very reason some of the scholars who utilize their techniques, myself included, have not hesitated to divorce themselves from Hillier and Hanson's explanative framework (Smith 1999; Gilchrist 1994; Markus 1993, 12-25).

Fortunately, Hillier and Hanson's techniques are quite appropriate for the study of Roman urban space. The Romans were acutely aware of the possibilities of the arrangement of space for creating and regulating social relations. One need only wander through one of the finely preserved amphitheaters or theaters to discover this awareness. Once in the *cavea*, or seating area, it is often impossible to walk from one section of the amphitheater or theater to the other. The visitor frequently needs to exit the building completely and enter through a different door in order to reach different sections of seating. These separate sections were reserved for members of different social classes, reservations that were often affirmed in legal codes.

Given the importance of spatial arrangements in structures for entertainment, it stands to reason that the arrangement of space in the urban context was equally important to the Romans. In this light, Raper's conclusions about Pompeii seem exceedingly odd. This study will employ the structuralist techniques devised by Hillier and Hanson and others to find patterns in the use of space at the Roman urban center of Empúries. Chapters 3 and 4 outline the available data and chapter 5 presents the actual analyses.

EMPÚRIES: CULTURE HISTORY AND ARCHAEOLOGY

Empúries, tu dorms! A dins nostres memòries,
vestigi que l'edat no és prou a destruir,
la plana que has escritar al cor de les històries
inextingible serva el teu record d'ahir . . .

. . . d'aquí que l'hom aspiri a las eternes cales.
Espera sols en Déu o tu qui l'has perdut!

Empúries, you sleep! In our memories,
traces which the ages are not sufficient to destroy,
the page that you have written to the heart of inextinguishable
history serves as your record of yesterday...

...Here man aspires to the eternal after world.
He trusts only in God, but oh you who have survived him!

Andrée Brugière de Grogot (1918)

3.1 Introduction

The above poem expresses some of the excitement caused by the initiation of annual excavations at the Greco-Roman site of Empúries. Publishing just ten years after the beginning of systematic and, for that day, thoroughly scientific excavations, Brugière de Grogot was not exaggerating to claim that the spirit of the site was being resurrected by the work of archaeologists. Although some information was available about the city from ancient sources, it was really the pioneering work of Catalan archaeologists that revolutionized the understanding of both Greek and Roman colonial efforts on the Iberian peninsula. The on-going investigation of the site has ensured that Empúries continues to maintain its position as an important center for the study of ancient Mediterranean urbanism.

The purpose of this chapter is to trace the cultural and archaeological history of Empúries, a task best accomplished by following the changing names of the site. At separate times it was known as Emporion, Indika, Emporiae, Municipium Emporiae, Sant Martí de Empúries, Ampurias. In the Middle Ages it even lent its name to the surrounding territory, the Empordà. These changes in nomenclature do not simply represent linguistic shifts; they signify, rather, important fluctuations in political and social control over the city, both as a living city in antiquity and the Middle Ages, and as an archaeological site in the nineteenth and twentieth centuries. This chapter examines the history of the site, beginning by placing it in its physical setting. The chapter then outlines the basic chronology of the site in antiquity concentrating in the cultural-historical context of the Roman period. Next, the chapter presents the modern archaeological history of Empúries. This is of particular importance because the evidence from these different excavations, the quality of which was wildly variable, forms the basis of the analysis of each individual category of space at Empúries in the following chapter. The chapter concludes with a brief description of the site as the tourist sees it today, giving a list of the most prominent features to help orient the reader to the site.

3.2 Empordà: The Hinterland of Empúries

The territory controlled by the city of Empúries in the early Imperial period corresponds roughly to the region now called the Empordà (fig. 2) (Mar and Ruiz 1993, 318). The Empordà is a depression defined in the east by the Mediterranean Sea, in the north and west by the pre-Pyrenees, and in the south by the Catalonian cordillera. At its widest, it measures approximately 55 km. north to south by 40 km. east to west. A humid Mediterranean climate prevails (Ager 1980, 283). With an annual rainfall of 750 mm. and a mean maximum temperature of 23°C the area is able to support evergreen forests and, at the higher altitudes on the northern, southern, and western edges of the Empordà, deciduous oak and beech forests. Today the main crops of the area are cereals. Four river systems, the Muga, the Fluvià, the Ter, and the Daró drain the plain (Pérez and Julià 1994, 91). Winds from the east and south make the area perfect for sailing towards or away from the Iberian peninsula, although the strong and cold northern *Tramontana* wind could often force sailors to wait in the Gulf of Roses for changes in weather. The Tramontana wind can blow steadily for as long as a week causing consternation to others than just sailors. There is a popular saying in L'Escala, the modern town near the site of Empúries, that those who act in a crazy manner have been "touched by the Tramontana."

The coast of the Empordà is not the most obvious place for the establishment of a major Greek or Roman colony. The area immediately around the site of Empúries lacks the fertile land one would normally associate with a *chora* or *territorium*, agricultural land controlled by residents of the city that provided necessary foodstuffs and other natural resources. As recently as the last century, prior to its being drained and turned into productive farmland, the territory around Empúries was filled with marshes and lakes. There is some reason to believe that conditions were the same in Roman times (Harrison 1988, 105). Strabo claims that only some of the territory held by the city was fertile, while the rest of it was known as the *Campus Iuncarius*, or "Rush Plain" (iii.4.9). The noun *iunceus*, meaning "reed," and the adjective *incosus*, meaning "overgown with reeds," have survived in English as the word "junk" (Jones 1960, 92, n. 1), a good adjective for how useful Strabo felt the Campus Iuncarius was. Based on his analysis of the ancient sources, particularly Strabo and Livy, Vallet concluded that Empúries was a "city without a territory" as the surrounding area was of little use for agriculture (Vallet 1967; Maluquer 1973; Morel 1981).

Borao further confirmed the poor quality of farmland around Empúries in his study of the Roman cadestration of a 500-km^2 region around the site (Borao 1987). Borao studied aerial photographs to determine the lines of cadastration, or property lines Roman surveyors laid out in the countryside. He found land divisions to be interrupted by the presence of marshes and lakes. In addition, these land divisions covered only half of the territory he surveyed. He noted that even in the areas that still bore evidence of Roman surveyors' work, there were few villas. In fact there are only three confirmed villas in the 500-km^2 area surrounding Empúries, with six additional sites that may possibly represent villas. Several of these, however, certainly dated to the third century A.D. or later, after the city of Empúries went into decline. This is not a pattern one would expect to find in a fertile territory. While these cadastral lines cannot be dated directly, their alignment, which is identical with the alignment of the Roman city, and the use of the *iugera*, a Roman standard of measurement suggest they date to after the arrival of the Romans. There is no basis for Plana's claim that the lines of cadastration date to the Greek period (Plana 1994, 143 ff.).

The city's position on the Gulf of Roses also leaves something to be desired for sea-faring peoples such as the Greeks and Romans. The harbor would have been quite small and exposed to the strong winds from the east. The impressive mole that still stands across part of the entrance to the harbor today is some indication of Greek and Roman attempts to protect the harbor from these winds. Roman dissatisfaction with the natural qualities of the harbor are further indicated by the evidence they built a second harbor more than 3 km south of Empúries at Riells-La Clota in the early second century B.C. To date there has been no systematic excavation of these facilities (Nieto and Nolla 1985).

Despite these drawbacks, the Empordà has much to recommend it for human settlement. The coast of the Empordà lies on the Gulf of Roses, making resources from the sea easily available to inhabitants. Today L'Escalas is justifiably famous across Europe for its anchovies. The Gulf of Roses is also an excellent place for ships to wait for favorable winds to cross the notoriously treacherous Gulf of Leon on their way to Marseille, the ancient Greek colony of Massalia. Nineteenth-century sailing manuals praise the "great refuge" of the Gulf of Roses for ships leaving or entering the Gulf of Leon and the ancient sources also indicate the Gulf of Roses was an important stop on sea routes linking southern Spain to France and Italy (Ruiz 1984; Avienus *Ora Maritimia* 519-565). The role of the Empordà in land communication was also extremely important, as one of the few passes through the Pyrenees lies on its northern border. The Via Augusta ran through the Empordà 12 km west of Empúries, but bypassed the city in order to avoid the marshes around the site (Dearden 1984; Strabo iii.4.8).

Another important feature of the Empordà is that it is rich in mineral resources. Deposits of copper, iron, silver, and lead are easily accessible from the sea. Other mineral deposits lie further inland but are easily reachable via navigable rivers. These rivers form another important asset of the region, providing fresh water and fish as well as facilitating communication between the Mediterranean and the cities and resources in the interior (Ruiz 1984).

At the site of Empúries two navigable rivers connected the Gulf of Roses with the plains at the foot of the Pyrenees (fig. 2). North of the city flows the Fluvià River, at whose mouth was the harbor of the city, and which allowed access by boat to the valleys of the Fresser and the upper Ter. Both of these regions still produce copper, silver, lead, iron, and gold. The Ter River enters the Mediterranean immediately to the south of the city. This river also gave access to the interior, particularly to the region of Anglès, an area rich in copper, silver, and lead (Ruiz 1984). The Ter was also a route of communication and transportation connecting Empúries to the important inland Roman and Medieval city of Gerona (Ruiz 1984). The importance of this river as a commercial and communication link between the two cities is stressed in the medieval legend of St. Felix. St. Felix is reported to have arrived in Catalunya from North Africa in the early fourth century on board a merchant vessel. After disembarking at Empúries he went on to Gerona where he was martyred (Almagro 1951b, 99-100).

The legend of St. Felix suggests the importance of Empúries as a regional center for the redistribution of imported goods from the Mediterranean to the countryside to as well as for products and raw materials from the countryside the broader Mediterranean world. The cargo excavated from the wreck Cala Culip IV may demonstrate the importance of Empúries as a center for redistribution. This ship was carrying a cargo of Baetican oil and southern Gaulish ceramics and may have been bound for Empúries at the time it went down (Nieto et al 1989; Wiseman 1996; Millett 1993). Two additional pieces of artifactual evidence for the use of Empúries as a transshipment port for goods between the Mediterranean and inland areas have been excavated at the site. The first consists of mid-first century A.D. graffiti found in the Roman villa 2b at the site. This graffiti depict four ships in some detail, two of which are clearly recognizable as large sea-faring vessels, while a third represents a smaller river vessel (Casanovas and Rovira 1994). The second piece of evidence consists of an inscribed lead tablet, a fifth century B.C. letter, discovered near the south gate of Neapolis, written by an Ionian merchant who instructed his agents at Empúries to send him merchandise (Sanmartí and Santiago 1987; Santiago 1990, 176). Unfortunately, the preserved fragments of the letter do not list what the merchandise was. Nonetheless, the Ionian instructed his agents to "repackage" the merchandise to prepare it for transport. Presumably he intended them to remove it from the packaging necessary to transport it by river boat or cart from the countryside and place it in whatever packaging was necessary for its loading on to a sea-faring ship (Sanmartí and Santiago 1987, 123).

3.3 Final Bronze / Early Iron Ages

The earliest evidence for human habitation at Empúries comes from an easily defensible island that stood in the Fluvià River, where the river reached the sea (fig. 1). Later in antiquity the Fluvià River silted up, leaving the island a hill overlooking the Mediterranean on which now stands the small village of Sant Martí d'Empúries. This village has been continuously occupied now for over two and half millennia. Evidence from recent excavations in Sant Martí have offered a tantalizing glimpse of the earliest incarnation of Empúries. Unfortunately, our picture of the early habitation at Sant Martí is very fragmentary because the village is still occupied and excavations have been limited to small areas (Almagro 1964). In the most extensive excavations to date, researchers excavated the narrow streets and tiny plazas as part of a plan to modernize the village's water and sewage systems (figs. 3 and 4) (Aquilué 1998, 10-13 and Aquilué et al. 1996, 52-64).

These excavations have shown that the island was first inhabited in the 9th and 8th centuries B.C. These settlers were followed, after a brief hiatus, by Iron Age Iberians in the second half of the 7th century B.C. The Iberians were eager to import Phoenician and Etruscan products, particularly amphoras of wine, from an early date. Thus they played a part, if only in a small way, in Phoenician attempts to organize trade routes that would give them access to mineral-rich areas in northern Spain and northern Italy (Aquilué 1998, 18-23).

3.4 Emporion

In stratigraphic layers dated to the early 6th century B.C. the frequency of Greek ceramics increases dramatically, perhaps as a result of the founding of the Phocean Greek colony at Massalia in the early sixth century. The introduction of Greek artifacts seems to have been rapidly followed by the establishment in the second quarter of the sixth century of a Greek colony on the island in the Fluvià, Ἐμπόριον (App. *Hisp.*, vi.2.7, vi.8.40, vi.40, viii.72; Polyb. i.82, iii.39, iii.76.1-4; Ptol. *Geog.*, ii.6.19; Skylax *Periplous*, 2 and 3; Steph. Byz.; and Strabo iii.4.8). The exact reasons for which this colony was established, and what the relationship between the Greeks and Iberians was are questions that are impossible to answer from the fragmentary evidence produced in excavations at Sant Martí. Nonetheless, the name of the site, Emporion (trading post), suggests that a central role of the colony was the exchange of local resources for imported Mediterranean goods.

Within a generation, the Greek settlement spread to the mainland. Strabo writes that the island continued to be occupied and referred to it as Palaiapolis, or "old city" (iii.4.8). Following Strabo's precedent, modern archaeologists have designated the site on the mainland Neapolis, or "new city" (fig. 5) (Puig i Cadafalch 1908, 161). There have been as few excavations into these early Greek levels on the mainland as there have been in Sant Martí. The trenches with excavated early Greek levels are concentrated on the southern edge of the city. The Greeks built large cyclopean city walls around Neapolis in the early fourth century; the gate in the southern portion of this circuit wall has been excavated (Sanmartí, Castanyer, and Tremoleda 1986, 1989, and 1990). Immediately outside this gate stood a sanctuary, almost certainly dedicated to Asklepios, which consisted of several altars. It has been suggested that the location of this sanctuary outside the city walls was intentional, creating neutral sacred space where the Greeks and Iberians could meet. The god of healing would certainly have had a broad appeal (Sanmartí 1993a, 21). The city was not just defined by its wall and sanctuary; the Greeks also minted coins. The Greek coin type, a silver drachma with a head of Artemis on the obverse and Pegasus on the reverse with the Greek name Emporion, was first minted in the fifth century B.C. Production of this type continued until the arrival of the Romans at the site (Mar and Ruiz 1993, 194-198; Villaronga 1977).

3.5 Indika / Untikesken

With so little known about pre-Roman Empúries from excavation, written texts are of immense value in understanding the early history of the city. Unfortunately, the literary sources can be difficult to interpret. Strabo and Livy describe Empúries as a *dipolis*, or double city, with neighborhoods for the Indicetani, the local tribe of native Iberians, and Greeks, separated by a wall (Strabo iii.4.8; Livy xxxiv.9.1, see also Plin. *HN*, iii.4.21; Ptolomeus *Geo. Hyph.* ii.6.19; Steph. Byz.; Avenius, *Ora Maritima* 523 and 533; and Sall. *Epistula Cn. Pompei ad Senatum* 4-5). The name of the Iberian community, Indika, is a Greek transliteration of the native name, Untikesken. Bronze coins from the site bearing the word Untikesken, written in Iberian characters, confirm the existence of an Iberian community (Villaronga 1977, 17; Almagro 1951b, 99-100). Finally a Flavian-era inscription mentions a group of *Indicetani*, proof that some sort of tribal organization still existed within the Roman-era municipium (Almagro 1955, 55-62; Fabré, Mayer, and Rodà, 1991, nos. 172, 173, 174; Mar and Ruiz 1993, 316-317). The inscription mentions a *legati atvocati Indicetanorum*, legal advocates in a case between the Indicetani and another group of Iberians, the Olossitani.

The exact relationship between the Indicetani and the Greeks is difficult to judge. Livy suggests a situation of mutual mistrust, in which the Greeks were forced to mount a guard every night on their walls to protect from attack from the Indicetani. Strabo presents a very different picture, claiming that the Greeks and Indicetani had joined together to build a common wall around their site for mutual protection. It is possible that Livy was relying on the accounts of M. Porcius Cato for his basic information. Cato wrote accounts of his campaign during the Iberian Revolt of 197–195 B.C., a period during which there would certainly have been a distrust of the natives on the part of the Greeks (Almagro Basch 1951b). Whatever the relationship between Greeks and Indicetani at the time of the Iberian Revolt, it can be certain that their relationship underwent many changes over time, and that the relationship was complicated by the arrival of the Romans. It is quite interesting that the first bronze coins bearing the legend Untikesken appear in the beginning of the second century, after the arrival of the Romans. These issues replaced the Greek silver issues, but maintained Greek symbolism with the representation of the head of Artemis and of Pegasus (Villaronga 1977).

A question that has plagued excavators is the physical location of Indika. No trace has been found in excavations south or west of Greek Neapolis. And yet the city could not have existed to the north or east because of the presence of the Fluvià River and the Mediterranean Sea (see fig. 1). Sanmartí argued that Indika could not have existed west of Neapolis as no excavation in that area has ever produced material dating to the period prior to the Roman arrival. Sanmartí concluded that Indika had to have stood directly south of the Neapolis south gates (Sanmartí 1978). Based on this reasoning, Sanmartí led excavations south of Neapolis in the early 1980s but found no evidence of an Iberian settlement. Instead he found the oldest material was associated with a Greek cemetery (Sanmartí et al. 1983-1984). The two remaining possibilities are that Indika was located further west or south of the Greek city. It may have stood in areas not yet excavated, or Strabo and Livy may have misunderstood a reference to the legal status of the Indicetani within the Greek city as a geographical reference outside of the city (see chapter 6, section 6.6).

3.6 Emporiae

Roman interest in Empúries began during the Second Punic War (219-201 B.C.), when Scipio Aemilianus used the city as a base for the Roman invasion of the Iberian peninsula in the attempt to stop reinforcements from reaching Hannibal, who was then ravaging the Italian peninsula (Polyb. iii.76.2). Cato used Empúries as a Roman military base as well during the Iberian revolt of 197-195 (Livy xxxiv.8.7, xxxiv. 9. 10; Appian vi.40). Despite Livy's claim that Cato located his camp some three miles from the Greek city (xxxiv.13.2), portions of a *praesidium* have been found located only a few hundred meters west of Greek Neapolis. This spot was continuously occupied for the next three centuries (Aquilué et al. 1984).

A settlement must have grown haphazardly around the gates of the Roman military camp. The settlement was organized into a regular city around 100 B.C. (fig. 6). An orthogonal street plan was laid out dividing the site into seventy rectangular *insulae*, or city blocks, each twice as long as it was wide. The size of each insula was approximately 35 x 70 m, the size of one Roman *iugerum* (Mar and Ruiz 1993, 329). Roman engineers constructed the city walls using poured cement, the latest in Italian architectural developments (Mar and Ruiz 1993, 263). At the center of the city, the *praesidium* and the area around it were turned into a forum. Because the Roman and Greek cities remained independent, the site became known to the Romans as Emporiae, a Latinized version of the Greek name with a plural ending to indicate the two separate cities. The name is attested in Livy (xxxiv.9.1, xxxiv.11.2, xxxiv.13.2); Pliny, (*HN.*, iii.4.21-22); Silius Italicus (iii.368-370 and iii.174-179). It also appears in epigraphic evidence (Fabré, Mayer, and Rodà 1991, nos. 22 and 34).

The exact legal status of this Republican Roman city, specifically whether it was a *colonia* or not, has been a subject of much debate. The question is an important one because a colonia was different from other towns. A colonia was considered an extension of Rome and its citizens had all the rights and privileges of Roman citizens, including the right to run for important political offices in Rome and, often, exemption from the land tax. A colonia was usually founded for soldiers retiring from the army after a successful campaign on lands of the former enemy (Garnsey and Saller 1987, 27-28). All arguments about whether or not Republican Empúries was a colonia are centered on the reading of one fragmentary inscription found in a secondary context in the Roman forum. The inscription reads "M. IVN/PRO/CO" and had been reused as a step allowing entry to the forum. Despite claims to the contrary, this inscription offers too little evidence for the determination of city's status. While "CO" can be read as an abbreviation for colonia, it can equally be read as "proconsul" when taken with the "PRO" above it. The context is simply too ambiguous to provide evidence for either argument (for a summary of the debate see Pena 1992, 65-77). The fact that the city held the legal status of *municipium* during the Imperial period, however, makes it highly unlikely that it was ever a colonia. A colonia had the greatest number of privileges of all types of Roman cities and once the status was granted, it was almost never revoked (Garnsey and Saller 1987 27-28).

3.7 Municipium Emporiae

Livy states that Caesar settled veterans at the site after his defeat of Pompey's forces in Spain (xxxiv.9.4). The enormous and rapid changes that began to take place after 45 B.C. at the site must certainly be ascribed to this new element among the elite of the town. Some time after the veterans arrived, probably in the early Augustan period, the Greek and Roman cities were legally joined. The new city was given the privileged status of *municipium*, which allowed the city to exercise a considerable amount of self-determination, including the election of its own magistrates and the creation of its own laws. Livy refers to this event (xxxiv.9.3-4) and it is confirmed by numismatic evidence. The legend *Untikesken* is replaced on the bronze asses after 45 B.C. by the legend *Municipi(um) Emporia(e)* (Villaronga 1977, series 17). A portion of a bronze tablet discovered in the forum shows the city had its own legal code (D'Ors 1967). Finally, public inscriptions dating between 32 and 2 B.C. show that the city counted seven different men as patrons, demonstrating that it was a significant urban settlement with important allies both on the Iberian peninsula and at Rome (Bonneville 1986).

The joining of the Greek and Roman cities and the subsequent prosperity of the *municipium* is reflected in the archaeological record at Empúries. During the pre- or early Augustan era the two cities were joined and walls separating them were dismantled. Luxurious gardens in existing villas were expanded into the new open space created by the destruction of portions of the city walls (Santos 1991). The area between the two cities had been used as a cemetery by the Greeks between the end of the fifth and the end of the third centuries B.C. Nonetheless, the new construction seems to have respected the existing graves (see chapter 4, section 4.6.3.2).

Another sign of the prosperity of the city was the construction of a large portico delimiting the space around the Roman forum and providing a backdrop for a centrally located temple (Aquilué et al. 1984). Over the next century the residents of Empúries added more temples to the forum and to Neapolis. In the latter, they constructed new temples to Asklepios and Serapis (Mar and Ruiz 1993, 178-179 and 285-294). Elite Emporitani also provided their community with a small amphitheater and a palaestra outside of the southern gate of the Roman city (Mar and Ruiz 1993, 341-343). Large numbers of amphora and fine-ware sherds found at the site from all around the Mediterranean testify to a vibrant economic life.

The fortunes of the city changed during the Flavian era (A.D. 69-96) for reasons that are not clear. At this time the building of monumental civic structures ceased while existing public buildings fell into disrepair. Sometime after A.D. 100 the east wing of the portico surrounding the forum collapsed and the structure was not repaired (Aquilué et al. 1984, 48). The large urban villas with their rich gardens were abandoned not long afterwards. Settlement receded into the original, more easily defensible walls of the island settlement, Palaiapolis (Aquilué et al. 1984, 48). Portions of Neapolis and of the Roman city show some evidence of continued use, of both a commercial and funerary nature. North African amphoras and fine wares dating to the second through fifth centuries have been found in primary contexts of shops inside the city and from secondary contexts in the cemeteries around the site. These provide evidence that Empúries continued to have an active port after the first century A.D. (Nieto 1981; Keay 1984).

New constructions at Empúries after A.D. 100 were few. In the fifth century a defensive wall was built around Palaiapolis (Keay 1984, 8-9). Perhaps as early as the fourth century, a Christian church was built in Palaiapolis, although the exact dating is problematic (Nolla i Brufau 1993, 216). A Christian funerary basilica was built in the ruins of a bath in Neapolis during the fifth or sixth centuries and graves were placed among the ruins of the northern half of the city (Almagro and de Palol 1962; Schlunk and Hauschild 1978, 162). Just outside the walls of Empúries a Christian church with a baptistery was built in the late fourth or early fifth century (Nolla et al. 1996, 233).

There is some epigraphic and historical evidence that the city continued to maintain a degree of regional importance, despite the diminution of its size. An inscription mentions a military detachment, a *vexillatio* from the seventh legion Gemin., which was stationed at Empúries between 163 and 191 (Fabré, Mayer, and Rodà 1991, no. 14.). A second inscription, dating to after 217, is the latest to mention a patron of the city (Fabré, Mayer, and Rodà 1991, no. 32). The fragmentary inscription commemorates the gift of costly metal decorations, probably intended for a statue of the deified Septimius Severus and his son Caracalla. Historical accounts indicate the importance of the town in the Late Antique period. Empúries was chosen as a bishop's see in either the fifth or early sixth century, one of only two episcopal cities, along with Tarraco, during this period in all of northeastern Spain (Almagro Basch 1951b, 107).

J. Puig i Cadafalch, a noted Catalan architect and archaeologist, suggested three possible explanations for the decline of the site after the Flavian era (Puig i Cadafalch 1908). The first suggestion, the Frankish invasion of the third century, is difficult to maintain as there is no evidence for destruction or disruption at the site during the third century and much of the site had already been abandoned by about A.D. 100. Puig i Cadafalch's second suggested explanation was that the harbor filled with silt. That this occurred can not be disputed because the harbor is now dry land. The silting of the harbor, however, must have occurred during the medieval period since the harbor was still serviceable as late as the tenth century (see section 3.8, below). Finally, Puig i Cadafalch suggested alterations in trade routes led to the collapse of the city. The large quantities of 2nd to 5th century A.D. imported pottery and amphoras found at the site discount this third explanation. Recently Mar and Ruiz have suggested that Vespasian's extension of Roman rights previously enjoyed only by the few select municipia, to all towns in Spain led to an erosion of Empúries's special status, an explanation that is certainly more plausible (Mar and Ruiz 1993, 415).

3.8 Sant Martí d'Empúries

The Empordà was little affected by the Moslem invasions of the early eighth century because the area was already depopulated and the Arabs only occupied the region for less than a century (O'Callaghan 1975, 106). The Carolingian conquest of Catalunya helped initiate the Christian *Reconquista*. The Carolingians made the Empordà a county in 812 and its first appointed count based himself on the island and former Greek colony (Aquilué i Abadías 1998, 39; Glick 1995, 106-107). The Frankish roots of the counts is evident in the dedication of a new church to Saint Martin of Tours, which then lent its name to the entire town (Almagro 1951a, 69). The port was apparently still open and in use as late as the tenth century. In 933 a Moslem general attacked Empúries both by land and by sea, sending ships into the harbor where he captured ships belonging to the count of Empúries (Nolla Brufau 1993, 224).

The city of Sant Martí suffered much destruction from artillery bombardments in 1468 during a thirteen-day siege led by King Juan II of Aragon who was suppressing one of the periodic revolts of the Generalitat of Catalunya (Aquilué 1998, 43). The inhabitants had to rebuild the city after this siege and the placement of streets and buildings does not seem to have respected the previous arrangement, with the exception of the church and its associated cemetery. Stones to aid in the rebuilding of the city were certainly quarried from the ruins of Neapolis and the Roman city. Two centuries later the site was used as a quarry once again with the construction of L'Escala and the fortification of two sites further afield, Roses and Perpignan (Mar and Ruiz 1993, 49).

The first significant construction to take place in Neapolis after the construction of the Christian basilica occurred over a thousand years later, in 1605. In that year a monastery dedicated to Nuestra Señorita de Gracia was founded on the site. The monastery building was constructed over the north-western end of the former Greek city (Mar and Ruiz 1993, 52). The monks used the ruins of Neapolis for the burial of their dead and converted one cistern into a small chapel (Mar and Ruiz 1993, 374). The Spanish government confiscated the monastery in 1835 after which the building was abandoned and fell into ruin (Mar and Ruiz 1993, 52). Other than the buildings of the monks and the village of Sant Martí, the areas covered by the former city of Empúries were only utilized for local agriculture.

3.9 History of Archaeological Investigation: Empúries Rediscovered

The Catalan antiquarian Pujades was the first modern scholar to connect the ruins around Sant Martí d'Empúries with the city mentioned in ancient sources. He included the first published eye-witness description of the site in his book of 1604 (Almagro 1951a, 164). The first recorded excavation campaigns using public funds took place intermittently over two years, from 1846 to 1848, and were concentrated in the area of the Christian basilica/bath complex. The excavations were one of the first acts of the fledgling Comisión de Monumentos de la Diputación de Gerona and helped supply the material that the organization would use to found its museum (Oliva Prat 1974). Private excavations and casual discoveries occurred throughout the 19th century, particularly in the area of villa 1. In 1849 farmers made the spectacular discovery of a figured mosaic depicting the sacrifice of Iphigeneia. The decision of the property owner, F. Maranges, to leave the mosaic *in situ* made Empúries an early archaeological tourist attraction (Barral 1986-1989). The Diputación de Gerona conducted one other excavation at the site in 1900, when agricultural activity again uncovered the remains of a building, what would turn out to be a temple in the Roman forum. The group uncovered a rich assortment of fragments of inscriptions and public statues (Oliva 1974).

In 1907 the Junta de Museus de Barcelona purchased land covering the southern half of ancient Neapolis. The next year Puig i Cadafalch led the first of many systematic excavations at the site (Puig i Cadafalch 1908, 150-151). The Junta de Museus, now the Museu d'Arqueologia de Catalunya, has sponsored excavations at the site nearly every year from that time to the present and, prior to 1936, managed to acquire most of the land covered by the remains of Neapolis.

Puig i Cadafalch's field director was E. Gandía, who made most of the decisions about how the site was to be excavated. Soon after he began to excavate at Empúries, Gandía decided not to dismantle the walls he encountered in order to excavate below them. As a result, most of the walls the visitor sees today in Neapolis date to the period of the abandonment of the site, the late first century A.D. Gandía also developed his own system for recording stratigraphy, an impressive accomplishment for the first quarter of the twentieth century (Cazurro and Gandía 1914). While Gandía published only one article about his work at the site, his notebooks can still be used to place artifacts he found in their three-dimensional location at the time of discovery.

Between 1908 and 1936 Gandía excavated all of Neapolis, with the exception of the port and the northeastern corner of the city. The latter fell victim to a plan of the Servicio Hidrológico Forestal del Estado to construct a road between L'Escala and Sant Martí and to stabilize the coastline by fixing dunes along the beach. In preparation for this work, the Servicio conducted excavations along the eastern edge of Neapolis in the early 1920s. Unfortunately, no record of this work, published or unpublished, survives. Today the northeastern corner of Neapolis is the only area of the Greek city not owned by the Museu d'Arqueologia de Catalunya and remains covered by the road and dunes (Mar and Ruiz 1993, 75-77).

The work of Gandía was interrupted by the Spanish Civil War, which had a severe impact on the site. Republican generals decided to locate a gun emplacement on the hill where Roman villas 1 and 2 stood in order to protect the Gulf of Roses (see fig. 6). Despite Gandía's objections, the gun emplacement was constructed, destroying the gardens of the villas and utilizing the cisterns of the villas for the storage of ammunition. Gandía lifted the mosaic of the Sacrifice of Iphigeneia as the guns were to be placed only a few meters away, and brought it to the museum in Barcelona for safe keeping. He also made certain that a museum, begun before the war in the ruins of a former monastery, was completed, thus offering the excavated material that could not be transported to Barcelona some degree of protection (Barral 1986-1989). Fortunately for the site, Nationalist forces never fired upon the guns.

3.10 Ampurias

No one who had been excavating at Empúries before the war continued to work there after 1939. Gandía died the same year the war ended. His assistant and chosen successor, P. Bosch Gimpera, went into exile in Mexico where he launched a highly successful archaeological career. Puig i Cadafalch, also in exile, turned away from archaeology to new interests, namely fighting Franco's suppression of Catalan nationalism. As part of that suppression, Franco outlawed publications in the Catalan language. During the Franco era the Greco-Roman city came to be called *Ampurias*, the Castillian version of its name (Mar and Ruiz 1993, 87).

Work began at Empúries almost immediately after the war ended. During the war the Republican government had appropriated most of the property within the walls of the Roman city for use by the army. The Franco regime honored that appropriation and allowed the Sociedad de Amigos de Ampurias, under the auspices of the Diputación y Ayuntamiento Barceloneses, to take control of Neapolis, the Roman city, and the road in between. Today only about one-third of the area inside the walls of the Roman city is still in private hands.

The director of the Sociedad, M. Almagro Basch, was a strong Nationalist who had the support of Franco's generals. They supplied him with Republican prisoners of war to renew work at the site (Mar and Ruiz 1993, 87). Almagro spent the beginning of his tenure at Empúries addressing problems that arose during the war. He did what he could to salvage archaeological remains from villas 1 and 2 as well as the space east of the villas, between Neapolis and the Roman city. Almagro also consolidated the remains excavated by Gandía, cementing many walls that were crumbling (Almagro 1940, 171-173 and 1941, 449-451). The quality of the mortar Almagro used was not high. Today, nearly fifty years later, the mortar has crumbled and deteriorated to the point where it is virtually indistinguishable from ancient mortar. Great caution must be exercised, therefore, when trying to determine the relative age of a building by examining its construction technique.

Finally, Almagro focused much attention on the necropoleis located south of the Roman city. These necropoleis were known to the people of L'Escala during the nineteenth century and were the focus of constant excavations, both by the owners of the properties and by clandestine excavators, all with the intention of selling the discovered artifacts (Cazurro 1908b). This practice was particularly common during the financial crises associated with the Spanish Civil War. Almagro did an impressive job of recovering what information he could from both looted and unlooted tombs and his publications on the necropoleis of Empúries are a landmark in Spanish archaeology (Almagro 1953 and Almagro 1955).

Almagro was a tireless investigator and initiated many new projects at Empúries. In 1947 he founded the Cursos internacionales de Prehistoria y Arqueología, a program for training a new generation of Spanish archaeologists. Graduates of the Cursos include many of Spain's currently practicing archaeologists. The first Cursos began as a collaborative excavation project with the Italian archaeologist Nino Lamboglia. Together they trained Spanish and Italian students in techniques of stratigraphic excavation in villa 2, the "decumanus A", and in areas of the Roman city as they investigated the forum (Almagro and Lamboglia 1959). In the late 1950s and early 1960s Almagro took advantage of the removal of graves from beside the church in Sant Martí to excavate the area below the graves, a rare opportunity to investigate the original Greek Palaiapolis (Almagro 1964). Throughout this work, Almagro found time to study and publish the material from his excavations in scholarly articles and books, popular guidebooks, and a newly created journal. Almagro founded the journal in 1940 and dedicated it to Spanish archaeology in general. The title he chose for it, *Ampurias*, reflected the importance of the site to Spanish archaeology.

Almagro's energetic approach to the site was not shared by his successor. E. Ripoll Perelló took over the direction of the site in 1964 (Mar and Ruiz 1993, 94). Ripoll continued excavations as part of the Cursos, concentrating work around the forum and beside the church in Sant Martí. Unfortunately, he published few of the results of his work. Later investigators published some of this material in specialist studies, but none of it has been published in a systematic manner. Ripoll did build up visitor and excavator facilities at the site, but Empúries lost its reputation as a center for dynamic and innovative archaeology (Mar and Ruiz 1993, 94).

3.11 Return to Empúries

The mid-1970s to the early 1980s was a tumultuous time in Spain. In 1975 Franco died, leaving the country to find its own way from dictatorship to democracy. In Catalunya, the Catalan language re-emerged and editors rechristened Almagro's journal *Ampurias* with its Catalan equivalent, *Empúries*. The directors of Empúries followed suit, inserting the Catalan spelling of the site in all new publications.

The lethargy of the 1970s at Empúries was shaken off in 1981 when Ripoll was promoted to the directorship of the Museo Arqueológico Nacional in Madrid (Mar and Ruiz 1993, 97). His replacement, E. Sanmartí i Grego, built a new team of young archaeologists and together they rejuvenated work at the site. Steeped in the tradition of New Archaeology, this group helped to introduce notions of hypothesis testing and the use of the Harris Matrix to all of Spanish archaeology through their instruction in the Cursos and publications of their excavations (Trocoli 1993, 47-56; Aquilué et al. 1984 26-30). Since the 1980s they have conducted a number of important excavations. The most important of these was the Roman forum excavation, which continues to this day. Other projects in the Roman city included the excavation of cardo B, the parking lot, and the southern city gate. In Neapolis they conducted a number of re-excavations of areas where Gandía had worked, including the Asklepieion, west wall, and Serapeum.

A positive trend that Sanmartí initiated was the restudy of material from earlier excavations. Although Gandía failed to publish many of the results of his excavations, he kept excellent notebooks. Researchers have used these notebooks to study specific deposits of finds (Barral 1986-1989; Casanovas and Rovira 1994; Campo and Sanmartí 1991, 153-172), certain classes of artifacts (Sanmartí 1978; Arxé 1982; Keay 1984; Campo and Ruiz 1986-1989; Barral 1986-1989; Mar and Ruiz 1993; Ruiz 1993), and the architecture of the site (Aquilué, Mar, and Ruiz 1983; Mar and Ruiz 1988). In particular, R. Mar and J. Ruiz de Arbulo have published an exemplary work that synthesizes all modern work at the site, including the unpublished notebooks of Gandía (Mar and Ruiz 1993). Their final chapter consists of a catalog of areas excavated by Gandía that were found to contain first century A.D. material complete with lists of all artifacts Gandía recorded finding, reproductions of Gandía's sketches of the artifacts, and identifications of ceramics using modern typologies.

The site benefited as well from Catalan government's preparations for the 1992 Olympics held in Barcelona. The Generalitat funded projects for new displays in the museum, the consolidation of portions of the ruins, the protection of the site through fences and a security system, the publication of popular books about the site, and the production of an award-winning audio-visual program. World attention focused on the site prior to the opening of the games when, in an elaborately choreographed ceremony, the boat bearing the Olympic flame landed at the site, symbolically re-igniting the torch of Greek civilization on the Iberian peninsula (Diputació de Barcelona 1993).

Empúries emerged from the Olympics in a fairly strong

position. The Curso continues to train new generations of Spanish archaeologists in modern archaeological techniques. The site's reputation for experimentation and innovation in archaeology is still strong. In 1998 the Curso included a new component in underwater archaeology, conducting explorations just off the coast at the site (Aquilué personal communication). Empúries is now one of the best organized and managed archaeological sites in the Mediterranean region.

3.12 Conjunt Monumental d'Empúries

The official name of the archaeological site is now Conjunt Monumental d'Empúries. It is one of Spain's most popular archaeological sites, with over 300,000 visitors per year from both Spain and abroad. In the past decade, a concerted effort has been made to present the main features of the site to the visitor (Pardo 1996). In addition to didactic signage and an audio-visual interpretation of the site's history, professional educators regularly present workshops for visiting schoolchildren.

Today tourists initiate their visit to the site south of Neapolis' southern gate where they park their cars (fig. 5). They enter the city through the gate and pass the Asklepieion and Serapeum. Along the paths that lead north are signs and multi-lingual recordings that describe, among other things, the "Torre Atalaya" (Watch Tower), a private peristyle house (structure 101), and a public market (structure 49). The paths lead them to the agora. Tourists generally browse the gift shop and stroll through the museum next, both of which are housed in the former monastery west of the agora. An outdoor snackbar near the museum gives visitors a chance to rest and refresh themselves. From the museum and gift shop, signs direct people to the Roman city (fig. 6). Walking up a hill into the Roman city, visitors encounter the villas 1, 2a, and 2b. They go south next from the villas to the forum. After inspecting the forum, some visitors walk south, through the southern gate. Outside of the gate are the remains of the amphitheater and the palaestra. A complete tour of Empúries takes about two and a half hours and can be quite exhausting in the summer sun.

4

CATALOG OF SPACE AT EMPÚRIES

...Iam illatis luminibus epularis sermo percrebuit, iam risus affluens et ioci liberales et cavillus hinc inde.

Tum infit ad me Byrrhena, "Quam commode versaris in nostra patria? Quod sciam, templis et lavacris et ceteris operibus longe cunctas civitates antecellimus, utensilium praeterae pollemus affatium. Certe libertas otioso, et negotioso quidem advenae Romana frequentia, modesto vero hospiti quies villatica. Omni denique provinciae voluptarii secessus sumus."

...Soon lamps were brought in and the table-talk increased, with plentiful laughter and free wit and banter on every side.

Byrrhena turned to me then and asked, "How do you like your stay in our home town? To my knowledge we are far ahead of all other cities with our temples, our baths, and our other public buildings, and besides we are amply provided with the necessities of life. Indeed we offer freedom for the man of leisure, the bustle of Rome for the travelling tourist of modest means. In short, we are the pleasure-seeker's retreat for the entire province."

Apuleius, *Metamorphoses* ii.1.9 (trans. Hanson 1989, 97)

4.1 Introduction

Apuleius places the above boast in the mouth of a native of a city in Thessaly, but a native of Empúries could have just as easily uttered the same boast to a visitor during the first half of the first century A.D. All the necessities of the Roman way of life, baths, temples, markets, as well as sumptuous private villas in which one could share fine meals with friends and associates, have been discovered at the site. Thus the site provides a splendid example of a typical provincial Roman city.

This chapter describes the structure of the site of Empúries by summarizing the data available about the site's buildings and architectural complexes. The primary sources of information are published excavation reports and R. Mar and J. Ruiz's excellent synthesis of archaeological investigations at the site, *Ampurias Romana* (1993). In addition to relying on the excavators' descriptions of structures, I also visited Empúries on three different occasions between 1995 and 1998 in order to examine every wall and building. In this way I was able to evaluate published interpretations and to formulate my own interpretations, particularly of poorly published areas.

One problem with attempting to describe the work of excavators over a period of more than 90 years is that there have been a number of different labeling systems used for identifying structures at Empúries, none of which have been applied universally to all buildings at the site. Thus a building may have two or more titles even within the same publication. The most comprehensive labeling system has been the one devised by Mar and Ruiz (1993). This system, therefore, is the one I have chosen to follow in this work. Mar and Ruiz designate each structure at Empúries with a unique number. They identified streets in Neapolis with a

unique letter and streets in the Roman city with the Latin terms cardo and decumanus, depending on the orientation of the street, followed by a unique letter. Where Mar and Ruiz failed to assign a structure number, the popular name of a complex is used in this text. For the sake of clarity, the other titles for buildings and streets assigned by excavators at different times, and still commonly used at the site, are given in a concordance, Appendices A-C. These building titles are in Latin, transliterated Greek, Catalan, or Spanish form, depending on the preferences of the excavator.

In addition to describing the different structures found at Empúries, this chapter also categorizes them according to their function. This is a traditional anthropological approach to describing architecture rather than the traditional classical archaeological approach which relies on form. The purpose of placing structures into functional categories was to make it possible to analyze the distribution of architectural complexes with similar functions across the site. The hypothesis which this system was designed to test was that there are patterns in the distribution of structures with the same functions across the site and that these patterns represent the underlying social structure of Emporitan urban society. This hypothesis was generated from my reading of the ancient sources on Roman cities which suggest that the distribution of structures with similar functions across the urban landscape had meaning to the inhabitants of those cities (see below).

Information about the excavation and function of every building at Empúries formed the basis for a computerized "space database" created using the database module available in the GIS program Idrisi 2.0 for Windows. I created an individual entry for each individual "space", that is to say each room or outdoor space (i.e. plaza, cemetery, etc.) at Empúries. Each entry recorded the space's categories of use based on the system outlined below, phases and periods of occupation, location within the city, as well as information about ease of access, period of excavation, and basis for the dating of stratigraphic layers. The completed database contained 1050 individual entries. Linking this database to digitized plans of the site, it was then possible to proceed with the analysis in chapter 5.

4.2 Categories for the Use of Space

H. Eschebach was the first to suggest that structures at a Roman city could to be categorized and studied by their function rather than their form. He drew a plan of Pompeii in which every structure was colored one of 12 shades to show it belonged to one of 12 functional categories (Eschebach 1970). This visual approach is quite useful for searching for patterns in the distribution of uses of space. Eschebach's plan of Pompeii makes it possible for one to see at a glance where all "common shops" were located and to search for patterns in their distribution. His idea also has enormous potential, particularly with the advent of GIS computer programs that make it easy to display a digitized site plan in a variety of colors and analyze the patterns in the distribution of those colors visually or statistically.

The problem, however, is that Eschebach's categories are too reductionist. His color-coded plan of Pompeii makes it difficult to see where structures with similar uses, for instance commercial structures, were located as these are divided into the categories of "common shops," "taverns," and "houses of trade," all of which are shaded differently. Patterns in the use of general commercial space are, therefore, obscured. The obvious way to overcome this difficulty is to create fewer, more encompassing categories such as "commercial space" into which all "common shops," "taverns," and "houses of trade" are placed and assigned the same shade on the plan of the site. Unfortunately, this leads to the opposite problem as one can not then search for patterns among specific uses of space by shading just "taverns" the same color.

Rather than choose between a "lumping" or "splitting" mentality for the categories of the use of space at Empúries, both approaches were used. Creating a four-tier hierarchy of the use of space, based partially on my reading of Vitruvius and other Roman authors, I assigned four levels of use to each room and architectural space at the site, moving from the more general to the more specific. For a complete list of the categories used in the hierarchy, see tables 4.1 and 4.2. These hierarchies are not intended to be comprehensive for all possible uses of space in all Roman cities. Rather, they are focused on the types of structures found at Empúries.

Entering this information into the space database, it became possible to link that database to the digitized plans of the site. This allowed for the display of very general information, such as the location of all private space at the site, or very specific information, such as the location of all public commercial bakeries. In addition, it became possible to abandon the idea of the hierarchy of uses and display the location of, for instance, all baths in the city, regardless of whether they were public or private baths. Finally, utilizing the dates for the use of each space generated from the dating of artifacts within stratified deposits, the computer could display very specific types of information, such as the location of all public commercial bakeries that were in use during the last quarter of the first century B.C. The database-map link provided a very powerful tool with which to search for meaning in the spatial arrangements of the city.

4.3 The Vitruvian Conception of Urban Space

In selecting the categories for the use of space and arranging them into the hierarchy represented by tables 4.1 and 4.2, I attempted to utilize categories that would have meant something to the ancient Romans based on both the literary and archaeological evidence. To determine how the Romans mentally categorized uses of urban space, I began by examining how Vitruvius' ten books of architecture are organized. Written during the reign of Augustus (27 B.C.– A.D. 14), Vitruvius was primarily concerned with urban architecture. While he addresses many issues of importance to the proper planning and construction of buildings, what is of interest here is the types of buildings he discusses and the order in which he discusses them in books i, iii, iv, v, and vi. This order reveals much about how Vitruvius and, presumably other Romans, mentally categorized urban space. Other Latin and Greek authors confirm Vitruvius' categorizations as will be seen below.

In organizing his work, Vitruvius describes a three tiered hierarchy for the use of space. The broadest divisions of the use of urban space in Vitruvius is between public and private, my category Use 1. He states, "building is divided into two parts; of which one is the placing of city walls, and of public buildings on public sites; the other is the setting out of private buildings" (i.3.1, trans. Granger 1955, 33). Thus his books i, iii, iv, and v concern public construction while book vi concerns private construction. Other authors agree that all space in a Roman city could be classified as belonging to either the *res publica* or *res privata* (Laurence 1994a, 68). Determining what land was public and what was private was the basis for many political and legal disputes described in literature and inscriptions (cf. Appian, *B. Civ.* i.1.7, id. i.1.9-i.2.16, id. i.4.27; Cic., *Off.* ii.21.73; id. *Att.* i.19; Livy v.55.3-5; Plut., *Vit. Tib. Gracch.* viii.7-ix.5; *CIL* I no. 585; and *CIL* X no. 1401).

In further subdividing categories of public buildings, Vitruvius makes a distinction between sacred and secular sites (i.3.1), my category Use 2. This is another very basic conception of space shared by other ancient authors (Laurence 1994a, 68; Crook 1967). The Romans assumed that once a space was declared sacred, it would always remain so (cf. Amm. Marc. xxvii.9.10; Livy v.52.13-17; id. vii.28.5; id. xlii.3.1-11, *Dig.* i.8; and Cic., *Verr.* ii.4.3).

19

Use 1	Use 2	Use 3	Use 4

```
                                                         ┌─── Tower
                                    Defensive ───────────┼─── Wall
                                                         └─── Storage

                                                         ┌─── Plaza
                                                         ├─── Portico
                                    Passage ─────────────┼─── Street
                                                         ├─── Hallway
                                                         ├─── Courtyard
                                                         └─── Stairway

                                    Administrative ───────── Meeting

                                                         ┌─── Bakery
                                                         ├─── Bath
                     Secular ───────Commercial ──────────┼─── Food
                                                         ├─── Market
                                                         └─── Unspecified

                                                         ┌─── Viewing
                                    Entertainment ───────┼─── Performing
                                                         └─── Storage

                                                         ┌─── Portico
                                    Educational ─────────┼─── Exercise
                                                         └─── Dressing

 Public ─────┤
                                                         ┌─── Ceremonial
                                    Sacred ──────────────┤
                                                         └─── Storage

                                                         ┌─── Courtyard
                     Religious ─────Passage ─────────────┼─── Stairway
                                                         └─── Portico

                                                         ┌─── Memorial
                                    Funerary ────────────┤
                                                         └─── Burial
```

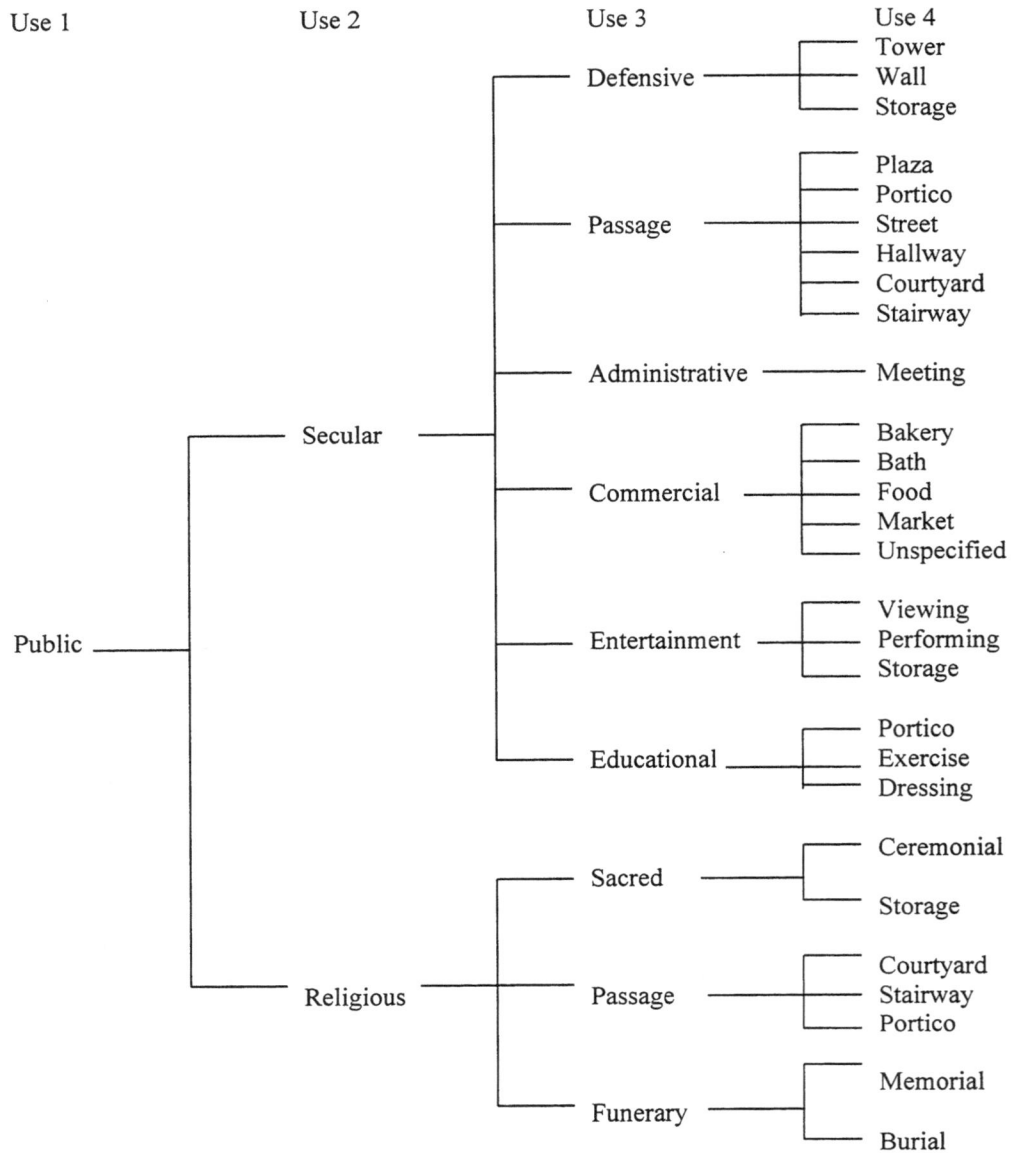

Table 4.1 Hierarchy of uses of public space

Vitruvius does not apply the same division of secular and religious construction to private buildings. Nonetheless, both the archaeological and the literary record have produced evidence for areas reserved for sacred space in private residences. Sometimes this space served a duel function, for instance the hearth had both a mundane use for cooking and heating the house and a religious one as the seat of the household god (cf. Plaut. *Aul.* 1-28). Other times the sacred domestic space would be marked by small niches in the wall that served solely a religious function (McKay 1975: 37 and 41). Occasionally there were also small altars placed in gardens or peristyles indicating that part of the space was reserved for religious use (see section 4.6.3.2 below). Thus the Romans seem to have also mentally categorized private space as either secular or religious. The omission from Vitruvius is to be explained from the simple fact that these niche shrines and altars required little if any architectural construction. Therefore, they would have been of little concern to an architect like Vitruvius.

The categorizations of the use of space under Use 3 also come from Vitruvius. Vitruvius does not place space devoted to the defense of the city into either the religious or secular categories in his introduction (i.3.1). This is probably because the Romans often conceived of the boundaries of the city as both a religious and a secular barrier (Grimal 1983, 345-346, see also below section 4.4.1). When he describes the construction of city walls, however, all religious connotations disappear and Vitruvius clearly considers them to be public secular structures laid out by the civic government for the physical defense of all citizens (i.5). Therefore, defensive space is classified in the hierarchy as a subcategory of public space.

Use 1	Use 2	Use 3	Use 4

```
                                                    ┌── Metal Working
                                                    ├── Kiln
                                    ┌── Industrial ──┼── Wine Production
                                    │                ├── Garum Production
                                    │                ├── Quarry
                                    │                └── Storage
                                    │
                                    │                ┌── Reception
                                    │                ├── Cooking
                                    │                ├── Dining
                                    │                ├── Garden
                  ┌── Secular ──────┼── Elite        ├── Passage
                  │                 │   Domestic ────┼── Bathing
                  │                 │                ├── Sleeping
                  │                 │                ├── Courtyard
                  │                 │                ├── Service
                  │                 │                └── Storage
                  │                 │
                  │                 │                ┌── Sleeping
                  │                 │                │
Private ──────────┤                 │                ├── Cooking
                  │                 │                ├── Dining
                  │                 └── Non-Elite ───┼── Garden
                  │                     Domestic     ├── Courtyard
                  │                                  ├── Passage
                  │                                  └── Storage
                  │
                  │                 ┌── Elite Domestic
                  └── Religious ────┤
                                    └── Non-Elite Domestic
```

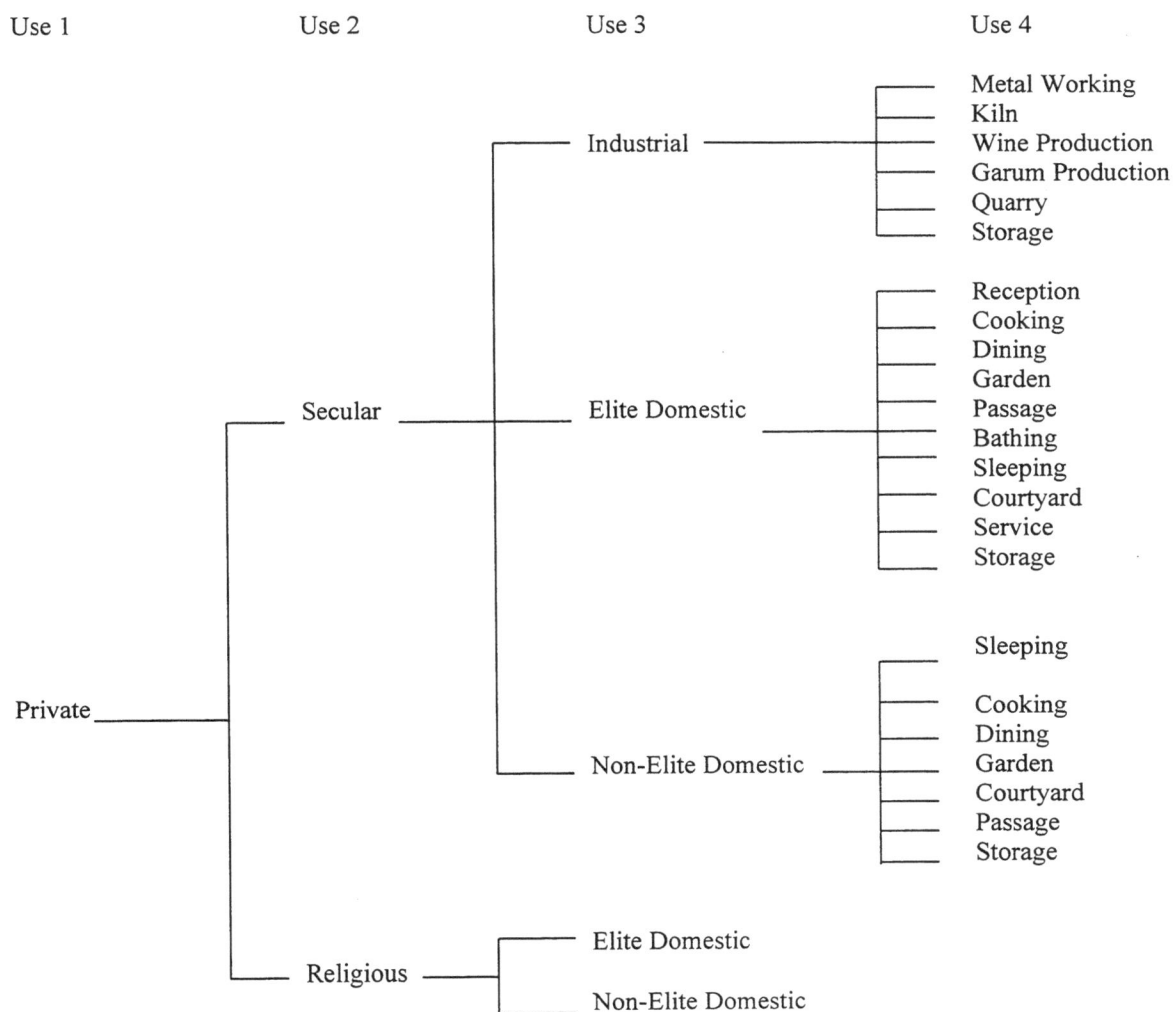

Table 4.2 Hierarchy of uses of private space uses of space

After discussing defensive construction, Vitruvius considers street networks or passage space (i.6). Following this, he turns his attention to other matters, not returning to public secular construction until book v, where he completes his discussion. Book v starts with a description of the forum and its associated structures such as the basilica, prison, and senate-house because, as Vitruvius explains, it is in the forum that, "…business, both of a public and private nature, is controlled by the magistrates" (v. pr. 5; trans. Granger 1955). Vitruvius clearly conceives of these structures as belonging to the same mental category, labeled in table 4.1 above as "administrative." Vitruvius follows his description of the forum with a long discussion of theaters and matters associated with them (v.3-9). This constitutes another distinct category of the use of public, secular space, one I have labeled "entertainment." It is not surprising that Vitruvius does not mention amphitheaters, as Rome's first permanent amphitheater, the Colosseum, was not built at Rome until after Vitruvius' time. His omission of the circus building is a little more difficult to explain.

The next section of book v concerns baths (v.10) and it is somewhat difficult, at first, to discern what mental subcategory of public, secular space this must represent. Baths were not a place for entertainment, so Vitruvius seems to be considering some new category of building. I suggest Vitruvius was considering commercial architecture at this point, as the bathers had to pay to enter the baths. It is interesting that baths are the only commercial structure Vitruvius describes in detail. He makes only one passing reference to one of the most ubiquitous types of commercial structures found in the excavation of any Roman city, the *taberna* or the one-room, all-purpose shop (vi.5.2). He also does not mention the *macellum* or market building.

Vitruvius rounds out his discussion of public secular space by mentioning the *palaestra* or gymnasium (v.11) and harbors and shipyards (v.12). Since the latter have not been excavated at Empúries, they have been omitted from table 4.1. A palaestra, however, has been discovered at the site. This was a structure used for instruction and physical exercise, therefore this use of space has been labelled "educational" in table 4.1.

Vitruvius devotes two books to temples and religious space (books iii and iv). While much in these books is devoted to the form of the temple and its precinct, it is still possible to discern categories for the use of religious space. Most importantly, Vitruvius seems to conceive of a category of space that is sacred. The cella, where the statue of the deity was placed, and the altar, set in front of the temple, were sacred areas that need to be visually joined during sacrificial ceremonies (iv.5.1 and iv.9). Contrasted with the ceremonial space is space available for people to pass through. Vitruvius mentions the portico of one temple designed to be wide enough to allow many people to comfortably await the end of a sudden rain shower if need be (iv.3.9).

One last religious use of space, which Vitruvius fails to mention, is funerary. This is perhaps because cemeteries were extra-mural or because funerary monuments were more sculptural than architectural. Nonetheless, every Roman city had space immediately outside its gates reserved for burials.

Under the rubric of private architecture, Vitruvius discusses primarily the houses of patricians, although he acknowledges that these must be constructed in a substantially different form from the houses of plebians (vi.5.2-3). Thus in the hierarchy of the uses of space private space is subdivided into the categories of elite and non-elite housing.

Completely absent from Vitruvius' work is any description of industrial structures. Nonetheless, industrial uses of space are prominent in the archaeological record. The placement of industrial architecture under the category of private space is based upon the evidence of relief sculptures as well as on literary evidence. According to this evidence it appears that work areas were off-limits to uninvited visitors and therefore were not considered public spaces. Based on his analysis of relief sculptures depicting workshops, T. Frank argued that iron working, felting, and commercial weaving all took place in workrooms that were separate from the rooms where the finished products were displayed and sold to customers. His evidence can also be read to imply that the production and sale of iron goods and textiles took place in completely separate structures from those where they were sold (Frank 1940, 187-188 and 262). Frank also mentions *Digest* xix.5.20.2 in which a silver smith is reported to have brought goods to a house for inspection and sale, which implies the site of production and the site of sale were separate (Frank 1940, 262). Classical Greek literature suggests that the Greeks shared this sentiment about the privacy of space devoted to production. Socrates is said to have taught his pupils who were too young to appear in the public squares in the workshop of his friend Simon the cobbler, thus implying that the workshop was not considered to be a public place (Camp 1986, 146)

The final subdivision of space, Use 4, is also based on both literary evidence for Roman ideas about the use of space and archaeological evidence, specifically as this evidence relates to the structures excavated at the site of Empúries. All of these divisions should be fairly intuitive to anyone who has studied the archaeological or textual evidence from Roman urban sites. Nonetheless, the textual evidence from Latin and Greek authors as well as the archaeological evidence form Empúries and other sites will be discussed in more detail throughout the rest of the chapter. As many readers may be unfamiliar with Latin and Greek architectural terms, a glossary is provided at the end of the text.

4.4 PUBLIC SECULAR SPACE

4.4.1 DEFENSIVE SPACE

Roman cities were surrounded by walls, which guaranteed and symbolized their right to self-government. Urban defensive space was made up of both the physical barrier of the city wall and a religious barrier called the *pomerium*. Founders of new cities created the pomerium during a ceremony in which they plowed a furrow where the city wall would be built. This barrier was inviolable (Livy i.44.3-5; Varro, *Ling.* v.143; Tac., *Ann.,* xii.23-24). According to legend, when Remus jumped over the freshly plowed pomerium of Rome, his brother Romulus made him pay the penalty in Rome's first fratricide (Livy i.7.2-3). While the pomerium and city wall may be considered both a religious and a secular barrier they are included under secular space in table 4.1. The daily impact of a defensive wall on the lives of residents and visitors to the city was much greater in the secular realm, defining the city and impeding movement, than in the spiritual realm. In addition, after the walls were built, they were not used in further religious ceremonies.

At Empúries Neapolis, the Roman city, and Palaiapolis were each enclosed by circuit walls. When Neapolis and the Roman city were legally united, the walls dividing the two cities were dismantled, and new walls were erected linking them. In Neapolis, walls have been excavated in the southern and western portions of the city. The Roman city walls have been excavated on the southern and eastern sides. Only one small portion of the Palaiapolis wall has been discovered.

4.4.1.1 Neapolis

The earliest extant walls around Neapolis were built in the first half of the fourth century B.C. The Neapolis wall only experienced one phase of expansion prior to the linking of Neapolis with the Roman city, implying that the size of Neapolis was, for the most part, fixed at the time of its foundation. Sections of the southern and western walls have been excavated, but no trace of an eastern or northern wall has been documented. Livy claimed that the Greek town was open to the sea, i.e. it lacked an eastern wall (xxxiv.9.2). It is impractical to test this claim through excavation. The area between the eastern end of the city and the Mediterranean is currently inaccessible as it is under 10 m high sand dunes. Nonetheless, it is suggestive that no trace of a city wall can be seen in photographs of the eastern edge of Neapolis taken prior to the implantation of the dunes nor in the plan drawn by Puig i Cadafalch in 1908 (Mar and Ruiz 1993, 81; Puig i Cadafalch 1908). Livy also claimed that there was only one gate to the city, presumably a reference to the southern gate (xxxiv.9.5).

Parts of the southern wall have been excavated by nearly all of the directors of the site of Empúries (Cazurro and Gandía 1914, 658-686; Almagro 1951a, 142-150; Sanmartí et al. 1986, 141-184; et al.; Sanmartí et al. 1989, 79-88) (fig. 7). The southern wall, dating to the early fourth century was made of cyclopean masonry and contained a gate in the center and a tower in the southwestern corner. Immediately outside the southern gate stood the Asklepieion. A second screening wall, called a *proteichisma*, was added in the second half of the third century B.C. Between 200 and 150 B.C., the southern wall was expanded to the south, incorporating the Asklepieion into the city (see section 4.5.2 below). The proteichisma was dismantled and the stones were probably incorporated into the construction of the new wall. Two towers were constructed flanking the southern gate and a third in the southwestern corner. Use of the southern gate appears to have continued until the latter half of the first century A.D. (Cazurro and Gandía 1914; Keay 1984). The closest parallel to the form of the city walls of Neapolis is the city wall of Tarraco (Tarragona), located less than 200 miles south of Empúries. These walls were built in the second century B.C. and were also of cyclopaean masonry. Despite these similarities, the walls of Tarraco appear to have been built by masons drawing on a Campanian tradition while those at Empúries were built by Greek masons during the fourth century B.C. and thus the similar appearance is probably coincidental (Dupré 1995, 356).

Gandía's excavation of the structures immediately inside the southern gate (fig. 7) produced an important discovery that provided the rare opportunity for identifying the use of tabernae. Gandía uncovered the remains of military equipment, including the metal parts of a special catapult known as a *scorpio*, the iron tips of 54 projectiles for use in the scorpio, and 1406 *glandes*, lead sling bullets, demonstrating that the one-room structures were used for the storage of military equipment. Their location so close to the main gate seems entirely appropriate, making them easily accessible to defenders on the wall and in the towers (Puig i Cadafalch 1911-1912a, 306; Puig i Cadafalch 1911-1912b, 671-672; Bosch Gimpera 1913-1914, 105-110).

Little remains of the west wall of Neapolis, most of it was destroyed by the construction of the monastery in the 16th century. The layout of the streets, however, suggests that there was a gate in this wall at the end of street 9 and that the street continued on towards the Roman city (see fig. 8). The only part of the western defenses that has survived relatively intact is the "Torre Atalaya" or "watchtower," and its associated structures, 16 and 17 (fig. 7). The tower stood on the highest point in Neapolis and, together with the other structures found in this area may have served as a military refuge from the first construction of the city. The tower was built in the mid-fifth century B.C. (Sanmartí and Nolla 1986, 160 and 189). The awkward nature of the terrain, a

characteristic that made this area desirable as a bastion of last resort, probably explains the lack of interest shown by the Emporitani in reusing the area for other purposes at a later date. At the base of the tower was a cistern, probably intended to aid the city's defenders (Puig i Cadafalch 1909–1910 709, fig. 11; Cazurro and Gandía 1913–1914; Mar and Ruiz 1993, 61 and 285).

Associated with the watchtower was a room, structure 17, found to contain 25 complete Mañá D Punic amphoras that were joined together by plaster to form a circular tank (Mar and Ruiz 1993, 61). Puig i Cadafalch noted that holes had been cut in the bottoms of the amphoras along the interior of the tank. He argued that water could be poured into the mouths of the vessels and emerge out the bottom after having been filtered by the sand or charcoal that may have once filled the amphoras. Puig i Cadafalch insisted that this water filter was associated with the Asklepieion, providing purified water for the rites which took place there (Puig i Cadafalch 1909-1910, 706-710). No parallel for the filter is known from any other Spanish site.

Puig i Cadafalch's interpretation of the feature is difficult to substantiate. The water filter is located in a space outside the *temenos*, or walled precinct of the Asklepieion, and to reach it would have required a rather awkward and lengthy trip. A much more plausible explanation for the use of the filter is that it was associated with the watchtower and filtered water from the cistern in the adjoining structure 16, making the water more drinkable in case of emergency. The filter was much more easily accessible from the watchtower than from the Asklepieion. The other rooms in structure 17 most likely served as storage for other military supplies.

4.4.1.2 Roman City (fig. 11)

The walls of the Roman city were constructed late in the second century B.C. when the city was reorganized and laid out on a grid plan (Barbarà and Morral 1982, 139; Mar and Ruiz 1993, 216). The base of the wall was made of a polygonal stone socle on top of which was placed a superstructure of *opus caementicum* (cement) poured into a wooden frame. The impressions of some of the crossbeams used to make the wooden frame can still be seen in the cement (Puig i Cadafalch 1908, 194).

The southern wall of the Roman city was pierced by two gates, one in the center of the wall's length, giving access to the *cardo maximus* or main north-south oriented street, and the other in the south-western corner. The central southern gate was adorned with a phallus, symbol of good luck and prosperity (Mar and Ruiz 1993, 212-216). The construction of this wall dates to the late second century B.C.

No trace of the northern or western walls has been securely located or excavated. Sections of the northern wall appear on a plan of the site drawn by Puig i Cadafalch (1908). On this plan there are some unlabeled lines with the proper orientation near the road to Sant Martí. In 1998 I inspected the ground in the area indicated on Puig i Cadafalch's plan. I did find some large pieces of cement similar to those in the other walls of the Roman city. These were not *in situ*, however, but suggest the wall had once stood nearby.

The Roman city was divided by an internal wall running across the entire width of the city, built at the same time as the rest of the city's walls, in the late second century B.C. (Mar and Ruiz 1993, 216). A little over half of the transverse wall has been excavated, although none of the information gained from these excavations has been published. The internal wall divided the Roman city into two unequal parts, the smaller to the north of the wall and the larger to the south. The excavated portion of the wall crosses three streets, blocking two of them but providing a gate for passage between the two halves of the city at cardo B. At an undetermined point in time, the eastern end of the wall was dismantled so that baths could be installed in villa 1.

At the time of the uniting of the two separate cities, new walls were built linking them and both the west wall of Neapolis and the east wall of the Roman city were dismantled. Little remains of these linking walls. In the north they have been completely destroyed by the construction of a road leading to Sant Martí and by a gun battery set up in this area during the Spanish Civil War (Mar and Ruiz 1993, 86-87). The southern linking wall was also affected by the construction of the road, yet parts of the foundation still stand at the southeastern corner of the Roman city and the southwestern corner of Neapolis. No evidence for the superstructure of this wall has survived. Only one feature has been excavated and published from along this wall, a storage pit used between the first and middle of the second centuries A.D. (Cazurro 1908a, 551).

It is curious that there is very little evidence for construction between these connecting walls. One would have thought that at the time of the joining of the two crowded cities, residents from both sides would have been quick to utilize the large amount of space made available. The owners of villas 1 and 2a took advantage of the destruction of the eastern wall of the Roman city to expand their houses to the east. In Neapolis, the owners of the structures 1 and 53 did the same, building into the newly opened space to the west (see sections 4.6.3.2 and 4.6.4.3 below). These expansions notwithstanding, there appears to have been no new construction in the intervening space. Indeed the Necropolis Martí, which was incorporated into the city by the construction of the connecting walls, shows no signs of having been disturbed at this time. Although the cemetery had ceased to be used in the third century B.C., the fact that there was no construction over the graves led Jones to conclude that the residents of the Imperial period at Empúries were aware of the existence of the cemetery and respected its integrity (Jones 1984).

4.4.1.3 Sant Martí

Little is known about the early defensive walls around Palaiapolis. Almagro excavated the only section of wall discovered thus far that pre-dates the medieval period. He believed that this section of the wall was of Greek construction, although he provided no evidence to support his claim (Almagro 1964, 97-98). This dating was challenged by Keay who argued for a fifth century A.D. date based on his revised dating of amphoras in the foundation trench of the wall found in Almagro's excavation (Keay 1984, 8-9). No other traces of the Greek or Roman wall around Palaiapolis have been found.

4.4.2 PASSAGE SPACE THE STREET NETWORK

Newly founded Roman colonies were often laid out with an orthogonal street plan, which provided the quickest and easiest way for organizing a new city. In contrast, the street network for older cities, particularly Rome and the cities of the eastern empire, grew naturally and often randomly with few straight lines. It seems to have been a source of embarrassment for Livy that Rome lacked straight streets meeting at right angles to be found in the western colonies (v.55.3-5).

The ancient street network of Palaiapolis is unknown but that of the late Republican and early Imperial Neapolis and the Roman city are well understood. The street network of Neapolis has been fully excavated while that of the Roman city is known through excavation and aerial photography. Streets in Neapolis are irregular, reflecting the growth of the original Greek colony while those in the Roman city were laid out in a regular grid pattern.

4.4.2.1 Neapolis (fig. 8)

The street network of Neapolis joined the most important points around the city. The principal streets led out from the agora. Street 2, the main north-south axis of Neapolis, linked the southern plaza and southern gate to the agora and harbor. The harbor was also linked to the agora via street 3, although this street was later blocked by Late Antique construction. Street 9 conducted traffic to the western gate. Other minor streets led from these main streets to the other portions of the city. Most of the streets were equipped with drains but few other public amenities. All were too narrow to allow for the construction of porticoes or sidewalks. Street 13 had a fountain and street 1 and the agora each had a well, otherwise water seems to have been drawn from private cisterns and the river.

The city had only two plazas, the agora (see section 4.4.3.1 below) and the southern plaza. The southern plaza gave access to the only two excavated religious complexes in Neapolis, the Serapeum and Asklepieion, both of which were reached by separate stairways from the plaza. The plaza was lined with shops on the north and was closed on the east by a complex of uncertain use. The plaza was created at the time of the expansion of the southern wall, during the first half of the second century B.C. (Sanmartí et al. 1989, 84).

The harbor of Empúries is one of the most poorly explored areas of the city. Aside from a mole at the harbor entrance, none of the facilities or associated buildings is known or has been excavated. Reconstructions of the ancient coast line indicate that there was little room directly north or northwest of Neapolis for the types of facilities one would expect in a harbor (Mar and Ruiz 1993, 332; Almagro Basch 1964, fig. 1). The most obvious place for such facilities is northeast of the city between the present ruins and the mole, in an area now beneath sand dunes and a modern road. Some walls now protruding from the dunes near the mole were constructed in a fashion very similar to the early Imperial buildings in Neapolis but, without excavation, it is impossible to know the function or date of these structures.

4.4.2.2 Roman City (fig. 10)

The orthogonal layout of the Roman city is a common feature of urban planning in the western provinces. On the Iberian peninsula similar layouts can be seen at many sites, including Baelo Claudia (Bolonia), Tarraco (Tarragona), Caesaraugusta (Zaragoza), and Italica (Santiponce) and others. The system was even adopted in some Iberian settlements, including Cabezo de Alcalá (Azaila) and Numancia (Soria).

The labeling of the streets in the Roman city at Empúries can be somewhat confusing. Classical archaeologists have adopted the Latin military and surveying terminology, designating all north-south streets cardines and east-west streets decumani. Originally Puig i Cadafalch improperly assigned the term decumanus to any north-south oriented street and cardo to any east-west oriented street (Puig i Cadafalch 1908, 184). Lamboglia and Almagro followed this system when assigning the labels decumanus A and decumanus B to the two eastern-most north south oriented streets (Almagro and Lamboglia 1959). In 1984, excavators at Empúries correctly relabeled the north-south oriented streets cardines or kardines and the east-west streets decumani, while maintaining the system of designating streets with letters (Aquilué et al. 1984, 367). The latter scheme is used throughout the present text. For a full listing of the names used by various scholars for the streets, see the concordance, Appendix B.

The Roman city was laid out on a grid plan at the same time the walls were built, the end of the second century B.C. The new construction represents a major reorganization of the city. The new streets covered over earlier houses, storage pits, and even a defensive tower (Almagro and Lamboglia 1959; Barbarà and Morral 1982; Castanyer et al. 1993). While the grid form has been recognized in aerial photographs, portions of only three streets have been excavated, cardines A, B, and C (Mar and Ruiz 1993, 216-218). The transverse wall appears to to have bisected all the cardines except cardo B. Gandía found threshold stones with pivot holes for a gate where cardo B intersected the wall. While he did not publish these, they can still be seen at the site. The walls uncovered by Gandía also prove that it blocked cardines A and C and presumably the other streets as well.

One of the principal streets of the Roman city, cardo C connected the southern gate with the forum. The street was lined with a portico of Tuscan columns (Puig i Cadafalch 1908, 185 and 1909-1910, 139). Two fragments of inscriptions found in the street were certainly in a secondary context, but probably came from public structures that once lined the street (Almagro 1952, 145; Pena 1981, no. 11). The street appears to have replaced an earlier street a few meters to the west that served the community and military camp prior to the reorganization and fresh laying out of the site (Barbarà and Morral 1982).

Decumanus C was another important street leading from the forum to the western city wall. Not enough of the wall remains to determine whether or not there was once a gate there. Until excavations are undertaken at the intersection of the wall and street to determine whether or not a gate was ever there, Pena's claim that this was the *decumanus maximus*, or the main east-west oriented street, is impossible to substantiate (Pena 1981). Decumanus C certainly did not meet a gate in the eastern wall as traces of the city wall remain, instead there may have been a gate one block further north along decumanus D. Decumanus D is the only street that is known to have linked the Roman city with Neapolis. Unfortunately, it is impossible to determine whether decumanus D exited the Roman city through a gate or whether the new path was created at the time of the dismantling of the west wall of the Roman city, as the area was destroyed during the Spanish Civil War.

4.4.3 ADMINISTRATIVE SPACE

The main administrative spaces at Empúries were the forum and agora, open plazas where groups of citizens could gather to discuss municipal and private business (cf. Cic. *Verr.* ii.5.58; Livy i.35.10; id. iii.44.6; id. iii.47.1; id. iv.6.9; Mart. *Ep.*, iii.38; Plaut. *Cur.* 474-475; Suet. *Aug.* 29). Types of structures associated with these spaces included the stoa and portico, that allowed people to escape the sun and rain, the basilica, a building where law cases were tried, and the curia, where the town council would meet. A few structures with an apparent civic use have been found outside of the agora and forum.

4.4.3.1 Neapolis (fig. 11)

The agora at Empúries is the only extant agora on the Iberian peninsula. The social and economic center of Neapolis, as well as a crossroads for the main streets, the agora stood in the approximate center of the city. It was reached from streets 2 and 9. Lined on its southern, western, and eastern sides with shops and houses fronted by porticoes, the agora was completed on its northern end with a two-story stoa, a long rectangular structure whose roof was supported by a wall in the rear and columns in the front. Excavators found the remains of several statue bases on the western end of the agora in addition to a well (Mar and Ruiz 1988). The well contained fragments of marble statuary and an inscription on a boundary stone with the word ΘΕΜΙΔΟΣ, the name of the

25

Greek goddess of justice.

This inscription led D'Olwer to suggest the agora was under the protection of the goddess, a suggestion followed by subsequent investigators (D'Olwer 1912, 675-676; Almagro 1952, no. 11; Mar and Ruiz 1993, 180 and 421). Such a conclusion is difficult to substantiate, however, as it is unprecedented at any other Greek site; one would expect the inscription to refer to a boundary of a shrine of Themis instead. A more plausible explanation, especially considering the discovery of the stone with other marble fragments, is that it had been brought to the agora from somewhere else to feed a lime kiln or for reuse after the city was abandoned. Gandía did not report the discovery of a lime kiln in this area, but he failed to report nearly all the post-Imperial structures in the agora as he had no interest in them.

The earliest construction date of the agora is not known. Originally it was approximately one-third its final size, the eastern two-thirds being occupied by houses. In the first half of the second century B.C. the houses were demolished and buried to make the open space necessary for the expansion of the agora (Cazurro and Gandía 1914, 681; Almagro 1947a; Almagro 1951a, 106 and 107, fig. 31; Mar and Ruiz 1993, 161). This open area was maintained in the Roman period until the end of the first century A.D. (Cazurro and Gandía 1914, 631; Mar and Ruiz 1993, 420-421; Campo and Ruiz de Arbulo 1986-1989, 154). A later structure, built in the middle of the agora, was probably associated with the conversion of the agora and stoa for Late Antique burials (Mar and Ruiz 1993, 160). Unfortunately excavators dismantled these later walls, without recording them or any associated artifacts.

The stoa, built at the same time as the expanded agora stood two stories high. The double aisle facing the agora stood in front of nine rooms and contained two cisterns. The stoa functioned as a meeting place for people engaged in political, commercial, and social business. The stoa at Empúries may also have served both as a monumental backdrop to make the agora more impressive and as a screen for the Tramontana wind, the fierce northerly wind that blows in the Catalonian region of Spain. It seems to have been abandoned at the end of the first century A.D., and was later reused for Late Antique burials (Puig i Cadafalch 1915-1920, 694-712; Almagro 1947b; Mar and Ruiz 1988; Mar and Ruiz 1993, 163-166).

Two other structures that seem to have served an administrative function are a bit more difficult to interpret. Both structures 69 and 102 have large rooms around courtyards and exterior façades of finely worked stone. In addition, structure 69 had a grand entryway flanked by two columns and reached by two low steps (Mar and Ruiz 1993, 344-345; Aquilué et al. 1983, 132). The size and decoration of these structures suggest they served an official function, although it is difficult to say anything more precise. Aquilué et al., speculated that structure 69 may have been an official storehouse (Aquilué et al. 1983, 132); the presence of stairs at the entryway, however, make its use for storage unlikely

as this would have hindered easy access to dollies and small carts.

Another stoa in Neapolis, structure 103, was much smaller than the stoa in the agora. Accessed from street 7, the stoa presented a façade of four or possibly five columns. The back wall was made of carefully cut limestone blocks fitted together with mortar (Mar and Ruiz 1993, 345). These blocks have a rough dressing similar to that of blocks in the Roman city wall, suggesting a Republican date for this structure. Inside the stoa still stand the remains of a base, probably for a statue.

4.4.3.2 Roman City (fig. 12)

The most important administrative space in the Roman city was the forum. The forum at Empúries was located in the south-central portion of the city (fig. 13). It consisted of an open area framed to the west, east, and south by an *ambulacrum*, or covered walkway, to the north it was bordered by an elaborate portico paved with mosaics built on top of a *cryptoporticus*, or semi-subterranean vault acting as a platform to raise the portico. To the east was also added a basilica and curia. The entire forum took up the space of four city blocks, the northern half of which was devoted to temples and the portico, while the southern half was reserved for open space, porticoes, and shops. The forum was built at the end of the second century B.C. in the area of the former military camp *praesidium*, or military headquarters. At this time only the northern cryptoporticus, central temple, probably dedicated to the Capitoline triad, and the southern shops were constructed (Aquilué et al. 1984, 237, 338, 339, and 342). During a remodeling in the early Augustan era, the eastern row of shops and the portico, along with the western basilica and curia, were added (Aquilué et al. 1984, 236; Arxé i Gálvez 1982, 58-60). Temples were added at various times to the forum, always in a line with the central temple (see section 4.5.3 below). The northern and northeastern edges of the forum were equipped with a tank, probably a cistern for public use. Several small rooms at the western and eastern entrances of the forum were probably used for storage of the equipment necessary for public business. Finally, the forum was adorned with a number of statues and inscriptions (Pena, 1981, nos. 2, 4, 7, 13-16; Aquilué et al. 1984, 116-132).

The Emporitani appear to have made a conscious decision to exclude commercial activity from the forum at the time of its remodeling in the Augustan era (Aquilué et al. 1984, 90). A similar decision seems to have been made with the remodeling of the forum at Conimbriga in the Flavian era (Alarcão and Etienne 1977; Mierse 1999, 213-220). At Empúries the doors of the existing shops in the southern façade of the forum were blocked and new doorways were made in the back wall, thus making them accessible only from the street outside of the forum and not from inside the forum. The new row of shops built at the same time along the west side of the forum were also only accessible from the street (Aquilué et al. 1986, figs. 6 and 7). Only one of these spaces could be entered from the forum, which suggests that it had an administrative, rather than a commercial, function.

At the same time the position of the doorways in the shops along the forum was changed, the entrance to the forum was modified, making it closed to cart traffic. The change may have had little impact on the shopkeepers around the forum as it would still have been easy for them to load and unload the goods they had to sell from carts or donkeys in the street. It would have had a large impact on the forum itself, however, making it a much quieter and safer place.

The latest public construction in the forum occurred in the Flavian era when two temples were added in line with the other temples (see section 4.5.3 below). Prior to the construction of the last temple, the western and northern wings of the cryptoporticus collapsed, allowing the new temple to be built partially overlapping the cryptoporticus (Aquilué et al. 1986, 234 and Aquilué et al. 1984, 109). The ruins of the northern cryptoporticus were re-utilized for the construction of several small shops, made accessible by the piling of broken and collapsed architectural members into a stairway. The forum ceased to be used in the third century A.D. (Aquilué et al. 1984, 231 and 330-333; Nolla 1974-1975, 163).

Basilicas and curias were necessary structures for municipal government. Legal cases and public meetings were held in the basilica (Plin. *Ep.* vi.33) while the curia was the meeting place of the town senate (Livy i.30.2; Varro *Ling.* v.155; vi.46). The basilica in the forum at Empúries was a long, narrow structure situated east of the eastern *ambulacrum*, separated from it by two steps. Typically the Romans would place the basilica on the side of the forum opposite the central temple, as is the case at Pompeii. The placement of the basilica on one side of the forum as it is done at Empúries is not unprecedented on the Iberian peninsula; see the fora of Conimbriga (Alarcão and Etienne 1977) and Sagunto (Aranegui 1987, 56-68). The builders took advantage of the wide streets of the Roman city at Empúries to build the basilica out into cardo B, giving it a bit more width. The western side of the basilica was delimited by a row of seven columns, thus allowing easy access from the forum. The substructure was of *opus incertum*, while the visible superstructure was of *opus certum*, a technique commonly used in Augustan period buildings at Empúries. South of the basilica, and only accessible from it was a small square room, approximately 9 X 8 m, which Aquilué et al. interpreted as a curia (Aquilué et al. 1984, 87-93). The basilica and curia were built as one unit in the Augustan period and continued in use through the third or fourth centuries (Aquilué et al. 1984, 184-196).

The public and administrative nature of these spaces is evident not only from their location, but also from the artifacts discovered in them. These include five pedestals for statues in the basilica and portions of a bronze tablet containing a *Lex Emporitana*, or municipal legal code for Empúries, found in the ambulacrum adjoining the basilica (D'Ors 1967, 293-298; Aquilué et al. 1984, 120). Fragments of stucco painted black, green, and red show that the basilica was handsomely decorated (Aquilué et al. 1984, 186).

One last administrative structure in the Roman city was located outside the forum (fig. 12). Although little of it has been excavated, its finely constructed podium and large size are still quite apparent. These features, as well as its location along cardo C between the southern gate and forum suggest a public function (Almagro Basch 1962, 7).

4.4.4 COMMERCIAL SPACE NEAPOLIS (fig. 14)

4.4.4.1 Bathing (fig. 15)

Baths were a common feature of a Roman city. They played a prominent role not only in hygiene, but in the urban social life as well. As many people went to the bath at some point in their day, it became a natural place to transact business, canvass for votes, and to meet friends (cf. Mart. *Ep.* iii.25; id. vii.34.5; id. xii.70; Procop. *Aed.* iv.10.20-22).

Only one public bath building has been excavated at Empúries, located in Neapolis. Unfortunately, the prominent remains of a Christian basilica and cemetery built in the Roman baths of Neapolis have made the area a focus for early investigators. The first recorded excavations in the area date to the 1840s; these resulted in the destruction of much stratigraphic information (Oliva 1974, 89). Puig i Cadafalch mapped the standing architecture but does not seem to have excavated in the baths (Puig i Cadafalch 1915-1920, 698-700 and 1913-1914, Plan 2). Almagro excavated two trenches with the intention of clarifying the stratigraphy; unfortunately nearly all of the datable artifacts he discovered belong to either before the Roman conquest or the Christian period (Almagro 1947b; Almagro 1951a, 115-117; Almagro 1952, 34-36). Almagro conducted other excavations here that were not published.

Palol first identified the public baths in Neapolis, although he had trouble specifying how all of the individual rooms were used (Palol 1957). Palauí and Vivó studied the baths with the aid of Almagro's unpublished excavation reports. They concluded that the baths were entered from street 3. They argued the bath consisted of a *palaestra* (open exercise yard), *apodyterium* (dressing room), *tepidarium* (warm bath), and a *calidarium* (hot bath). The calidarium was equipped at its western end with a small pool or *alveum* and a washing basin, or *labrum*, the remains of the base of which are still visible today. Palauí and Vivó also argue the bath contained a steam bath. They posit that the most logical place for the furnace was north of the alveum and west of the steam bath, although there is no architectural or artifactual evidence to support this claim. At some point, the steam bath was abandoned and the space was cut off from the rest of the bath by a new wall of opus caementicum. On the basis of similarities in form to urban baths at Musarna in Etruria and Baetulo (Badalona) in Catalonia, Palauí and Vivó dated the first phase of construction to between the end of the second century and first century B.C. They placed the second phase when the opus caementicum wall was added in the Augustan era and argued that the baths continued in use until the second century, although they offered no direct evidence for this range of dates (Palauí and Vivó 1993).

While Palauí and Vivó's interpretation is quite interesting, it is certainly faulty on this last point. The second phase of the use of this space does not represent the alteration of an existing bath in the Augustan era, but part of the space's later conversion into a Christian basilica. An understanding of the origins of the north wall of the calidarium is crucial for understanding its purpose and period of use. This wall is made of one enormous slab of poured opus caementicum, unlike any other wall in Neapolis. Sanmartí recognized, however, that this type of construction is found only in the wall of the Roman city, and claimed that the slab was originally part of the Roman wall and was simply dragged down to Neapolis for reuse (Sanmartí 1996-1997, 460-461). A comparison of figure 16, the north wall of the caldarium with figure 17, the southern Roman wall, shows the similarities between the two walls. The similar construction technique and the notches left by beams placed across the top to help stabilize the wooden frame into which the cement was poured are quite evident. Figure 18 shows the base of the wall and demonstrates quite clearly that it has been placed on top of the *opus signinum* pavement of the bath. Sanmartí assumed that the movement of this slab to Neapolis had to have taken place after the joining of the two cities, in the Augustan era. This would have been the time that fragments of the city wall would have become available for other uses, although one can not be certain how long after the joining of the two cities this event took place.

The niches in the wall, however, do provide one clue for the dating of this remodeling. These were not a feature of the use of the wall as part of the Roman city wall, as similar niches do not appear on any other surviving fragments of the city wall that remain in situ. Palauí and Vivó assume these had to have been added as part of the bath, because analogous niches exist in other baths from the Imperial period. There is, however, a much closer analogy. Immediately north of the calidarium is a room that unquestionably dates to the Christian phase of the structure and probably served as a *diaconion*, or room for the storage of utensils used in the Christian ceremony. In the east wall of the diaconion is a niche identical to that in the north wall of the calidarium, thus suggesting that these features as well as the wall itself, date to the Christian period (see figs. 19 and 20). The two niches are of approximately the same size, are placed at the same height in the wall, and are both plastered on the inside. Therefore the opus caementiucum wall could not have been an original feature of the bath and Palauí and Vivó's "steam bath" must be seen as just another part of the calidarium.

The conversion of the baths to a Christian basilica dates to the fourth or fifth century A.D. At that time an apse was constructed at the eastern end of the calidarium and the entryway was taken over to create a rectangular nave. The entryway stood to the south of the nave, while the small square diaconion, stood to the north (Sanmartí and Nolla 1993, 37). Access to the basilica was gained by descending a flight of stairs and a corridor, perhaps a symbolic way of re-enforcing the funerary nature of the building. The basilica at Empúries bares a strong resemblance to the basilicas of North Africa, the area from which the first Catalonian Christians probably came (Sanmartí and Nolla 1993, 37; Almagro and Palol 1962). The African origins for Christianity at Empúries are further emphasized by the medieval legend of St. Felix, a Christian martyr who traveled from North Africa to Empúries on board a merchant vessel in order to seek converts in Catalunya. Almagro believed that the grave at the base of the apse was a martyr's grave, containing all or part of St. Felix's body (Almagro Basch 1951a and 1951b). Christians turned the surrounding abandoned ruins into a cemetery that they used from the fourth to the seventh centuries (Puig i Cadafalch 1931a; Puig i Cadafalch 1931b, 150-151; Almagro and Palol 1962, 41; Oliva 1974, 89-90, fig. 1; Nolla 1993, 216; Almagro 1951a, 115; Mar and Ruiz 1993, 80).

4.4.4.2 Market (fig. 14)

Commercial activity in Roman cities was concentrated in the forum or in a market building called a *macellum* (cf. Livy xxvii.11.16; Plaut. *Aul.* 373-375; id. *Amph.* 1012; Suet. *Iul.* 43). Empúries is one of only two sites excavated on the Iberian peninsula known to have a public market, the other being of Baelo Claudia (De Ruyt 1983, 267). The Neapolis macellum consisted of four rooms that opened onto a large courtyard that contained a large cistern. The courtyard was directly accessible from street 2. Two other rooms had separate entrances from the street 2 as well. The western end of the building was built into a steep slope. This would have made it possible for the building to have a second story, directly accessible from the street 8 (Mar and Ruiz 1993, 344; Aquilué, Mar, and Ruiz 1983, 134). Street 8 was equipped with a drain that emptied into a second drain which conducted water into the *macellum*, down the courtyard wall, and out into street 2. The steep terrain that separates the level of the two streets by about 4 m in height made this arrangement possible. Of all the public drains known at Empúries, this is the only one that leaves a street and runs through a building.

De Ruyt has pointed out that the form of the Neapolis *macellum* is typical of *macella* across the Roman world. It is centrally located next to the agora, has the usual *macellum* layout of one-room spaces opening onto a central courtyard, and contains a public water supply (De Ruyt 1983, 313-326). The peculiar feature of the drain running through the building and the form of its construction confirms the public nature of this building. The walls were made of small squarish blocks and the foundation is of opus caementicum, features found only in other public buildings in the forum of the Roman city and in the Temple of Serapis. These buildings date to the end of the first century B.C., suggesting a date for the construction of the macellum.

4.4.4.3 Unspecified Shops (fig. 14)

The most ubiquitous type of commercial structure in any Roman city was the small shop or *taberna* (cf. Dion. Hal. *Ant. Rom.* iii.67.4; Livy i.35.10; id. iii.44.6; id. iii.48.5; id. vi.25.8-10; id. ix.7.8; id. xxvi.11.7; id. xxvi.27.2-4; id.

xxvii.11.16; id xxxv.40.8; id. xxxix.44.7; id. xl.51.5; id. xliv.16.11; and Varro *Ling.* viii.55). Anderson has called the taberna "...one of the most significant determinants of the nature of human space in Rome and in the cities and towns of the Roman world" (Anderson 1977, 334). These one- or two-room structures were employed for multiple uses at nearly all urban sites across the Roman world. They were typically accessed from a street, usually a major thoroughfare or plaza. Most tabernae probably served a commercial function, although some were used for storage (see section 4.4.1.1, above). In addition to their commercial function, they probably also were homes to the shop proprietors (Stambaugh 1988, 166). It is usually impossible to assign a more specific use to these structures, other than shop, and it is difficult to gauge in what type of commercial activity the occupants were engaged.

Mar and Ruiz interpret 50 of the structures in Neapolis as tabernae. To this list I have added seven structures based on my own examination of the architectural remains at the site. Each of these seven structures fits the definition given above, they consist of one or two rooms and open directly on to the street, but not any other structure. Despite their small size, some of the tabernae in Neapolis could be well decorated. Excavators have uncovered fine pavements and painted fragments of wall plaster in a few of the tabernae (Mar and Ruiz 1993, 349, 426; Campo and Sanmartí 1991). Most probably served a commercial function, although the remote location of structures 11-14 suggests they were for storage (Aquilué, Mar, and Ruiz 1983, 132; Mar and Ruiz 1993, 349). The tabernae located near the southern gate of Neapolis also stored equipment (see section 4.4.1.1 above). Structures 2 and 66 were built attached to elite houses (Mar and Ruiz 1993, 349). The house owners probably rented out these rooms for retail businesses.

4.4.5 COMMERCIAL SPACE ROMAN CITY (fig. 21)

4.4.5.1 Bakery (fig. 13)

Bakeries, or *pistrina*, met the urban need for the grinding of grain and the baking of bread (Ter. *And.* 219; Suet. *Aug.* iv; Varro *Ling.* v.138). The only bakery discovered at Empúries to date was located in the southwestern corner of the forum in the Roman city. The identification is based on the discovery of a mill powered by animal traction, a *mola asinaria*, and an associated oven. No published report of the excavation of this area exists, but stratigraphic evidence from other rooms within this complex indicate that it was built sometime in the first century B.C. (Aquilué et al. 1984, 80; Mar and Ruiz 1993, 353).

4.4.5.2 Prepared Food (fig. 13)

Roman cities frequently had small shops or, *thermopolia*, where one could purchase prepared hot food (Juv. viii.168). Aquilué et al. discovered a thermopolium just north of the forum, unfortunately they have published no plan and little

information about it. It was part of the macellum immediately north of the forum (see section 4.4.5.4 below). Its structure was found to have two doors giving access from cardo D, a counter top, and marble steps that led to a second story, probably the residence of the proprietors of the shop. A small oven and the reported discovery of at least two wine amphoras have led to the suggestion that warm food was sold here. The one-room nature of this thermopolium is unusual. Similar shops at Ostia and Pompeii usually had two rooms, one for the preparation and storage of food and a second for the customers to sit and enjoy their purchases (Anderson 1997, 329). The space belonged to a row of one-room stalls that were built during the Augustan era (Mar and Ruiz 1993, 352). The date of the abandonment of this structure is possibly quite late. Keay reported that a complete amphora found here was a Mauritanian Dressel 30, or Keay I b, which he dated to the last half of the third century (Keay 1984, fig. 19).

4.4.5.3 Meeting (fig. 13)

The *collegium*, or merchants' meeting house, is one of the best explored and published of all the commercial establishments at Empúries. The space was part of a complex of rooms built along the westren end of the forum in the Augustan era that continued in use through the third century. It consists of a single room with entry from cardo D and has a polychrome mosaic paving depicting the garlanded heads of banqueters as well as fragments of painted stucco in green, red, black, and white. The fine nature of the decoration of this space, the mosaic depicting banqueters, and the location of the space beside the forum led Aquilué to conclude that it was not a shop, but a meeting place for the members of a particular *collegium* or corporation (Aquilué et al. 1984, 93-97 and 224-230 and Mar and Ruiz 1993, 353). This interpretation is open to question. The presence of banqueting rooms was common among the collegia of Ostia, however none of the collegia are as small as that at Empúries, which consists of just one 5 X 5 m room. Furthermore, all other collegia had associated shrines, which the space at Empúries does not (Meiggs 1960, 324-330 and Hermansen 1981, 60-61). Fortunately for the purposes of this study, its form and location are clear signs that it had a commercial use; whether that use was as a taberna or a collegium has no effect on the analysis in chapter 5.

4.4.5.4 Markets

Like Neapolis, the Roman city also had a market building or macellum. Mar and Ruiz refer to it as the *Macellum de les cisternes públiques*. Unfortunately, this area has neither been fully excavated nor properly published. It consisted of two rows of single rooms with individual access from the central passage that separated them. At least one of the rooms, the thermopolium, had a second story, so it can be assumed that all did (see section 4.4.5.2, above). In the southeastern portion of the market stood a large cistern. This cistern had originally stood beneath the praesidium of the Roman military camp and survived as a public cistern in the subsequent conversion of the area into the city's forum. The construction of the macellum appears to date to the same period as the reforms to the forum during the Augustan era (Aquilué et al. 1984, 103). The macellum continued in use through the third century (Nolla and Aquilué 1984, 51-57).

Retail business was transacted not only in tabernae or the macella, but in the open air in temporarily constructed booths as well. Rome had many fora that were devoted to the sale of specific goods often from temporary booths (cf. Plaut. *Cur.* 474; Varro *Ling.* v.146; Livy. xxi.62.2; id. xxi.63.3; id. xl.51.5; Tac. *Ann.* ii.49; id. xii.24; Columela viii.17.15).

Empúries also seems to have had an open-air market. The two blocks south of the forum were left under-developed. The only structures discovered were a row of shops on either side of cardo C and a large unexcavated structure, probably for public use (see section 4.4.3.2 above). Almagro originally interpreted these two blocks as the central administrative forum of the Roman city, despite the unprecedented presence of shops lining a street in the middle of the area (Almagro 1962, 5-8 and Mar and Ruiz 1993, 93-94). Later, after uncovering the remains now interpreted as the forum, investigators assumed that this area had been left reserved for commercial activity in the form of an open-air market (Aquilué et al. 1984, 22). Unfortunately, Almagro never fully published a record of his excavation activities in this area and no work has been carried out there since the early 1960s.

4.4.5.5 Unspecified Shops

In general, the tabernae in the Roman city were larger than those in Neapolis. They were located either as freestanding structures along cardo C and in front of the forum, or embedded in villas 1, 2a, or 3. The tabernae lining cardo C are curious in that there were no other structures on this block, suggesting a large amount of open space along one of the main streets of the city (Almagro 1962, 6). The form of construction consisted of roughly squared small blocks set in courses, joined by mortar. This technique, *opus certum*, was common in structures dated to the Augustan era at Empúries, possibly offering a date of construction for these tabernae.

Villa 3 contained a total of 9 tabernae, 6 opening into cardo B and three into cardo A. Several of these were paved with *opus signinum* and two contained the base of stairs, suggesting the entire structure had a second story. Published ceramics, unfortunately with neither stratigraphic associations nor with precise locational information, suggest that all of the spaces which made up the structure were used between the first and fifth centuries A.D. (Arxé 1982, 43; Keay 1984, fig. 46, 5; Nolla 1974-1975, 160). A drain running from a cistern elsewhere in the structure underneath all three shops in the eastern façade may indicate that they were all owned by the same person or by the city and were rented out to individuals.

The shops surrounding the forum were built in two stages. The southern row was constructed at the end of the second

century B.C. as part of the original forum construction. At that time the doors of these shops faced into the forum. With the reforms of the Augustan era, a second row of tabernae was added on the western edge of the forum and the southern row of tabernae were altered so that access was only from the street, not from the forum (Aquilué et al. 1984, 93-97). It is difficult to assign a specific use to any of these tabernae, with the exception of the bakery and the collegium (see sections 4.4.5.1 and 4.4.5.3 above).

4.4.6 ENTERTAINMENT SPACE (fig. 22)

The only space excavated at Empúries known to have been devoted soley to an entertainment function was the amphitheater. There has been no theater or other structure for entertainment located at the site. The amphitheater provided popular, if bloody, spectacles for Roman urbanites throughout the Roman world including the Iberian peninsula (Golvin 1988; Tac. *Ann.* iv.62; id. *Hist.* ii.67; Suet. *Aug.* 29; id. *Tib.* 40; id. *Calig.* 18; id. *Ner.* 12; id. *Vesp.* 9; id. *Tit.* 7). Individual gladiators could become popular with crowds and their careers could be followed as avidly as modern sports figures. At Empúries, the discovery of a small bone figurine depicting a gladiator with the name "Pardus" scratched on it show that the Emporitani were no different than other Romans in their admiration of successful gladiators (Almagro 1952, 180).

Located outside the walls of the Roman city, the amphitheater of Empúries was a modest structure with a stone socle that provided a foundation for a wooden superstructure. Sanmartí estimated its capacity to have been 3343 spectators. Access to the central arena was through two longitudinal entrances and by one central entrance. The east entrance was the main entrance to the arena, the *porta triumphalis*; doorjambs provide evidence for two leaves which would have been opened to allow the combatants to enter or leave the arena. The monumentalization of the east end is probably because it stood near the south gate of the Roman city, which opened onto cardo C. Spectators would have entered the cavea, or seating area, via wooden stairs from the exterior of the structure. The space between the supports for the cavea provided for one-room tabernae accessible from the area outside of the amphitheater. Sanmartí believed that all of these structures were for the storage of the equipment used in the games; it is also probable, however, that some were used as small shops, particularly on the day of a performance. The amphitheater dates to the mid-first century A.D. (Almagro 1941, 449-451; Almagro 1945, 99-75; Almagro 1955-1956, 1-26; Golvin 1988, 121; Sanmartí et al. 1994, 119-138; Mar and Ruiz 1993, 341-343)

In two of the tabernae Almagro found two cremation graves, one of which had been looted. Almagro dated the graves to shortly after the construction of the amphitheater, based on the shape of an *unguentarium* found in one of the graves (Almagro 1955-1956, 15). As one of the graves contained a mirror, Almagro assumed it belonged to a woman and posited that these graves could have been those either of the patrons who paid for the construction of the amphitheater or popular gladiators who died in the ring (Almagro 1955-1956, 17). After restudying the ceramics from the graves, however, Sanmartí came to the conclusion that they date, in fact, to the period prior to the construction of the amphitheater. Sanmartí argued the graves dated to the period of Augustus and that they belonged to the nearby cemetery (Sanmartí, et al. 1994, 134).

4.4.7 EDUCATION (fig. 22)

The only structure identified at Empúries as having an educational function was the palaestra, discovered just outside the southern gate of the Roman city, and east of the amphitheater. Although a space devoted to physical exercise might appear to a modern observer as a place for recreation, this activity in fact formed a central part of education in Greek and Roman cultures (Pl. *Resp.* iii.403c-404b; Jaeger 1943-1945; Gwynn 1926). While private tutors in the home would normally give education in literature and rhetoric, public lectures in palaestrae were also common (Verg., *Aen.* 6.642). The palaestra at Empúries is the only freestanding palaestra known on the Iberian peninsula. There are other palaestrae known in Spain and Portugal, but all are attached to baths (i.e. the baths of Reina Mora at Santiponce; the baths of Trajan at Conimbriga; the baths at Baetulo (Badalona)). The palaestra at Empúries consisted of a central open courtyard surrounded by porticos on four sides, the southern side of which has been completely destroyed by later agricultural activity. Two sets of three stairs, one in the northeastern and one in the northwestern corners of the courtyard allowed access to the exercise yard. In the middle of the western portico there was a room of which only the foundations are preserved today. Almagro speculated that this small space, only 10 x 3 m, provided a place for the men to disrobe before entering the palaestra grounds. A more likely interpretation, however, is that the space was used as a small lecture hall. Palaestrae with lecture halls were common in the eastern Mediterranean during the Hellenistic and Roman periods (Delorme 1960). There are no other rooms associated with this structure. Construction of the building appears to date to the same period as the amphitheater, the second half of the first century A.D. (Mar and Ruiz 1993, 341-343; Almagro 1955-1956, 20).

4.5 PUBLIC RELIGIOUS SPACE

Public religious space could take many forms in the Roman world. Ceremonies were performed at small shrines, at statues, and in front of temples. Unfortunately, the only evidence for public religious activity that survives at Empúries are the temples; no small shrines have been discovered. Evidence for temples has been found in all three parts of the site, Sant Martí, Neapolis, and the Roman city.

4.5.1 Sant Martí / Palaiapolis (figs. 3 and 4)

Sant Martí's only church has stood in the same location for

at least 1100 years, and probably longer. The current structure was reconstructed in the sixteenth century, but an inscription preserved in the front façade of the building indicates that there were two earlier reconstructions in the thirteenth and tenth centuries (Almagro 1951b, 7). An altar table built into a wall of the church, which dates stylistically to the fifth or sixth century, suggests that a church stood on this location from an even earlier date (Nolla 1993, 216). A cemetery dating to between the fourth and seventh centuries discovered to the north of the church also suggests there was a church on this site at an early date. The pre-Christian history of this site is open to conjecture. A large column and part of a relief showing two back-to-back winged sphinxes, both found to the north of the present church, suggest that a monumental structure once stood in this area (Puig i Cadafalch 1915-1920, 707; Almagro 1951a, 67; Almagro 1964; Sanmartí and Nolla 1993). If this structure were a temple it was probably the one dedicated to Artemis of Ephesus to which Strabo makes an oblique reference (iii.4.8). There have been no excavations inside the church.

4.5.2 Neapolis (fig. 23)

Asklepieion (fig. 24)

The Asklepieion was excavated between 1908 and 1911. Puig i Cadafalch published the basic interpretation outlining the development of this sanctuary and few investigators have modified his interpretations. The identification of the sanctuary as one of Asklepios, the Greek god of healing, comes from the discovery of a marble statue in the area as well as ceramic feet and toes that may be votive offerings of a kind common in Asklepieia (Puig i Cadafalch 1911-1912a, 311 and 317). The life-size, nearly complete statue is an extraordinary piece. The torso is made of Parian marble, the lower body, of Pentelic marble, and the serpent at his feet is made of marble from the Pyrenees (Álvarez i Pérez and Bru de Sala, 1983-1984, 300). There has been a long debate over the dating of the statue; currently the third century B.C. is the most widely accepted date (Mar and Ruiz 1993, 171). The presence of a Greek statue on the opposite side of the Mediterranean from the apparent site of its production and its embellishment by a local artist is intriguing. Sanmartí and Nolla suggest the Romans brought it to Empúries after their conquest of Greece, although it is, in fact, impossible to know when the statue arrived Empúries (Sanmartí and Nolla 1993, 27).

The sanctuary of Asklepios went through three phases of development. In the first phase, dating to before the second century B.C., the area consisted of two altars, one a double altar and the second a large altar of the Hellenistic type. Both altars were approached via stairs from the west. A temenos wall surrounded the double altar. Between the altars stood a well approximately 3 m deep (Mar and Ruiz 1993, 174-176). There is no direct evidence that this sanctuary was dedicated to Asklepios at this period, but given the statue of the god was found associated with temples in a later phase, it is logical to assume that the dedication of the sanctuary was the same in the earlier period. The sanctuary stood outside of the city walls during this phase, a placement which may have been one way the Greeks attempted to sustain good relations with the local Iberians (Sanmartí 1993a, 21). There is some epigraphic evidence that Iberians used the sanctuary during this period (Almagro 1952, 71-73).

The second phase dates to the first half of the second century B.C. (Puig i Cadafalch 1909-1910, 707; Mar and Ruiz 1993, 177). This was the period of the extension of the Neapolis southern wall (see section 4.4.1.1, above), a process which incorporated the sanctuary into the city. It is interesting that after the extension of the south wall, the Asklepieion was on the edge of town. It was common for temple precincts of Asklepios to be placed on the edge of, or away from, cities as is seen at Corinth, Rome, and Pergamon (Kerényi 1959). The Asklepieion at Empúries has a second feature in its placement common to temples of Asklepios: it is placed beside or on the acropolis of the site. Such a placement is also seen at Carthage and Athens (Walton 1979, 36).

The Neapolis sanctuary itself was greatly modified once it was brought into the city. A terrace wall was built at its eastern end, allowing for the construction of a level surface raised well above the newly constructed street that bordered the precinct to the east. The Hellenistic altar and the double altar were buried by the newly created terrace, and two small tetrastyle temples were built (Puig i Cadafalch's "cel-la P", and "cel-la M"), both with pavements of *opus signinum*. Gandía discovered the lower half of the statue of Asklepios in cel-la M, suggesting the temple had been dedicated to Asklepios (Casellas 1911, 284; Albertini 1911-1912, 467). The only vestige of the earlier sanctuary to survive was the well, which was incorporated into the *pronaos* of cel-la P. Access to the temples was gained from the southern plaza via a tall stairway, reminiscent of the Hellenistic Asklepieion at Kos. It could also be reached via a narrow passageway and stair which led between the temples and behind cel-la M to the open area around the watchtower (Puig i Cadafalch 1911-1912a, 307-310; Mar and Ruiz 1993, 176-178).

During the third phase, the precinct experienced more radical changes. A new temple (Puig i Cadafalch's "cel-la C") was built in the southern portion of the precinct. Unfortunately, only the foundations of a cella and a *pronaos* reached by a stairway remain. An altar was built just south of this temple, almost directly above the double altar, which was buried in the terrace. A large cistern was added in front of the temples destroying the stairs of the Hellenistic altar that were still preserved within the terrace. Another addition was a portico in the northern portion of the precinct, which was equipped with a drain that allowed water from this area to be fed into the cistern (Puig i Cadafalch 1911-1912a, 307-310; Mar and Ruiz 1993, 178-179). This may have been an *abaton*, the place where the sick slept in hopes that Asklepios would send them a dream in which he outlined their cure. The abaton in the precinct of Asklepios in Epidaurus is placed in a similar position, immediately north of the temple (Mar and Ruiz 1993, 182; Sanmartí and Nolla 1993, 26). This phase probably dates to the first century B.C. temple (Mar and Ruiz 1993, 179).

The Asklepieion was richly decorated with marble. Casellas recorded the discovery of many fragments of marble statuary and architectural embellishments (Casellas 1911; Mar and Ruiz 1993, 62). While much of this material certainly decorated the precinct, some was likely moved there after the Asklepieion was abandoned. A lime kiln located a short distance north of the temple precinct may indicate that some farmer or mason had gathered the marble fragments together in this area to burn (Mar and Ruiz 1993, 171).

Serapeum (fig. 25)

The story of the identification of the Serapeum at Empúries is as much an epigraphic as it is an archaeological one. Excavation began in the precinct in 1908 and within three years enough had been uncovered to allow for its identification. Puig i Cadafalch was able to connect the porticoes and temple in this plaza to the god Serapis by the discovery of a dedicatory inscription. This inscription was found at the southern gate of Neapolis and records the erection of a temple portico to Serapis (Puig i Cadafalch 1911-1912a, 314; Mar and Ruiz 1993, 285 and 292). The same year Gandía uncovered this inscription he found another bilingual Greek and Latin inscription in the cistern near the watchtower (section 4.4.1.1). It was not until the 1950s that Almagro realized the two inscriptions were part of the same stone and was thus able to restore a major portion of the inscription (Almagro 1952, 18-19). The different find spots of the two pieces of the stone can be attributed to the movement of marble up to the lime kiln for burning. Several scholars have made contributions to the reading of this stone, the most important of which was made by Vidman, who argued that there was enough room in the first line for the insertion of the name of Isis (Vidman 1969, nos. 767 and 768). The currently accepted reading of the inscription is that a native of Alexandria, Numa, son of Numenius, dedicated a temple to Isis and Serapis adorned with porticoes and statues (Fabré, Mayer, Rodà 1991, no. 15).

The precinct went through three phases of construction. The area was included within the walls of Neapolis when the southern city walls were extended to the south at the end of the second century B.C. (see section 4.4.1.1 above). This expansion provided room for the construction of a large terrace, which was entered via stairs from the southern plaza. At the western end of the terrace the open space next to the tower was enclosed. It is impossible to say what structures stood on the terrace as it was altered by later construction (Mar and Ruiz 1993, 286).

During the second phase, builders raised the level of the terrace by almost 2 m, constructed a Doric portico around the terrace, and converted the space at the western end into two rooms. Presumably the portico circled the terrace on all four sides; the eastern side, however, did not survive the construction of the modern road to Sant Martí (Mar and Ruiz 1993, 286-290; Puig i Cadafalch 1911-1912a 316-320). The western end of the plaza was provided with a finely-made drain for collecting and distributing water. Elaborate water collection and distribution systems are common in sanctuaries of Isis and Serapis (e.g. Pompeii) because water was thought to have important symbolic and magical qualities (Takács 1995, 151). These modifications are difficult to date, but they surely occurred between the end of the second and the end of the first centuries B.C. (Mar and Ruiz 1993, 229; Sanmartí 1978, nos. 99-103).

In the final phase of construction, workers, probably in the employ of the Numa mentioned in the inscription, rebuilt the portico several meters further west to make room in the western end of the plaza for the temple dedicated to Serapis. The temple stood on a podium made of an opus caementicum core, sheathed in well-cut blocks. The temple was a small tetrastyle, prostyle building approached from the sides by two stairways (Mar and Ruiz 1993, 390-392; Puig i Cadafalch 1911-1912a, 320-322). There is no stratigraphic data available to help date the construction of the building, but the *cyma reversa* molding on the podium is identical to the molding on the podium of the central temple in the forum which dates to the Augustan era. The temple of Serapis, therefore, is almost certainly Augustan in date as well (Mar and Ruiz 1993, 292). Mar and Ruiz speculate that the rooms on the western end of the plaza were dedicated as a second sacred space to the cult of the goddess Isis. As evidence, they point to the similarity in layout of the plaza, with its portico and small rooms in the west, with the Serapeum on Delos and Temple E, also thought to be a Serapeum, at Soli on Cyprus (Mar and Ruiz 1993, 293).

The cult of Serapis was popular on the Iberian peninsula. Although the Serapeum at Empúries is the only structure found to date associated with Serapis, a number of inscriptions discovered in modern Spain and Portugal testify that individuals and groups of devotees worshiped the god (Wagner and J. Alvar 1980, 329). Wagner and Alvar argue that worshippers of the god were nearly always either Italian immigrants or highly Romanized natives (Wagner and J. Alvar 1980, 333). In the case of Empúries, however, the presence of an Alexandrian mentioned in the dedicatory inscription, in a trading port supports the idea proposed by Takács that the cults of Isis and Serapis were spread along lines of commerce (Takács 1995).

4.5.3 Roman City Forum (fig. 13)

The only known temples in the Roman city of Empúries are in the forum. Nine temples stand in a row in the forum's northern half. Behind the temples was an open space from which it was possible to reach the cisterns, or a *nympheum*. This back area was completely cut off from the rest of the forum during the late Republican period by a low wall open only at the point of the central temple and altar (Mar and Ruiz 1993, 282-283). The wall was later replaced by the row of temples. Several small fragments of statuary found in this area may actually have fallen from porticus behind the temples when it collapsed (Aquilué et al. 1984, 115-121).

The largest and the oldest of the temples in the forum is the central one, probably dedicated to the Capitoline triad. Set in the middle of the forum, it is aligned with the southern

entrance to the forum, cardo C, and the southern gate. The temple sat atop a podium made of opus caementicum covered by a façade of cut stones sheathed in stucco. The tetrastyle temple was made of opus caementicum, which was also covered by a façade of stone. The column capitals were of the Corinthian order. The single cella was paved with a floor of *opus signinum*, the design of which does not survive. Access to the temple was from a frontal stairway; later stairs were added on the eastern and western sides. A large altar stood in front of the temple (Aquilué et al. 1984, 48-62 and 241-252; Aquilué et al. 1986, 228-230; Mar and Ruiz 1993, 218-224 and 282-285). The temple and altar were built at the end of the second or beginning of the first centuries B.C. The area continued to be used through the third or fourth centuries (Aquilué et al. 1984, 265-268).

Later the other eight temples were added to the forum in a seemingly haphazard fashion. There appears to have been no attempt to arrange these later temples in a symmetrical fashion about the axis created by the central temple. All of the temples post-date the construction of the central temple. The two temples on the western side of the forum were the last two constructed. These last two temples were built overlapping the base of the cryptoporticus. This indicates that the temples' constructions post-date the collapse of the cryptoporticus, and that they were thus built in, or after, the Flavian era. With the exception of the central temple, there are no published records of the excavation of these structures (Aquilué et al. 1984, 109). An inscription found near the later temples records the construction of a temple and the dedication of a statue to the goddess Tutela, a guardian deity. The proximity of the temple and inscription led Pena to conclude that one of the late temples was dedicated to Tutela (Pena 1981, 14-16). Fabré et al. argue against this identification because the lettering of the inscription is of an Augustan date, prior to the temple's construction (Fabré et al. 1991, no. 17).

4.5.4 Cemeteries (fig. 26)

Another required feature of Roman cities was the cemetery. Typically located outside the city walls, cemeteries were considered sacred places where one could offer sacrifices to the dead (Juv. i.170-171; Plaut., *Cas.* 353). They were also places where one could communicate with malevolent spirits. The discovery of curse tablets placed in a glass cinerary urn and buried in the Necropolis Ballesta show the Emporitani performed magical ceremonies in their cemeteries as well (Almagro 1955: 60-62; Fabré et al. 1991, 159-163).

Excavations in the lot adjoining the church in Sant Martí in 1955, 1962, and 1975 revealed the existence of a cemetery. Only the 1955 and 1962 excavations have been properly published (Almagro 1964); the 1975 excavation was partially published as a part of Keay's analysis of the late-period amphoras at Empúries (Keay 1984). This area was disturbed at various times in its history and the area of excavation was constricted by surrounding buildings, making interpretations difficult. Nonetheless, it seems clear that the lot was used as a cemetery between the fourth and sixth centuries.

The only cemetery found within the walls of Neapolis also dates to the Late Antique and early medieval periods. There were numerous Late Antique and modern graves found in the northern half of Neapolis. Most of these graves had been dug in or near the Christian funerary basilica that was installed in the public baths after the city had been abandoned (see section 4.4.4.1 above).

During the Republican and Imperial periods, the majority of the dead were interred outside the walls of the city. There were a number of cemeteries located primarily south of the Roman city and Neapolis. Of these, only one preserved a monument above ground, the Necropolis at Castellet. Most of the cemeteries were destroyed and looted during the end of the nineteenth and first half of the twentieth centuries. Almagro salvaged what he could in excavations during the 1950s. Although most of these cemeteries probably formed part of a few larger cemeteries, Almagro excavated different parcels of privately owned land, naming the cemeteries after the owners. Almagro found the earliest graves in the Bonjoan, Les Coves, Granada, Martí, Mateu, Parralli, and Portichol cemeteries to date to the fifth and sixth centuries B.C. (Almagro 1952; Almagro 1953; Keay 1984). Sanmartí et al. found a fourth to third century B.C. cemetery immediately outside the gates of Neapolis under the modern visitor's parking lot (Sanmartí et al. 1983-1984). The Bonjoan, Les Coves, and Granada cemeteries continued in use through the Augustan era while the Parking Lot, Martí, Mateu, Parralli, and Portichol cemeteries fell out of use. Other extra-mural cemeteries were created during the Roman era at Ballesta, Castellet, Las Corts, Estruch, Mitjavila, Nofre, Patel, Pí, Rubert, Sabadí, Torres, and Viñals (Almagro 1952, 101; Almagro 1955; Keay 1984). The Castellet, Estruch, and Rubert cemeteries were the latest to be used; new graves continued to be dug into the fifth and sixth centuries (Almagro 1955; Keay 1984).

4.6 PRIVATE SPACE

4.6.1 INDUSTRIAL

Manufacturers in the city met many of the needs the Emporitani had for goods. Evidence has been found for the production of iron goods, ceramics, and fish sauce. In addition, there are several industrial establishments that are difficult to identify. Manufacturing seems to have taken place both inside and outside the city's walls.

4.6.1.1 Metal Working (fig. 27)

Structure 29 was a small two-room structure in Neapolis. The room closest to the street contains the remains of a forge made of uncut stones. Quantities of iron slag found in this same room suggest the forge was used for the production of iron goods (Mar and Ruiz 1993, 71, fig. A, 410). The forge was semi-circular and faced the eastern wall with an opening

to the south. The adjoining space could have been either the residence for the artisan who used the forge or his storeroom and workshop. The use of cement in the construction of the walls suggests that it dates to the Augustan era or later.

Structure 57 was an elite house in Neapolis whose peristyle was modified for metalworking. The space was built around a tiny peristyle courtyard entered from street 2 by way of a *fauces*, or hallway. The courtyard was equipped with a cistern, a 10-meter-deep well, and a portico supported by four columns on a side. Two rooms were accessible from the courtyard. At some point a forge was added to the courtyard, probably taking advantage of the proximity of the cistern and well for water. One other piece of metallurgical equipment included a sluice, probably for washing raw ores. Mar and Ruiz interpreted a bronze spear head found in the courtyard as one example of the artisan's production, indicating that the forge was used for bronze working (Mar and Ruiz 1993, 387; Puig i Cadafalch 1915-1920, 703).

In the early 1980s, Sanmartí conducted an excavation in the visitor's parking lot of the site, immediately outside the southern gate of Neapolis in the hopes of locating remains of the original Iberian settlement, Indika. He did not find an Iberian city, but he did find an interesting succession of structures. Originally a Greek cemetery, the area was converted to use by the Romans immediately after their arrival. In the second century B.C., a building was constructed on top of the Greek graves with *opus africanum* walls, a technique common in Campania in the early second century B.C., the date of the building's construction (Sanmartí et al. 1983-1984, 134; Keay, 1983-1984, 151). The building was abandoned and re-utilized for metal working in the late second century B.C. (Sanmartí et al. 1983-1984, 146-149). The metalworking equipment included two circular furnaces, several sluices for washing raw ores, and a well. In addition, quantities of lead waste and a small silver ingot suggest the area was used for the production of silver. Unfortunately, too little of the structure was excavated to allow for an explanation of how the metalworking was organized. The metalworking establishment was buried in the mid-first century A.D. when a press was constructed over its ruins (Sanmartí et al. 1983-1984, 150; Keay, 1983-1984, 151).

Other industrial establishments were also located outside the walls of Empúries. In the 1990s Sanmartí noted curious piles of slag, often filling natural cavities in the stone, immediately outside of Neapolis, at the base of the mole protecting the entrance to the harbor, and on the promontory of Les Coves. He interpreted these as the remains of bloomeries for the smelting activities that transformed raw iron ore to refined metal. Iron smiths utilized these fissures and holes in the rock for ventilation and as ducts to draw off purified iron during the initial smelting of raw iron ore. Sanmartí believed these to be evidence for ancient iron working, although this activity could not be dated (Sanmartí 1995, 163-164). Their position on top of the stones which form the base of the mole at least prove that they post-date the construction of the mole (Sanmartí 1995, 158).

4.6.1.2 Ceramics Kilns (fig. 27)

Four ceramics kilns have been found in Neapolis. The remains of the pair located in the north of the city, structure 72, clearly post-date the abandonment of Neapolis as they were constructed over the remains of buildings of the city. The pair of kilns may have been contemporary with the use of the site for a monastery in the 16th century.

The other two kilns in Neapolis were located near each other on either side of the western wall. The kiln located within the city had a rectangular plan with two firing chambers. Heat generated by the two chambers must have been transmitted up through holes in the floor of the chamber above where the pottery was placed for firing. The walls that enclosed this kiln are still preserved and show that there was only a small space at the mouth of the double chambers for feeding fuel to the fire. Space was also available for loading and unloading the ceramics from the upper chamber. There can be no doubt that this kiln was used until the late first century B.C. (Puig i Cadafalch 1915-1920, 704-705; Mar and Ruiz 1993, 410). The kiln located outside the city wall probably dates to the same period as the double-chambered kiln because it had a similar rectangular base, although it had only one chamber (Puig i Cadafalch 1915-1920, 705-706). Both kilns were probably abandoned and buried at the time of the dismantling of the city's west wall and the expansion of the large domestic building, structure 1.

Another kiln seems to have been located in the Roman city, just north of villa 1 beside the city wall. Excavators discovered two walls of a structure in 1967 when they were preparing this area for the installation of a large metal water tank to supply the administrative buildings at the site. The identification of the area within the two walls with the production of amphoras is based almost completely on artifactual rather than structural evidence. Dressel 8 amphoras made of a local fabric have been found at Empúries in 1st-century A.D. contexts. Many bear a stamp that reads "ANTH." Presumably the Dressel 8 "ANTH" amphoras were produced somewhere at Empúries. Nolla suggested that the owner of villa 1 was involved in the production of these amphoras. He pointed out that most of the published Dressel 8 Ampuritana amphoras were discovered in villa 1. He also published data from the water tank excavation in 1967 documenting portions of a wall running north-south for about 7 m. with a second wall made of bricks meeting it at a right angle. Inside this space, he reported the discovery of several complete Dressel 8 Ampuritana amphoras along with numerous fragments, 11 of which bore the stamp "ANTH." No other stamp was found on the fragments. Ceramic fragments discovered in the complex suggested it dated to the first century A.D. Nolla concluded that the Dressel 8 "ANTH" amphoras were produced very near the spot where the water tank was installed (Nolla 1974-1975, 180-182).

Additional data tend to support Nolla's conclusion. In the 20 years since he published, despite considerable excavations in different areas around the site, there has been no report of the excavation of a Dressel 8 Ampuritana amphora nor an amphora with the stamp "ANTH" in any structure other than villa 1. Also, in 1996, as part of an unpublished magnetometry survey of a small portion of the Roman city at the intersection of cardo B and decumanus G (fig. 11), K. Kvamme discovered an enormous magnetic anomaly composed of two circular areas, together measuring slightly less than 20 meters across. The high magnetic readings indicate that the area was burned. The burn spot may represent the position of a structure that burned down in part or in full. Another possibility, however, is that it represents a pair of kilns, each some 10 meters in diameter. Roman kilns of such a large size are known in Catalunya (Revilla Clavo 1995; Nolla and Casas 1984). Unfortunately, this hypothesis will remain only a tantalizing possibility until it can be tested thorough excavation.

4.6.1.3 Garum Production (fig. 27)

In 1917 and 1934 Gandía excavated structure 31, which has come to be interpreted as a fish salting or garum factory (Mar and Ruiz 1993, 409-410; Sanmartí and Nolla 1993, 33). It consisted of a patio and a series of tanks lined with hydraulic cement situated on two sides of the patio. Around the other two sides of the patio was a portico. Traces of stucco still visible on the walls inside the portico may indicate that they were decorated. The building was clearly constructed in a space that had had an earlier use; the construction of the portico cut a neighboring cistern in half. There are no stratigraphic data available for this area. Gandía mentioned finding a fragment of a southern Gaulish terra sigillata cup Dragendorff form 29 and a fragment of a Thin Walled Ware vessel, which could indicate the space was used through the end of the first or beginning of the second centuries A.D. (Mar and Ruiz 1993, 409-410).

The layout of the structure 31 is similar to garum factories on the Iberian peninsula (Ponsich and Tarradell 1965). At the site of Roses, just a few miles north of Empúries, a similar structure consisting of a courtyard surrounded by five tanks on two sides was discovered dating to the fourth or fifth centuries A.D. Rather than a portico, however, the Roses garum factory had a courtyard outside the patio with the tanks (Nolla and Nieto 1982).

4.6.1.4 Quarries

Most structures at Empúries were built of local limestone. Sanmartí found evidence for the extraction of limestone blocks from the bedrock at several places along the coast including Les Coves and around the port. Extraction along the edge of the water would have facilitated movement of the stone to its final destination. Naturally, it is impossible to date these cuts into the bedrock as there are no associated archaeological remains; it seems quite logical, however, that these resources would have been exploited during the construction of the city (Sanmartí 1994, 144).

4.6.1.5 Unidentified Industries in Neapolis (fig. 27)

Four other structures in Neapolis appear to have had an industrial use, although it is difficult to determine what exactly that use was. Gandía discovered a large quantity of coral fragments in structure 54. Unfortunately structure 54 is in an extremely poor state of preservation because of erosion, the reuse of the structure for modern burials, and the construction of the monastery. The use of the structue is difficult to interpret, but the large quantity of coral suggests some industrial use (Mar and Ruiz 1993, 407).

Aquilué was the first to propose an industrial purpose for structure 107, but he failed to speculate on what that purpose may have been (Aquilué et al. 1983, 132). The structure is a confusion of wall foundations, drains, and tanks, the latter providing the evidence for the industrial nature of the building. The west wall was extremely well made in *opus certum* and at its highest preserved point the wall contains a course in *opus vittatum*. A piece of a figured mosaic showing fish was also discovered in this structure, obviously in a secondary context, covering the opening to a cistern. It is uncertain whether this was part of a pavement originally in the structure or from some other part of the site. The fine technique of the wall construction may indicate an Augustan date for the construction of the building. Stratigraphic excavation suggests it was abandoned during or after the second half of the first century A.D. (Cazurro and Gandía 1914, 677).

The excavators at Empúries have not identified two other structures with industrial uses. One is a single-room taberna which probably opened onto street 2. On the southern wall stood a tank approximately half a meter high and lined with hydraulic cement. This tank could have been used for a number of functions, including washing or dying. The second structure is in the space enclosed by the structures 83, 84, and 85/86 and consists of the remains of two circular furnaces made of stone and clay (Mar and Ruiz 1993, 412). Both were double-chambered furnaces, one with the chambers beside each other and the other with the one chamber inside the other. Access to the furnaces was from a short street. The date of the furnaces is uncertain. There is no hint, however, that the construction of the furnaces violated the integrity of any of the surrounding houses or streets, a circumstance that suggests they were built while these structures were still inhabited, sometime before the end of the first or beginning of the second century A.D.

4.6.1.6 Unidentified Industries in the Roman City (fig. 28)

The Roman city has two structures which seem to have served some industrial purpose. One, in villa 3, contained a tank lined with hydraulic cement that stood about a half a meter high. The space was installed in the back of two tabernae, which may have been associated with its use. The tank could have been used for a variety of purposes, including the dying and washing of fabrics.

While excavating the cardo B, Lamboglia found a tiny portion of a building that he interpreted as having an industrial purpose. Located directly across the street from the forum in the Roman city, the structure contained part of a tank with a canal leading off of it just inside the building. Lamboglia dated the construction of this tank to the end of the second or beginning of the first centuries B.C. and the abandonment of it to the Augustan period (Lamboglia 1955, 208-210).

4.6.2 ELITE AND NON-ELITE DOMESTIC SPACE

Elite domestic structures on the Iberian peninsula have been the subject of only a few general studies (Balil 1970 and 1971; Gorges 1979). Hispano-Roman villas are often indistinguishable in plan from, and share architectural features with, their counterparts in Italy. Indeed, villas 1, 2a, and 2b are identical to villas of Pompeii, Cosa, and any number of other Italian sites. Synthetic works on Roman houses in Spain have, however, focused almost exclusively on the *villae*, or elite houses, and not on the dwellings of the non-elite. This is unfortunate as many non-elite houses have been excavated on the Iberian peninsula (cf. Numancia, Augusta Emerita, Roses, Toletum, Conimbriga) and offer an enormous potential for investigations of a wide range of issues.

With the near-total excavation of Roman Imperial levels in Neapolis, as well as the excavation of three residential blocks in the Roman city, it is possible to discuss the residences of both the elite and the non-elite at the site. The basic problem, however, is distinguishing between the two. Mar and Ruiz label domestic structures with courtyards as elite housing while those without courtyards they consider to be non-elite housing. Thus they determine all tabernae to be the housing of the non-elite while all other domestic structures to be elite dwellings (Mar and Ruiz 1993, 348). This distinction is problematic for a number of reasons, the most obvious of which is that it ignores the evidence from ancient literature about how the Romans themselves conceived of elite and non-elite housing.

The evidence from Vitruvius is quite informative on Roman attitudes towards partician and plebian housing. He states that patrons needed houses with enough space to receive their clients, best done in an entryway called an *atrium*, and space to talk with them, in the peristyle among other places. The visit of the client to the patron's house was part of the daily ritual of *salutatio* that was usually conducted in the morning. The visit reinforced the bonds between the patron and client and gave each the opportunity to ask for and receive small gifts, loans, and favors (Cic. *Fam.* vii.28.2 and xi.20.3; Sen. *Brev. Vit.* 14, 6; Mart. i.70; Sall. *Cat.* xxvii.1). The clients, according to Vitruvius, had no need of a peristyle or atrium in their houses because they did not receive clients (6.5.2-3). Juvenal notes a further distinction in the size of elite and non-elite housing, contrasting the cramped living space of the poor clients in Rome with the spacious houses of the wealthy patrons (iii.183-198).

In trying to determine whether excavated domestic structures at Empúries should be considered the dwellings of the elite or non-elite, I have considered both form and size. The presence of a peristyle, atrium, or both is used as one sign that a domestic structure belonged to a member of the local elite, while their absence is used as a sign that the structure belonged to a non-elite member of local society. Size of the structure is used as another indication of the status of the owner. I have selected a cutoff of 150 m^2 and above as an indication of an elite house, and 149 m^2 or less as an indication a non-elite house. The smallest area of a domestic structure at Empúries with a clearly definable atrium or peristyle is 151 m^2 (see table 4.3). Finally, I have also considered the presence of elaborate decoration as another indication that one was receiving clients and guests in one's home. Mosaic pavements are the best surviving type of decoration at Empúries, therefore I have used their presence in a domestic structure as an independent indication of an elite structure. To determine the status of a domestic space, therefore, and to account for the uncertainties of preservation, I considered a structure an elite dwelling if it had any two of these three factors: presence of an atrium or peristyle, an area 150 m^2 or larger, and a mosaic pavement or fragments of painted plaster in at least one room. All other structures lacking two or more of these three characteristics I have labeled non-elite. Possible residences in shops are not considered in this discussion as these are discussed above (see section 4.4.4.3).

Since 1908 excavators have uncovered a total of 38 domestic structures at Empúries. Of these, I have designated 15 as elite and 23 as non-elite houses, each presented in separate sections below. To ease in the presentation of the excavation data, I discuss the domestic structures following the designations of Mar and Ruiz who analyzed the houses at Empúries based on architectural style.

4.6.3 ELITE DOMESTIC SPACE (figs. 29 and 30)

4.6.3.1 Atrium Houses (fig. 31)

The typical atrium house was built around a small, enclosed courtyard or atrium. Most of the atrium was roofed, with the exception of the central section that was open to the sky. The open section, the *copluvium*, allowed light to enter the house and heat to escape. When it rained, the roof channeled the rain through the copluvium where it would fall into a shallow basin in the floor, called the *impluvium*. The water would then be collected in a cistern below for later use. The atrium was usually reached directly from the street via a short hallway, called the *fauces*. The fauces was usually flanked by two *alae*, literally "wings", small rooms where a slave porter may have monitored the main door to the house (Plaut. *Curc.* 76-77). Sometimes a small room opened off the atrium directly opposite the fauces. This room, called the *tablinum*, often contained a table, or *cartibulum*, which held small gifts for the patrons or their clients. The rooms of the

rest of the house opened off the atrium as well. One of these rooms was usually more finely decorated than the others, indicating that it was the *triclinum* or dining room. It would be in this room that the owner of the house would serve his guests fine meals (Vitr. *De arch.* vi; McKay 1975, 32-34). Atrium houses are fairly common on the Iberian peninsula (George 1997, 33; Gorges 1979).

Four atrium houses have been excavated in Neapolis. There is evidence that two of these, structures 7 and 85/86 contained a second story. Structure 85/86 is unusual in that it was built partially into a hill. As a result, on the ground floor there are rooms on only three sides of the atrium, while on the second story there were rooms on all four sides. The eastern end of structure 85/86 was severely damaged by the construction of the road to Sant Martí in the modern era, making it impossible to determine the original size of the house (Mar and Ruiz 1993, 375). Nonetheless, the surviving surface is larger than 150 m^2, allowing it to be placed in the category of elite domestic structure.

In the Roman city there were two atrium houses. Although one of these, villa 2, was originally thought to be one unit, Nieto showed that it was in fact two completely separate houses, each inaccessible from the other. Nieto designated the northwestern villa 2a and southeastern one 2b (Nieto 1979-1980, 313). Nearly all-subsequent authors have followed this convention, including the present one. Unfortunately, Mar and Ruiz switched the labels and consistently refer to villa 2a as 2b and visa versa (Mar and Ruiz 1993: 390-397).

Villa 2a experienced major changes over time (fig. 31). Originally the entrance to a *hortus*, or garden, stood across the atrium from the fauces rather than the traditional tablinum. The hortus was later taken over by the neighboring house, villa 2b, whose owner installed several dining rooms, a bath, and a peristyle in the space, all of which were sealed off from villa 2a (see section 4.6.3.2 below). The owner of villa 2a kept one small corner of the garden and built what was probably a dining room, finely decorated with a pavement of *opus tessellatum* and walls that were stuccoed and painted (Nieto 1979-1980, 313; Santos 1991, 31-33; Mar and Ruiz 1993, 241-242).

There is no good stratigraphic information for this structure, so dating of the building and alterations must be based on other observations. The initial construction of the building post-dates the laying out of the grid plan in the Roman city at the end of the second or beginning of the first century B.C. as it is oriented to this grid. The owner of villa 2a probably gave up his garden to his neighbor in the mid-first century A.D. The peristyle installed in the hortus by the new owner is typical of the time of Nero (Mar and Ruiz 1993, 394). The villa remained in use through the end of the third century (Nieto 1979-1980, 319).

Table 4.5 Total areas of the domestic structures at Empúries in m^2

Stuctures less than 150 m^2		Structures greater than 150 m^2	
structure 10	40	structure 79	151
structure 18	40	structure 42	160
structure 53	46	structure 85/86	170
structure 70	50	structure 5	171
structure 74	52	structure 7	187
structure 87	61	structure 52	193
structure 84	64	villa 3 (Atrium House)	206
structure 32	81	structure 80	220
structure 23	82	structure 1 (phase 1)	238
structure 56	83	structure 34	243
structure 43	83	structure 75	262
structure 94	91	structure 83	266
structure 35	93	structure 57	291
structure 9	96	structure 19	381
structure 76	106	villa 2a (phase 2)	472
structure 82	110	structure 101	509
structure 50	113	structure 1 (phase 2)	568
structure 20	117	villa 1 (phase 1)	782
structure 28	122	villa 2a (phase 1)	1004
structure 55	136	villa 2b (phase 1)	1064
structure 33	140	villa 2b (phase 2)	1596
structure 41	148	villa 1 (phase 2)	1769
		villa 1 (phase 3)	2569
		villa 2b (phase 3)	2637
		villa 1 (phase 4)	3283

Overall average = 454 m^2
Average including only initial phase of multi-phase houses = 211 m^2
Average including only final phase of multi-phase houses = 314 m^2

Another of the buildings in the Roman city has been labeled *Casa Romana* or villa 3, an unfortunate misnomer as the structure did not have a single unified use, but rather contained a number of adjoining commercial and residential structures, often built with party walls. It is one of the most confusing and poorly published structures at Empúries and has never been studied in great detail.

The five rooms in the northeastern corner of villa 3 appear to form an independent unit that was an atrium house. Four rooms open off of a central atrium. The entire unit is larger than 150 m^2 and is richly decorated with mosaics and wall paintings (Mar and Ruiz 1993, 349). Unfortunately, little more can be said of the structure as its excavation has not yet been published.

4.6.3.2 Atrium and Peristyle Houses

In addition to having an atrium, some elite houses at Empúries also had a peristyle or a courtyard surrounded on three or four sides by a colonnade. The peristyle originated in Italy and was a fairly typical feature of elite domestic structures at Pompeii. During the first century A.D., the peristyle spread all over the Roman Empire, becoming a more popular feature of domestic architecture on the Iberian peninsula than in any other region of the Mediterranean

(Smith 1997, 183).

Three domestic structures with atria at Empúries also contained peristyles. What is interesting is that in all three cases, the peristyle was an addition to an already existing atrium house, supporting other evidence that the atrium preceded the arrival of the peristyle on the Iberian peninsula. In the case of structure 1 in Neapolis, the construction of the peristyle and its dependent rooms was made possible by the dismantling of the Neapolis west wall and by the burial of two kilns which had stood beside the city wall. The peristyle was built over these buried structures. The date of the extension of the house, therefore, must be Augustan, when the two cities were joined, a date confirmed by the pottery found in association with the abandoned kilns (see section 4.6.1.2 above). The house ceased to function in the latter half of the first century A.D. and was later reused for Late Antique burials (Puig i Cadafalch 1913-1914, plan 2; Puig i Cadafalch 1915-1920, 701-702; Aquilué et al. 1983, 133; Santos 1991, 21).

The two peristyles in domestic structures in the Roman city were also built as additions on to existing atrium houses. The owners of both villas 1 and 2b appear to have acquired all or part of their neighbor's property in order to add extensively to their homes, building new peristyles, atria, dining rooms, slaves quarters, baths, and various other rooms whose functions have not been identified. The owner of villa

2b built one peristyle to the east, over the remains of the dismantled eastern wall of the Roman city during the Augustan era (fig. 31). Later the owner seems to have acquired most of the garden of villa 2a, building another peristyle, dining rooms, and a bath. Inside the peristyle, excavators discovered a painted altar dedicated to the god of healing, Aesculapius, the Roman counterpart to the Greek Asklepios (Nieto Prieto 1971-1972, 285-390). This altar is the only secure testament to domestic religion known from Empúries. These additions seem to have occurred in the middle of the first century A.D. (Nieto 1979-1980, 322-325; Santos 1991 32; Mar and Ruiz 1993, 339-342; Balil 1970, 90-101). The last addition to the house was an extensive garden to the east. Associated with this garden were a number of rooms. The largest of these had three entries and was positioned for what must have been a magnificent view of the garden and the sea. This may have been a summer dining room, catching the cooling breezes from the sea beyond (Nieto 1971-1972, 322-325).

The expansion of villa 1 followed a similar pattern to that of villa 2b. The owner seems to have acquired the house and property immediately to the south of villa and had all of the existing structure except for a cistern dismantled. In other episodes of expansion, new parts of the villa were added to the east, over the disassembled city wall, and to the north (Santos 1991, 217; Mar and Ruiz 1993, 339-342 and 390-397; Nieto 1979-1980; Balil 1972, 90-101; Sanmartí and Santos 1986-1989, 294-296).

What is striking about all three of these villas is their great size and sumptuous decoration. In its final phase, villa 1 was the largest house yet excavated at Empúries, covering an area of more than one city block or nearly 3300 m². Villa 2b was the next largest domestic structure at the site followed by villa 2a in its initial phase. Structure 1 was the fourth largest domestic structure at the site, about half the size of villa 2a. Much of structure 1 was destroyed by the construction of the monastery in the 16th century, however, so it may have been much larger originally. Traces of painted plaster found in all three of the atrium and peristyle houses indicate the walls were painted and, in the case of villa 1, covered with excellent figured frescoes (Nieto 1977 and 1979-1980). The finest pavements found at Empúries were also found in these three structures. Two *opus signinum* pavements with the Greek words ΞΑΙΡΕΤΕ (good luck) and ΕΥ(Τ)ΥΧΕΩ (I am blessed) were found in dining rooms in structure 1 (Puig i Cadafalch 1915-1920, 701-701). Figured mosaics were found in villa 1, one with an elaborate scene depicting the sacrifice of Iphigeneia, another showing a bird removing the lid of a jewelry box, and a third showing a theatrical mask (Ripoll 1972, 50-51 and Puig i Cadafalch 1911-1912c, 885). Without a doubt, the most prominent citizens in Empúries lived in these three houses.

4.6.3.3 Peristyle Houses

The peristyle is feature that could also stand on its own in a house at Empúries, and is not always found in association with an atrium. At Pompeii peristyles often contained gardens (Jashemski 1979). It is difficult to say whether or not those at Empúries also contained gardens as they were excavated before archaeologists were aware of the necessity to search for evidence of gardening within peristyles.

In Neapolis there are three domestic structures that have peristyles but no atria. Of these, only one, structure 19, has been excavated below the stratigraphic level of use and abandonment. These excavations proved that the peristyle in structure 19 was an addition to the house that required the demolition of some existing rooms (Mar and Ruiz 1993, 387-388). Unfortunately, this remodeling is impossible to date. Nonetheless, since this peristyle and the others in the atrium and peristyle houses at the site were all added to existing structures, it seems that the peristyle was a feature that became popular in the Augustan era or later at Empúries. Peristyles became popular at other sites on the Iberian and Italian peninsulas during the same time period (Smith 1997, 83).

4.6.3.4 Central and Lateral Patio Houses

The central and lateral patio houses differed from the atrium houses in that one immediately entered an open patio upon crossing the threshold to the house. This patio was open to the sky and usually had a cistern below it, although it lacked the impluvium typical of the atrium house. The other rooms of the house opened off of the patio. As the names imply, the patio was located in the center in central patio houses, and off to the side in lateral patio houses (Mar and Ruiz 1993, 354, 403-407).

Three of the patio houses in Neapolis are larger than 150 m² and contain mosaic pavements and so are categorized here as elite domestic structures. Much of one of these, structure 52, was damaged by the construction of the monastery, so we will never know if it had an atrium or peristyle. Even in its damaged state, however, it has more than 150 m² of surface area and a small dining room paved with an *opus signinum* mosaic with the inscription ΗΔΥΚΟΙΤΟΣ, or "sweet sex" (Sanmartí and Nolla 1996-1997, 38). Artifacts excavated from all of these houses indicate that they were abandoned in the late first or early second centuries A.D. (Mar and Ruiz 1993, 445, 452).

4.6.4 NON-ELITE DOMESTIC SPACE (fig. 32)

4.6.4.1 Lateral Patio Houses

The small, square lateral patio house with two or three rooms opening off of the patio is one of the most common types of non-elite domestic architecture found at Empúries. Mar and Ruiz identify 12 lateral patio houses, all in Neapolis. Excavators discovered traces of painted stucco in structures 4 and 43, and traces of mosaics in structures 23, 28, 32, and 43, indicating that some lateral patio houses could be finally decorated despite their small size. Only one of these houses, structure 10, contained evidence of a second story (Mar and

Ruiz 1993, 354-355), the rest certainly had only one story.

The most controversial of the non-elite lateral patio houses is structure 43 (fig. 33). Accessible from the agora, it stood on the corner where street 9 entered the agora. Its entryway was peculiar as steps leading up from the level of the agora gave access to two rooms via different doors. These two spaces are clearly part of one structure: an interior door connects them, a drain in one led to a cistern in the other, and the walls are bonded. Artifacts from the levels of abandonment of this house suggest that the structure was abandoned in the late first or early second century A.D. (Mar and Ruiz 1993, 357).

Interpretations of structure 43 vary widely. Nonetheless, there is no artifactual evidence to support Mar and Ruiz's conjecture that structure was both a residence and place of business for the selling of luxury items (Mar and Ruiz 1993, 357). Equally difficult to sustain is Puig i Cadafalch's interpretation of the structure as a curia (Puig i Cadafalch 1934). While it is appropriately located, its form is simply too peculiar for such a function. Despite the oddity of the two entryways, the structure is identical to the other three-space square domestic structures in Neapolis in all other respects leaving little doubt as to its domestic nature (compare figs. 33 with 34).

4.6.4.2 Central Patio Houses

Ten non-elite central patio houses were discovered in Neapolis. On average, these were larger than the lateral patio houses, had more rooms, and had a greater variety of shapes. All of the central patio houses had only one story, with the exception of structures 20 and 35. Only two of the central patio houses, structures 35 and 55, have preserved mosaic pavements.

Unlike the elite houses, none of these non-elite houses have an associated taberna. In their interpretation of the room in the northwest corner of structure 22, Mar and Ruiz claim the room must have been a taberna as it was accessible only from street 8 and not from inside the rest of the structure (Mar and Ruiz 1993, 366-367). Both their plan of the city, however, and my own examinations on the ground indicate the room was clearly accessible from the patio and not from the street 8. Thus, I have included this room as part of the domestic space of structure 33.

4.6.4.3 Other Types of Houses

Only one domestic structure in Neapolis can not be classified in to any of the categories mentioned above. Structure 53 is one of the most poorly preserved of the domestic structures at Empúries, most of the walls were destroyed by the construction of the monastery. Presumably the remaining walls were part of rooms in the eastern end of a house that was built over the foundations of the dismantled west city wall and therefore must date to the Augustan era or later. Little more can be said as there have been no publications of the excavations in the structure. Undoubtedly this structure had some type of patio or atrium, but no evidence for it has survived.

4.7 Empúries After the 1st Century A.D.

Some time in the late first or early second centuries A.D., most of Empúries was abandoned for reasons that remain obscure. Activities that took place in the centuries after the abandonment were usually on a small scale and did little to disturb the existing archaeological remains, the only exception being the construction of the monastery in the 16th century which disturbed much of the western part of Neapolis. The abandonment of the site makes it possible to state with relative certainty the function of nearly every excavated structure in the second half of the first century A.D. This is a blessing to the archaeologist interested in the structure of Roman urban space; Empúries provides a snapshot of a Roman provincial city at one moment in time. In the next chapter this snapshot is analyzed to see if any patterns in the use of space exist or whether the distribution in the use of space is random, and whether or not there is information on the social structure of the city embedded in the use of space.

5

ANALYSIS OF SPACE AT EMPÚRIES

...Praeter istos, quorum, si nihil aliud, rectae voces sunt, alipilum cogita tenuem et stridulam vocem, quo sit notabilior, subinde exprimentem nec umquam tacentem, nisi dum vellit alas et alium pro se clamare cogit. Iam libari varias exclamationes et botularium et crustularium et omnes popinarum institores mercem sua quadam et insignita modulatione vendentis.

...In his, quae me sine avocatione circumstrepunt, essedas transcurrentes pono et fabrum inquilinum et serrarium vicinum, aut hunc, qui ad Metam Sudantem tubulas experitur et tibias,nec cantat, sed exclamat).

...Still, at least these are natural sounds—not like the hair-plucker, who's always whistling and screeching to make people take notice of him. He's never quiet unless he's working; and then he's plucking armpits, and his victim does the yelling for him! Then there are people selling drinks, sausages or pastries, and the men advertising food-shops; each one shouts his wares with his own particular cry.

...Outside (but just as distracting) there are carriages hurrying past, a carpenter up that street, a blacksmith down this one—and last but not least, the maker of musical instruments down on the corner, always testing his oboes and trumpets, making a terrible noise and never producing a real tune at all.

Seneca, *Epistulae Morales* 56.1-2 and 4 (trans. Nichols and McLeish 1974, 41)

5.1 Introduction

In a letter to a friend Seneca describes the sounds that distracted him while working in his residence in Rome. Granting Seneca a certain amount of hyperbole, the letter is still interesting for the great variety of uses of space Seneca suggests took place within the range of his hearing. In addition to the activities listed above, (hair-plucking, the selling of various foods and drinks, carpentry, black-smithing, and instrument making), there are other activities mentioned elsewhere in the letter including bathing and barge transportation. This letter suggests a great mixing of uses of space within the city of Rome. The interesting question is whether or not within this mix there was some pattern.

An increasing number of archaeologists would assert the confusion of uses of space implied by Seneca represents the true picture, that Roman cities had little patterning in their use of space (see Introduction). The work of Richard Raper at Pompeii, discussed in detail below (section 5.3), has led to the generally accepted view that few areas of Pompeii were segregated for specific uses and that there is no meaning in the placement of structures across most of the city. The present chapter challenges this view by examining the evidence from Empúries. Using techniques developed by both archaeologists and sociologists for the analysis of urban space, it will be argued that the use of space at Empúries, was, in fact, highly structured.

Trying to find patterns among the locations of similar types of archaeological remains is not a new concept. Archaeologists have been using GIS to help explain the location of sites within a landscape by looking for correlations between the location of sites and natural phenomena such as the presence of fresh water, direction of a slope, or visibility of a site (cf. Wansleeben 1988; Peterman 1992; Kvamme 1992.). More recently archaeologists, particularly prehistorians, have been attempting to use GIS to reconstruct the social landscape of a territory (cf. Zubrow 1994; Allen 1996; Maschner 1996; Ruggles and Medyckyj-Scott 1996; Van West and Kohler 1996; Blasco Baena, and Recuero 1995). Yet there has been very little examination of intrasite social phenomena. The Roman city, itself a constructed social environment, presents the perfect opportunity for a case study of the location of spaces within a site that have been generated primarily through social phenomena.

The problem with any attempt to analyze the social environment is that it is usually much more difficult to reconstruct than the natural environment. This is less true for the Roman city, where the placement of buildings and the urban layout offer clues to the social system that created them. The architecture itself was one of the major factors in the construction of urban social behavior by directing and limiting movement through space (Hillier 1996, 14). The challenge is to find ways of quantifying the evidence of remaining architecture in some way so that it can be tested to determine what commonalities exist among structures with similar functions and what differences exist among structures with varying functions. The resulting patterns represent, to a large degree, rules or societal norms about the use of space within the city.

This study begins by examining the layout of Neapolis using the GIS program Idrisi 2.0 for Windows in order to determine whether or not it has a regular layout. Next, three different factors, clustering/dispersion, the nature of the street, and visibility, are tested to determine whether they played a role in the distribution of uses of space. A pair of tests examines whether or not structures with the same use

Analysis of Space at Empúries

were clustered or dispersed around the city. Another suite of tests seeks correlations among certain uses of space and streets with similar defining characteristics. The visibility of structures across the city is also tested to determine if visibility was a factor that influenced their location.

5.2 Neapolis Street Network and Topography

While this chapter concentrates on social space in the early Imperial period, we must first briefly consider one of the non-cultural factors had an influence on the layout of Empúries. One of the questions that has generated much discussion is how much topography influenced the original layout of the Greek Neapolis in the 6th century B.C. Originally, Puig i Cadfalch and Schulten argued the street layout of Neapolis was in fact regular, and represented a conscious application of the ideas of Hippodamus of Miletus who argued for the regular arrangement of streets in an orthogonal pattern (Puig i Cadafalch 1934, 22; Schulten 1931, 138). While the pattern is not exactly regular, they point out that there are three parallel streets north of the agora and two south of it that are crossed at right angles by a series east-west oriented streets. Balil was the first to challenge this idea, arguing the layout was too irregular and that the Greek colony was built before the Hippodamean layout became popular. The Hippodamean plan was applied to existing cities only when they had suffered severe destruction and were being rebuilt, something which never occurred at Empúries (Balil 1970, 319-320). Balil's opinion has prevailed, with subsequent investigators agreeing that the layout is too irregular to be Hippodamean and must, therefore, represent an adaptation to the terrain.

The controversy over the Hippodamean layout has hinged mainly on an examination of the street plan. Proponents of both sides have pointed to a map of the street layout and state that the Hippodamean or natural layout is self-evident. Balil is the only one to have introduced a new argument by pointing to the timing of the layout. He failed to note, however, that the orthogonal layout was used in Greek colonies long before Hippodamus advocated its use (Owens 1991, 29).

I have come to agree with Balil that the layout of Neapolis was meant to adapt to the terrain and was not intended to be orthogonal. Taking advantage of a digitized contour plan, I overlaid the street plan of Neapolis and discovered nearly every street in Neapolis either follows the contour lines or meets them at a right angle (fig. 35). There can be little doubt, then, that topography had a major impact on the direction of the street layout.

Only two areas do not conform to this general rule, the southern temple precinct and Mar and Ruiz's reconstruction of the direction of the street 3. The deviation of the contour lines shown by the southern plaza may have more to do with the fact that this area was heavily terraced in antiquity, an action which would have remade the contour map. This is the only area in Neapolis where the contours were remade to fit to the architecture, not the other way around.

In the northeastern portion of the site, Mar and Ruiz may

have reconstructed the direction of the roads incorrectly. If street 3 was really as long as Mar and Ruiz project, then it must surely have had a bend in it. This is the pattern with street 2A, which is approximately the same length as Mar and Ruiz's reconstruction of street 3. The other option is that it simply was not as long as Mar and Ruiz suggest, ending at its intersection with street 11.

5.3 Clustering/Dispersion of Use

There are numerous ways to analyze a set of spatial data in search of patterns, although an appropriate one must be found based on the data being analyzed. One of the more useful methods of analysis, pioneered by Raper to analyze the use of space at Pompeii, is a test for the clustering or dispersion of structures. Raper employed a grid of a uniform size that he placed over the study area so that he could count the frequency of objects of interest within each grid cell. Raper took advantage of the map of Pompeii published by Eschebach in which Eschebach designated one of 12 categories of land use to every excavated space in the city (Eschebach 1970). Raper drew a grid on Eschebach's map, dividing the site into squares. Each square in Raper's grid corresponded to a 100 x 100 m square on the ground at Pompeii. Raper then made an overlay, which was equivalent to one of these 100 x 100 m squares, and subdivided it so that every square represented one square meter on the ground. Placing this overlay on top of each square of his gridded version of Eschebach's map, Raper noted which of Eschebach's categories of land use each 1 x 1 m square covered. By counting the number of squares within each 100 x 100 m square that had the same use, he was able determine the percentage of space within that 100 m square devoted to each category of land use. Summing these percentages from all the 100 x 100 m squares and dividing by the total number of 100 m squares needed to cover all Pompeii, he was able to obtain percentages for the city as a whole. Raper then calculated the mean for each of the categories of use for the entire city and compared the mean to the results from each individual 100 x 100 m square, looking for the degree of variation from the mean. He came to the conclusion that there was no significant variation in land use in most parts of the city. Space devoted to commercial, public, and residential use was evenly distributed around the city with no patterning in any particular section of the city. Raper found just two exceptions to this general rule. Public structures were clustered around the forum and some shops lined the streets leading to the forum. Otherwise, he concluded that the use of space was randomly distributed (Raper 1977).

Another possible explanation for these results, however, is that the absence of patterning was more a result of Raper's methodology than an actual absence of patterns in the ancient use of space (Bates 1983). Key to his analysis is the size of the grid cell. Weak patterns can be obscured when the size of the grid cell is too large while strong patterns can be weakened by fragmentation when grid cells are too small. Raper used a 100-m square to ease his calculations. The problem with the 100-m square is that it has absolutely no relevance to how the ancient Pompeians viewed their city. Each square encompassed a number of insulae or city blocks; therefore variation between individual insulae would not be detected.

A central goal of this study was to run a quadrat analysis on the data from Empúries to see if patterns in the clustering or dispersion of different uses of space could be detected. Quadrat analysis is nearly identical to the type of analysis employed by Raper with the only difference being that point data are counted rather than area data. The advantage to counting point data is that it can be done rapidly with a computer using most GIS software.

The size of the grid square to be used in this study was selected by averaging the areas of each of the insulae in Neapolis, producing a figure of 30 m on a side. Developments in computer technology since Raper's day made it possible to run much more sophisticated analyses of the frequency counts of the grid squares than he used. Patterns could be described with a variance/mean statistic, which could be tested with the Student's t-test to determine whether or not there was a significant pattern of clustering or dispersion. Unfortunately, not enough of the Roman city has been excavated to make this form of analysis feasible so the quadrat analysis was undertaken for Neapolis only.

The quadrat method followed here was suggested by D. Unwin (1981, 38-40). The process can best be explained through an example from Neapolis. Figure 29 shows a plan of Neapolis where every space determined to be an elite domestic space in the previous chapter is hatched. As it is the distribution of whole structures around the site, not just individual spaces, which are of interest, a single dot was digitized in the center of each elite domestic structure to represent that structure (fig. 36). Then a grid was placed over the map of Neapolis (fig. 37) and the computer counted how many dots fell within each grid square (fig. 38). The resulting frequencies for each cell are represented by shading the grid cell darker to represent a higher frequency of elite houses (see fig. 39). The resulting frequencies are also represented in table 5.1.

In order to determine the variance/mean ratio, the number of elite structures (n) were multiplied by the number of cells with that frequency (f). In this case 20 cells had structures, but no elite structures (20 x 0 = 0), 9 cells had one elite structure (9 x 1 = 9) and one cell had two elite structures (1 x 2 = 2). By summing this number (11) and dividing by the sum of the frequency of cells (30), it is possible to calculate the mean, 0.367 elite structures per grid cell (see table 5.1). With the mean calculated, the other half of the variance/mean ratio was determined by calculating the variance. This is done by determining the deviation from the mean by subtracting the mean from the number of elite structures (n-mean). This figure is then squared and multiplied by the frequency $(f(n-mean)^2)$. The sum of these is then divided by the sum of the frequency minus 1.

$$Variance = \frac{\Sigma(f(n-mean)^2)}{f-1}$$

The result is the variance (table 5.1). The calculation of the variance/mean follows simply by dividing the variance by the mean. The closer this figure is to one, the more the pattern appears to be randomly generated. A variance/mean

figure greater than one indicates clustering while a variance/mean figure less than one indicates dispersion.

Table 5.1 Calculation of variance/mean ratio for the elite domestic structures in Neapolis

Number of Elite Structures (n)	Freq. of cells (f)	No. of points (nf)	Deviation from mean (n-mean)	$(f(n-mean)^2)$
0	20	0	-0.367	2.689
1	9	9	0.633	3.610
2	1	2	1.633	2.668
	30	11		8.967

$$Mean= \frac{\Sigma (nf)}{\Sigma (f)} = \frac{total\ number\ of\ points}{total\ number\ of\ cells} = \frac{11}{30} = 0.367$$

$$Variance= \frac{\Sigma (f(n-mean)^2)}{\Sigma f-1} = \frac{8.967}{29} = 0.309$$

$$Variance/mean\ ratio = \frac{0.309}{0.367} = 0.843$$

The strength of the pattern produced can then be tested with a Student's t-test. The Student's t-test is the observed variance/mean ratio minus one divided by the standard error of difference. The standard error of difference is calculated by the formula

$$[2/(k-1)]^{0.5}$$

where k equals the number of cells (Unwin 1981, 55-56). Thus for the elite houses in Neapolis the calculation is

$$t = \frac{0.843 - 1}{[2/(30-1)]^{0.5}} = \frac{-0.157}{0.263} = -0.597$$

In order to check for the significance of this statistic, one also needs to calculate the degrees of freedom, which is the number of cells analyzed minus one, in this case

$$degrees\ of\ freedom = k - 1 = 30 - 1 = 29$$

in which k equals the number of cells. Checking these figures against a table of critical values for the Student's t-distribution shows that the figure -0.597 at 29 degrees of freedom is not significantly different from a non-patterned distribution. Therefore, we must assume that the elite domestic structures in Neapolis are not clustered together nor dispersed from one another in a statistically significant manner. Below all tests employ 29 degrees of freedom, therefore any Student's t-distribution that is greater than two represents a result significant at the 5% level or less, meaning there was a 95% chance the pattern was generated by design and only a 5% chance it was generated by coincidence.

Mercifully, the quadrat analysis module in the GIS program Idrisi 2.0 for Windows allows for a very rapid calculation of variance/mean ratio and Student's t-test of significance. It also allows for the creation of a mask that has the computer analyze only the grid cells that contain data. Cells that lack data, particularly those on the edge of the map, are ignored. This analysis was run on each of the categories of land use listed in Uses 1 through 3 (tables 4.1 and 4.2 and summarized again in table 5.2). The categories in Use 4 of tables 4.1 and 4.2 were not analyzed because this study was interested in the use of space at the level of the individual building within the city, not at the level of individual rooms within buildings.

Table 5.2 Summary of categories of use of space

Use 1	Use 2	Use 3
Public	Public Secular	Defensive
		Passage
		Administrative
		Commercial
Entertainment		
		Education
	Public Religious	Sacred
		Funerary
Private	Private Secular	Industrial
		Elite Domestic
		Non-Elite Domestic
	Private Religious	

5.3.1 Use 1

According to the quadrat analysis, the public space in Neapolis is significantly clustered (see table 5.3). Visual inspection suggests that the highest frequency of public structures is clustered around the agora, not a surprising discovery and one which certainly confirms Raper's caveat that there was patterning in the use of space around the forum of Pompeii (fig. 40). Concentrations of public structures elsewhere indicate significant public activity in other parts of the city as well. Private space does not appear to be clustered or dispersed in any significant way (fig. 41).

Table 5.3 Results of the quadrat analysis of Use 1 in Neapolis

Category of Use	Variance/ Mean	T-test	Level of Significance
Public	1.97	3.71	<0.001
Private	1.10	0.39	Not significant

Degrees of Freedom = 29

5.3.2 Use 2

As there was no space in Neapolis that could be securely identified as having a private religious function, all of the private secular space corresponded exactly to the private space analyzed above, thus making its analysis unnecessary. There was, however, public space in Neapolis devoted to both religious and secular use. By breaking the public space into secular and religious, it is possible to determine the contribution of each component to the distribution of public space as a whole. Both religious and secular space proved to be clustered at significant levels (see table 5.4). Public religious spaces are concentrated at the southern edge of the city (fig. 23). A similar clustering may also be found in the Roman city where all excavated temples have been found only in the forum. It is interesting that these blocks were reserved for temples and no other use such as residence or commerce. As demonstrated by the remodeling of the forum to exclude tabernae (see chapter 4, section 4.4.3.2), the Emporitani seem to have formed strong opinions about which type of activities should be excluded from religious space beginning in the Augustan era. The distribution of public secular space is also significantly clustered, apparently in areas where there were no religious structures (fig. 42).

Table 5.4 Results of the quadrat analysis of Use 2 in Neapolis

Category of Use	Variance/ Mean	T-test	Level of Significance
Public Religious	1.64	2.45	<0.05
Public Secular	2.25	4.76	<0.001

Degrees of Freedom = 29

5.3.3 Use 3

The quadrat analysis of the categories in Use 3 suggested that there was no significant clustering or dispersion of the administrative, industrial, and elite domestic space in Neapolis (table 5.5). A visual inspection of the maps showing these distributions also fails to reveal any particularly striking patterns (figs. 12, 27, and 29). Naturally, there are administrative structures around the agora, just as one would expect, but that is not the only place where these are located. Industrial spaces are located both on the edges of the city and in the interior, close to and away from domestic structures, etc. The only suggestion of a pattern is the dearth of administrative, elite domestic, and industrial structures near the temples, suggesting that religious use of space was not to be mixed with these other uses of space. Such a pattern is unusual in the Roman world and is not seen at other urban sites. The sample size for both categories is so small, however, that this could account for the lack of an obvious pattern. Otherwise, it is difficult to know how to account for this oddity.

The distribution of commercial space is significantly clustered, according to the quadrat analysis (table 5.5). The greatest concentrations appear to be in and near the agora and along street 2, one of the main streets in Neapolis (fig. 14). The low concentration of shops in the northern quarter of the city is odd, as one might have expected more shops close to the port. This may confirm the conclusion in chapter 4 that the majority of the port facilities were in the northeastern sector of Neapolis and are now covered by a modern road and sand dunes. The lack of commercial structures in the southern portion of the city is quite striking. The reason may lie in the apparent reluctance of the Emporitani to mix religious uses of space with other uses. Finally, the quadrat analysis indicates that non-elite domestic structures are significantly clustered together as well (table 5.5). The map of their distribution shows that the greater concentrations of non-elite houses avoid the temple precincts in the south of the city and the agora (fig. 33).

Table 5.5 Results of the quadrat analysis of Use 3 in Neapolis

Category of Use	Variance/ Mean	T-test	Level of Significance
Administrative	1.28	1.05	Not Significant
Commercial	2.93	7.34	<0.001
Industrial	1.09	0.34	Not Significant
Elite Domestic	0.84	-0.60	Not Significant
Non-Elite Domestic	1.74	2.84	<0.01

Degrees of Freedom = 29

Not all of the categories of spatial function from the Use 3 category were analyzed. There were no spaces reserved for educational or entertainment functions in Neapolis. Information about defensive space is fragmentary, given the absence of excavation in the northern and eastern portions of the city and the nearly complete destruction of the western wall. Thus any results would have reflected the activities of the 16th century monks and the 20th century excavators rather than the 1st century Emporitani. Passage space was also not analyzed with the quadratic technique as the methods outlined below (section 5.5) are more appropriate for the analysis of streets and plazas. Finally, religious space was not analyzed. All graves dating to the Imperial period were located outside of the walls of the city, so any analysis of internal religious space would have been identical to the spaces analyzed under Use 2, public religious space.

Although the data are too fragmentary for any type of robust analysis, it is still interesting to look at the areas immediately outside the city walls of Empúries to see how space was used there. One striking thing about the areas outside Empúries is the indication of activities that took place only outside of the city and nowhere else. The most obvious is burial of the dead. It was, of course, common for Greeks and Romans to bury their dead outside the walls, there were even legal

prohibitions against disposal of the dead within city walls (Gonzázlez 1990, 26-27). More unusual, however, are the presence of the palaestra and amphitheater. The only two spaces known in the entire city to have been dedicated solely to public educational and entertainment purposes were actually placed outside the city walls. Naturally the palaestra was not the only place for educational activities. Private tutors and instructors would certainly have been engaged by the wealthier Emporitani to come to their homes to instruct their children, which would, of course, have left no archaeological traces. The placement of the palaestra and amphitheater outside the city walls must represent a conscious decision on the part of the Emporitani, as there was enough space available inside the city walls to house both of these structures. The two blocks directly south of the forum, for instance, were left almost completely empty. Gladiatorial combat could be dangerous, for instance the riot in the amphitheater at Pompeii led to a number of deaths (Tac. *Ann.* 14.17). The Emporitani may have wanted to keep such dangers outside the city walls.

The other interesting thing to note about activites outside the city walls is that industrial activities of quarrying and metal refining that took place along the coast of the Mediterranean Sea. There may have been two practical reasons for this, it was easier to transport quarried stone via sea and the breezes off the sea must have fed the fires in the bloomeries.

5.3.4 Summary

It appears that certain categories of the use of space were clustered together at Empúries. Public structures showed a particularly strong tendency to be located near other public structures. More specifically, public commercial structures always appeared together as did public religious structures. Among private structures, non-elite domestic structures had a tendency to be placed together. Finally, there is an interesting mix to the use of some spaces and segregation of others. Elite and non-elite domestic, commercial, industrial, and administrative spaces were all mixed together to a lesser or greater extent in the same areas. Public religious space, however, was segregated from other functions, mixed only with defensive uses of space in Neapolis and administrative use of space in the Roman city forum. In addition, certain activities were exclusively extramural, including public educational, entertainment, and funerary uses of space.

5.4 Clustering / Dispersion of Use by Block

While quadrat analysis is an effective and time-efficient way for analyzing urban space, the use of artificial grids poses two problems. As discussed above, the size of the grid can have an enormous impact on the results. Using a larger or smaller grid size can clarify or obscure patterns in the data. The other problem is the use of the artificial grid in no way represents how the ancient inhabitants conceived of their city.

An attempt was made above to compensate for these problems above by using a 30-m grid cell, the average size of the insulae in Neapolis, but this grid was still laid randomly over the plan of the city, not corresponding to any particular block. In an attempt to overcome these drawbacks the quadrat analysis was run again using the exact same procedure, changing just one factor in the analysis. Rather than use the artificial grid, the insulae themselves were used as the units of measurement. In this way it was possible to test the hypothesis that ancient inhabitants of Empúries considered the individual block to be a significant unit for organizing space. Technically, the quadrat analysis should only be run using areas of equal size, which the blocks in Neapolis definitely are not. In exchange for consistency, however, this method allows for the investigation of how the Emporitani may have conceived of the urban space surrounding them. The great disadvantage to this method is that it is impossible for a GIS program to examine irregularly sized and placed quadrats. As a result, all of the calculations had to be done by hand, a very time-consuming process.

5.4.1 Use 1

The results of the modified quadrat analysis on structures categorized as Use 1 are presented in table 5.6. In both cases, the results suggest that public and private space were clustered in blocks together to a highly significant degree (figs. 40 and 41). Most blocks in Neapolis seem to be dominated by one of these categories of the use of space, making them predominantly public or private. These results demonstrate that there were patterns to the distribution of both public and private space throughout the city, not just the public space as the quadrat analysis using the artificial grid suggested.

Table 5.6 Results of the quadrat analysis by block of Use 1 in Neapolis

Category of Use	Variance/ Mean	T-test	Level of Significance
Public	4.64	9.97	<0.001
Private	8.38	20.22	<0.001

Degrees of Freedom = 15

5.4.2 Use 2

The quadrat analysis by block confirms the results of the quadrat analysis with the artificial grid for the structures classified under Use 2. Religious structures in Neapolis seem to be clustered on the same two insulae, while secular structures are also clustered in insulae other than those reserved for religious purposes (figs. 23 and 42). This is a further suggestion that the Emporitani took the separation of structures with religious use from the other structures very seriously.

Table 5.7 Results of the quadrat analysis by block of Use 2 in Neapolis

Category of Use	Variance/ Mean	T-test	Level of Significance
Public Religious	5.53	12.42	<0.001
Public Secular	24.45	64.22	<0.001

Degrees of Freedom = 15

5.4.3 Use 3

As with the quadrat analysis by grids, the analysis by blocks suggests that there was no significant distribution to the administrative and industrial structures in the city (figs. 12 and 27). None appear to be clustered together or dispersed in any statistically significant manner. The analysis also confirmed that commercial and non-elite domestic structures were clustered together on the same blocks (figs. 14 and 33).

The most interesting finding, however, is that there was a significant pattern picked up in this analysis in relation to the elite domestic structures which was not noted by the quadrat analysis using the artificial grid. The analysis indicated that elite houses were significantly distributed in a dispersed pattern. The distribution of elite domestic structures in figure 29 shows a rather striking pattern. Not one insula has two elite residences, and every elite residence is separated from all other elite residences by at least one street. It seems that the elite Emporitani did not want to live near one another.

Table 5.8 Results of the quadrat analysis by block of Use 3 in Neapolis

Category of Use	Variance/ Mean	T-test	Level of Significance
Administrative	0.73	-0.74	Not Significant
Commercial	9.19	22.44	<0.001
Industrial	0.45	-1.51	Not Significant
Elite Domestic	0.05	-2.59	0.02
Non-Elite Domestic	7.20	16.99	<0.01

Degrees of Freedom = 15

5.4.4 Summary

The results of the modified quadrat analysis were very interesting. They reproduced and confirmed the results of the quadrat analysis using the artificial grids. The results using the city insulae, however, were of much greater statistical significance, suggesting blocks played a role in the organization of space at the site. In addition this method made it possible to identify patterns the analysis using regular grids failed to note, namely that private space was clustered together on the same block and that elite domestic structures were dispersed evenly across the site.

5.5 Nature of the Street

One can say that any city street has a "feel" based on how wide it is, how straight or curved, whether it intersects many or few other streets. The problem for anyone studying urban environments is how to translate this amorphous feeling into concrete terms that can be studied and measured. In this section the system of streets at Empúries is analyzed using forms of circuit analysis. After establishing how to describe the streets of the city using these techniques, tests are described that determine whether or not buildings that were put to similar uses were located along streets with similar attributes and descriptive statistics. In cases where correspondences exist, it is assumed that the particular variable being measured had meaning to the ancient Emporitani and that it was a factor in the choice of that street as the location for a structure with a particular use.

For the purposes of this analysis not all categories of the use space in Neapolis and in the Roman city were considered. Categories that had an expected frequency of five or less were disregarded because this is the minimum expected frequency commonly accepted as necessary for the chi-square test, the statistical test used here to measure significance (Unwin 1981, 56). The remaining categories analyzed included Use 1: public and private space; Use 2: public secular space; Use 3: administrative, commercial, industrial, elite domestic, and non-elite domestic space.

In order to perform the tests described below, it was also necessary to re-label some of the streets. Whenever a street had a bend of 90 degrees or more, or was made impassible at some point, it is considered to have become a separate street beyond the obstacle. Therefore, Mar and Ruiz' labels for the streets at Empúries have been modified (figs. 43 and 44). For instance, the transverse wall divides Mar and Ruiz' cardo D in half and so the southern half is labeled cardo D2 here, while the northern half is labeled here as cardo D1.

In Appendix D it is possible to see the totals for each use category organized by street identification number. Thus, the number 16 under the column "Commercial Ob." (observed) and row 2A indicates that it was possible to enter sixteen commercial spaces directly from street 2A. Using the total number of spaces devoted to specific uses in the entire city, it was possible to produce an "expected" number for each use along each street. This was done by multiplying the total number of structures devoted to each use by the length of each individual street and then dividing by the sum of all the street lengths studied. For example, there are a total of 107 known spaces devoted to commercial use throughout Empúries. When this figure is divided by 1519, the total length in meters of all excavated streets at Empúries, it produces a figure of 0.0704 commercial spaces per meter:

$$\frac{107 \text{ commercial spaces}}{1519 \text{ meters}} = 0.0704 \text{ commercial spaces/meter}$$

Street 2A has a total length of 108.3 meters. By multiplying this length by the number of commercial spaces per meter, it is possible to produce an expected value of 7.6 commercial spaces along street 2A assuming a uniform distribution of commercial enterprises throughout the city.

0.0704 commercial spaces/meter x 108.3 meters = 7.6 expected commercial spaces

This figure represents how many commercial spaces should be expected along street 2A if there were no pattern to the distribution of commercial spaces in the city. Both the expected and the observed values for each street are given in Appendix D. The length measurements for each street are given in table 5.9.

Table 5.9 Lengths of the streets used in the analysis in meters

Neapolis			Roman City	
street 1A	27.4		cardo A2	73.5
street 1B	8.7		cardo B	89.5
street 1C	23.1		cardo C3	34.5
street 1D	10.9		cardo D2	77.0
street 1E	81.8		decumanus B	44.5
street 1F	25.2		decumanus D	22.0
street 1G	7.0			
street 1H	16.1			
street 1I	27.0			
street 2A	108.3			
street 2B	53.1			
street 2C	27.4			
street 3	78.3			
street 4	53.5			
street 5A	35.7			
street 5B	23.9			
street 6A	16.1			
street 6B	18.3			
street 7	30.4			
street 8A	17.4			
street 8B	15.7			
street 8C	13.0			
street 9	50.0			
street 10	61.8			
street 11	38.3			
street 12	29.1			
street 13A	46.5			
street 13B	24.8			
street 14	16.5			
street 15	31.3			
street 16	21.7		Sum	1519.0
street 17	24.8		Minimum	8.7
street 18	22.2		Maximum	108.3
Agora	58.7		Mean	37.0
So. Plaza	34.0		Stand. Deviation	24.4

Street lengths were measured from a digitized plan, including only the portions of the streets that actually contained excavated structures. To compensate for the problem unique to the Roman city at Empúries, where excavations were carried out only on one side of some streets, the lengths of all such streets were divided in half. Once the observed and expected frequencies had been generated in this manner, the chi-square statistic could be used to test a null hypothesis that uses were randomly distributed in relation to each of the descriptive statistics. This technique violates strict statistical application of the chi-square test, as the same data should not be used to generate the expected values against which the observed values are to be tested. Such a use of the chi-square statistic is frequent in archaeology, however, in cases where there is no comparable data set from which to draw the expected values. Ideally, the data from another Roman urban site of the same time period and in the same area would be analyzed to produce all of the expected values. Comparisons with other Roman cities in Spain are of little help, however, because no other site has been excavated to the same degree as Empúries. Comparisons with other more fully excavated Roman cities are equally fruitless because the most comparable, Pompeii and the Roman cities of North Africa, have very significant historical and cultural differences from Empúries. These differences could account for differences between the frequency of expected counts generated at these other sites and the observed ones at Empúries.

In the following sections five techniques for statistically describing the nature of individual streets are outlined. They are then applied to the data from Empúries. The tests that proved significant are used to form a definition of what factors helped determine the location of a specific type of structure along a specific type of street.

5.5.1 Depth

The sociologists Hillier and Hanson have developed a descriptive statistic for urban street networks that allows one to study the attitudes of the residents of the city towards non-residents. They label their statistic "depth" (Hillier and Hanson 1984, 104). Borrowing the idea of "steps" from network analysis, Hillier and Hanson count the number of streets one needs to pass through in order to reach a street of interest from a point of origin. In the simplest case, they start from outside the city and record the number of steps required to reach each street in the city. Streets with a low depth would have been easy to reach from outside of the city while streets with a high depth would have been more difficult to reach from outside. Residents of the city would have placed structures in which they wanted to interact with non-residents at a shallow depth while structures which they did not want outsiders to find would have been located along streets with a higher depth.

Street access and depth can be represented in what Hillier and Hanson call a "justified map" of an urban system (Hillier and Hanson 1984 93-94 and 106). The justified maps of both Neapolis and the Roman city are presented in figures 45 and 46 respectively. For the map of the Roman city only the streets that were lined by excavated structures and for which the nearest city gate could be located were mapped. Several of the streets, especially in the northern half of the city, must have ended in a gate but as all evidence of the wall above the

ground has disappeared, it is impossible to be certain where these gates stood and, therefore, the "depth" of those particular streets. It should also be noted that these plans only represent each street's relation to the nearest exit from the city and not necessarily the relationship between all streets within the city. The depth counts are represented in tabular form in table 5.10.

Table 5.10 Depths of the streets used in the analysis

Neapolis		Roman City	
street 1A	5	cardo A2	2
street 1B	5	cardo B	2
street 1C	4	cardo C3	1
street 1D	3	cardo D2	2
street 1E	2	decumanus B	2
street 1F	2	decumanus D	1
street 1G	3		
street 1H	4		
street 1I	2		
street 2A	3		
street 2B	2		
street 2C	2		
street 3	2		
street 4	4		
street 5A	4		
street 5B	6		
street 6A	4		
street 6B	5		
street 7	4		
street 8A	3		
street 8B	5		
street 8C	4		
street 9	1		
street 10	3		
street 11	3		
street 12	3		
street 13A	4		
street 13B	3		
street 14	5		
street 15	4		
street 16	3	Sum	126.0
street 17	4	Minimum	1.0
street 18	1	Maximum	6.0
Agora	2	Mean	3.1
So. Plaza	2	Standard Deviation	1.3

Using these "depth values," the streets were sorted into categories according to depth, then the sums of the resultant use values for each depth were tested against the expected values using the chi-square statistic (tables 5.11-5.13). Thus, for example, streets with a depth of five in Neapolis include 1A, 1B, 6B, 8C, and 14. The expected number of commercial structures for each of these streets is 1.9, 0.6, 1.3, 0.9, and 1.2 respectively. It is a physical impossibility, of course, to have 1.9 commercial structures, there are either one or two buildings. Nonetheless 1.9 commercial structures is a statistical reality and the use of the real numbers allows for greater accuracy when testing for significance. By summing these five figures, the figure of 5.9 is derived as the total number of commercial structures that one would have expected to see on streets with a depth of five if commercial structures were distributed randomly about the city with reference to the factor of depth. The observed frequency of non-elite domestic structures at a depth of five is zero. When the observed and expected are tested for significance using the chi-square test, the result for a depth of five is 5.9, not significant. The figures in tables 5.11 and 5.12 give the observed vs. expected counts of structures while those in table 5.13 represent a test of all the levels of depth together, rather than just the one depth of 5 illustrated here. The degrees of freedom mentioned in table 5.13 are necessary in order to test significance. The degrees of freedom are calculated by subtracting one from the total number of categories used, in this case six categories minus one.

Table 5.11 Frequencies of observed (Ob.) vs. expected (Ex.) structures in categories Use 1 and Use 2 in relation to depth

Depth	Public		Private		Pub. Sec.		Pub. Relig.
	Ob.	Ex.	Ob.	Ex.	Ob.	Ex.	Ob.
1	20	10.3	5	4.2	20	9.9	0
2	74	53.8	16	22.0	69	51.6	5
3	20	25.6	18	10.5	20	24.6	0
4	3	23.5	8	9.6	3	22.6	0
5	1	6.7	3	2.8	1	6.5	0
6	4	1.9	0	0.8	4	1.8	0

Table 5.12 Frequencies of observed (Ob.) vs. expected (Ex.) structures in category Use 3 in relation to depth

Depth	Admin.		Comm.		Industrial		Elite Dom.		Non-elite	
	Ob.	Ex.	Ob.	Ex.	Ob.	Ex.	Ob.	Ex.	Ob.	Ex.
1	0	0.6	19	9.1	0	0.5	4	1.7	1	1.9
2	5	3.1	63	47.2	1	3.1	8	8.8	8	10.1
3	1	1.5	18	22.5	2	1.5	5	4.2	10	4.8
4	1	1.3	2	20.6	4	1.3	2	3.9	2	4.4
5	0	0.4	1	5.9	0	0.4	1	1.1	2	1.3
6	0	0.1	4	1.7	0	0.1	0	0.3	0	0.4

The analysis of depth produced some important results. The categories public and public secular uses of space (figs. 47 and 48 respectively) proved to have strongly significant distributions in relation to depth. Structures in the categories public and public secular appeared in higher than expected numbers at depths of two and three. The only major anomaly in the general trend for public structures are the four public spaces on the street 5B with a depth of six. All four are part of structures 11-14 and have been categorized above (section 4.4.4.3) as tabernae. Their unusually great depth may be an indication that they were used for storage rather than commercial activity. As there are no contextual data associated with these structures, it is also possible that they date to the Late Antique period, after much of Neapolis had been abandoned. Although I did not calculate the figures for public religious spaces because their frequencies were too low to be statistically significant, it is interesting to note that all of the streets giving access to these spaces fit the general trend of public structures. All religious spaces are in areas that have shallow depths, appearing on streets with a depth of only two.

Table 5.13 Analysis of the distribution of uses of space in Neapolis and the Roman city in relation to depth

Category of Use	Chi-square	Level of Significance
Public	42.92	< 0.001
Private	8.23	not significant
Public Secular	41.11	< 0.001
Administrative	2.52	not significant
Commercial	42.01	< 0.001
Industrial	7.79	not significant
Elite Domestic	4.58	not significant
Non-Elite Domestic	8.55	< 0.13

Degrees of Freedom = 5

On the more specific level of Use 3, the categories of commercial and non-elite domestic space produced significant chi-square statistics. Commercial spaces tended to be located in concentrations greater than expected on streets with lower depths, with the exception of the four tabernae discussed above (fig. 49). Non-elite spaces were located in greater than expected numbers on streets with the mid-range depth of three (fig. 50).

5.5.2 Integration/Segregation

Hillier and Hanson do not place much value on the use of the depth statistic alone, but rather use the concept of depth as the basis of more sophisticated statistical manipulation. They invented a descriptive statistic they call "real relative asymmetry" that indicates how integrated or segregated a particular street is from the rest of the street network (Hillier and Hanson 1984, 108-113). In turn, this statistic also indicates how well the particular street being measured integrates and segregates the rest of the streets in the system.

The integration/segregation statistic allows for a more nuanced labeling of streets than has been practiced for streets in Roman cities in the past. Traditionally streets located in a central position in the city, usually linking a city gate to the forum, are considered to be important thoroughfares while others are considered to be side streets. The integration statistic allows for the quantification of such impressions; streets with a high integration statistic would have acted as important thoroughfares linking areas within the city while streets with a low integration statistic would have acted as side streets segregating areas of the city. Structures located along integrated streets would have had a high profile within the city; they would have been seen and passed by many people who were going about their daily business. Structures located along segregated streets would have had a lower profile; they would have been seen and passed by fewer people in the course of a day.

The integration value is derived by summing the number of streets needed to pass through in order to go from an original street of interest to every other street in the city. The total number of streets minus one, the street from which one is counting, is then divided by this sum. In this way, one calculates the mean depth of every street in the system from the original street. For example, the counts for the number of steps necessary to go from street 18 to every other street in Neapolis are provided in table 5.14. The calculation of the mean depth for street 18 is

Mean = $\frac{\Sigma(\text{depth of all streets from 18})}{(\text{total number of streets - 1})}$ = $\frac{163}{(36-1)}$ = 4.66
Depth

Hillier and Hanson then recommend multiplying the mean depth by a constant, where k equals the number of streets in the system, in order to make all integration statistics vary between zero and one.

$$\text{Relative Asymmetry} = \frac{2(\text{Mean Depth-1})}{k-2}$$

$$\text{RA of street 18} = \frac{2(4.66-1)}{36-2} = 0.215$$

Table 5.14 Depth counts of to every street in Neapolis from street 18

street 1A	4
street 1B	5
street 1C	4
street 1D	5
street 1E	5
street 1F	5
street 1G	6
street 1H	6
street 1I	6
street 2A	2
street 2B	4
street 2C	5
street 3	4
street 4	3
street 5A	3
street 5B	5
street 6A	3
street 6B	4
street 7	3
street 8A	6
street 8B	8
street 8C	7
street 9	4
street 10	5
street 11	5
street 12	5
street 13A	7
street 13B	6
street 14	4
street 15	3
street 16	6
street 17	6
Agora	3
So. Plaza	1
Port	5
Sum	163

In the example of street 18, the integration statistic is 0.215, which is greater than be zero but less than one. Finally, Hillier and Hanson recommend dividing the relative asymmetry statistic by a "D-value." In order to make figures between systems of different sizes comparable, producing a figure they label "real relative asymmetry" (RRA). The "D-value," or "diamond-shaped pattern value" is the relative asymmetry value for a space at the base of a justified map that has k spaces at the mean depth, k/2 at one step above and below the mean, k/4 at the next step above and below and so on until there is only one space at the shallowest and deepest points (Hillier and Hanson 1984, 111-113). This figure will be between zero and two. The D-value for a system of 35 streets, such as Neapolis, is 0.163; in the above example for street 18 in Neapolis, then, the RRA is 1.320

$$\text{RRA} = \frac{0.215}{0.163} = 1.320$$

The RRA values for all streets at Empúries are given below in table 5.15.

In order to study Empúries in this manner, the last division by the D-value is necessary as Neapolis and the Roman city need to be considered as separate systems. While they were joined into one city during the Augustan era, the street system still remained segregated at that time. In Republican period Neapolis there was only one street, 9, that led west from Neapolis towards the Roman city. After the joining of the cities, this apparently remained the only street that led to the west. Even though several other streets were no longer blocked by the impediment of the west wall, they were still blocked by other construction or by the sloping terrain. The same is true for the east wall of the Roman city. The one street that certainly left the Roman city during the Republican period and led east to Neapolis was decumanus D. This street was almost certainly linked to street 9 in Neapolis. With the unification of the two cities the situation did not change. The majority of the other streets in the Roman city were blocked by prior construction, making it impossible for them to have been extended towards the east. The only two streets that may have, in theory, been extended east are decumanus B and decumanus C2. Both were located south of Neapolis, however, so their extension would simply have caused them to intersect with the southern connecting wall. In addition, the base of the eastern wall of the Roman city is still preserved where these two streets met it and there is no indication that the wall itself was ever dismantled in this area. Finally, it is important to note that there is very little evidence for new construction in the space that was incorporated into the city when the connecting walls were built. As discussed in chapter 4 (section 4.6.3) several of the villas expanded into the space that had been between the two cities, but there is no evidence for completely new constructions. Indeed the cemetery Martí, which was used until the third century B.C. and was located between the two cities, shows no signs of having been disturbed after it was incorporated into the city. This fact led Jones to conclude that the Augustan era Emporitani were aware of the old cemetery's existence (Jones 1984, 237-260). Even though walls enclosed the area between the two cities, it still seems to have been treated as a liminal area. Thus Imperial period

Empúries needs to be seen as one city made up of three spatially segregated neighborhoods including Neapolis, the Roman city, and Palaiapolis. While we know virtually nothing about the organization of space in Palaiapolis, it was certainly segregated from the other two neighborhoods as it was on an island.

To interpret the RRA values, Hillier and Hanson suggest that high values indicate streets that are segregated from, and act to segregate, the system. The results for the example above, street 18, show that it was a segregated street. This stands to reason as it is at the edge of the city. In addition, this high RRA value indicates that street 18 served to segregate the street network of Neapolis. It gave access to only one other street in the city. Conversely, street 2A has a low RRA value, indicating that it was integrated into the street network in Neapolis, as it is centrally located. Street 2A also served to integrate the streets in Neapolis as it was possible to access many streets directly from 2A.

finely detailed description of each street. With the RRA values, therefore, the continuum was created by selecting the mean to divide between integrated and segregated and then subdividing these categories by averaging the low value and the mean for integration and the high value and the mean for segregation (tables 5.16-5.18). With all streets assigned to one of these four categories, correlations were sought between the uses of spaces along the streets and their level of integration. The degrees of freedom needed to test for significance were calculated by taking the number of categories, four, and subtracting one, making the degrees of freedom three.

Table 5.16 Frequencies of observed (Ob.) vs. expected (Ex.) structures in categories Use 1 and Use 2 in relation to RRA

RRA	Public		Private		Public Secular		Public Relig.
	Ob.	Ex.	Ob.	Ex.	Ob.	Ex.	Ob.
Highly Integrated	39	21.2	7	8.7	37	20.4	2
Integrated	75	71.6	34	29.4	72	68.7	3
Segregated	3	21.1	9	8.7	3	20.3	0
Highly Segregated	5	7.9	0	3.3	5	7.6	0

Highly Integrated RRA =	0.27–0.63
Integrated RRA =	0.64–0.98
Segregated RRA =	0.99–1.36
Highly Segregated RRA =	1.37–1.78

Table 5.15 RRA values of the streets used in the analysis

Neapolis		Roman City	
street 1A	1.12	cardo A2	0.64
street 1B	1.24	cardo B	0.27
street 1C	0.95	cardo C3	0.85
street 1D	0.91	cardo D2	0.64
street 1E	0.75	decumanus B	0.45
street 1F	0.92	decumanus D	0.45
street 1G	1.20		
street 1H	1.24		
street 1I	1.26		
street 2A	0.64		
street 2B	0.65		
street 2C	0.96		
street 3	0.82		
street 4	0.93		
street 5A	0.88		
street 5B	1.47		
street 6A	0.96		
street 6B	1.32		
street 7	0.97		
street 8A	1.05		
street 8B	1.73		
street 8C	1.38		
street 9	0.61		
street 10	0.96		
street 11	0.96		
street 12	0.94		
street 13A	1.43		
street 13B	1.07		
street 14	1.31		
street 15	0.99		
street 16	1.09	Sum	40.17
street 17	1.30	Minimum	0.27
street 18	1.32	Maximum	1.73
Agora	0.57	Mean	0.98
So. Plaza	0.97	Standard Deviation	0.31

Table 5.17 Frequencies of observed (Ob.) vs. expected (Ex.) structures in category Use 3 in relation to RRA

RRA	Admin.		Comm.		Industrial		Elite Domestic		Non-elite Domestic	
	Ob	Ex.	Ob	Ex	Ob	Ex.	Ob	Ex.	Ob	Ex.
Highly Integ.	3	1.2	34	19	1	1.2	4	3.5	3	4
Integr.	4	4.1	66	63	3	4.1	14	12	16	13
Segreg.	0	1.2	2	18	3	1.2	2	3.5	4	4
Highly Segreg.	0	0.5	5	7	0	0.5	0	1.3	0	1.5

Highly Integrated RRA =	0.27–0.63
Integrated RRA =	0.64–0.98
Segregated RRA =	0.99–1.36
Highly Segregated RRA =	1.37–1.78

Hillier and Hanson divide the RRA values into only two categories, integrated and segregated. Rather than depend on binary categories only, a continuum of four categories moving from highly segregated to segregated, to integrated, to highly integrated is preferable. This allows for a more

In the broad categories of Use 1 and Use 2, the level of integration proved important in the categories of public and public secular space, producing very significant chi-square figures (figs. 51 and 52). Both had unexpectedly high numbers of spaces in the integrated and highly integrated categories. Use 3 produced a higher than expected number of commercial spaces which appeared in integrated and highly integrated categories (fig. 53). Although public religious space was not calculated, it is interesting that all religious spaces occur in the category integrated and highly integrated, just as the other public spaces do.

Table 5.18 Analysis of distribution of uses of space in Neapolis and the Roman city in relation to RRA

Category of Use	Chi-square	Level of Significance
Public	31.62	< 0.001
Private	4.34	not significant
Public Secular	29.32	< 0.001
Administrative	4.27	not significant
Commercial	28.69	< 0.001
Industrial	3.43	not significant
Elite Domestic	2.43	not significant
Non-Elite Domestic	2.21	not significant

Degrees of Freedom = 3

5.5.3 Access

Another descriptive statistic that Hillier and Hanson use is "E-value" or "control statistic" (Hillier and Hanson 1984, 107). The control statistic indicates how much a street controls access to its immediate neighbors. Like the integration statistic, this is a way of separating important streets from side streets. A main thoroughfare in a city exerts strong control over its neighbors as traffic is more likely to travel along the main street simply because it is possible to reach more destinations than by travelling along a side street. Thus the control statistic describes whether or not a street facilitates movement within the city.

Every street has a certain number (n) of intersections with other streets. Hillier and Hanson argue that each street therefore gives an amount of control (1/n) to each of the streets it intersects. To calculate control, one need simply sum 1/n for all the streets that intersect the street of interest. For example, in Neapolis street 6A intersects two streets, 2B and 6B. In turn, street 2A intersects seven streets (n=7) while street 6B intersects only one (n=1). The control value for 6A therefore equals 1.14

$$\text{Control (6A)} = \frac{1}{7} + \frac{1}{1} = \frac{8}{7} = 1.14$$

The control values for all the streets studied are given below in table 5.19.

Hillier and Hanson interpret the control figures produced in this manner by examining whether they are greater than or less than one, greater than one indicating a street which exerts a strong control over the streets it intersects, less than one indicating the opposite. The access values of the streets

at Empúries have a mean of 1.01, confirming that 1 is a good dividing line between strong and weak control. Once again, a shaded continuum was created by subdividing the two categories and averaging the lowest value with the mean and using that to create the categories very weak and weak control, and the highest value with the mean to create the categories very strong and strong control. Thus street 6A would fall into the category strong control. As there are four possible categories, the degrees of freedom needed to test for significance is three (four minus one).

Table 5.19 Control values of the streets used in the analysis

Neapolis		Roman City	
street 1A	2.00	cardo A2	1.35
street 1B	0.66	cardo B	2.03
street 1C	1.50	cardo C3	0.34
street 1D	0.53	cardo D2	1.18
street 1E	2.75	decumanus B	1.28
street 1F	0.75	decumanus D	1.11
street 1G	1.00		
street 1H	0.83		
street 1I	0.58		
street 2A	3.75		
street 2B	1.82		
street 2C	0.75		
street 3	1.16		
street 4	0.47		
street 5A	0.47		
street 5B	0.33		
street 6A	1.14		
street 6B	0.50		
street 7	1.14		
street 8A	0.70		
street 8B	0.50		
street 8C	1.00		
street 9	1.12		
street 10	1.42		
street 11	0.75		
street 12	1.17		
street 13A	0.50		
street 13B	1.20		
street 14	0.50		
street 15	0.14		
street 16	0.20	Sum	41.40
street 17	0.33	Minimum	0.14
street 18	0.50	Maximum	3.75
Agora	0.81	Mean	1.01
So. Plaza	1.14	Standard Deviation	0.70

The results of comparing the access statistic to the location of the categories of use produced significant results only between the location of public and public secular structures and streets that had a very strong control over access to their neighbors (tables 5.20-5.22). On the more specific use level, the location of the use of commercial space was significantly located with regard to the variable control. More commercial spaces appear in the streets with a very strong control over access to other streets than were expected.

Table 5.20 Frequencies of observed (Ob.) vs. expected (Ex.) structures in categories Use 1 and Use 2 in relation to control

Control	Public		Private		Public Secular		Public Religious
	Ob.	Ex.	Ob.	Ex.	Ob.	Ex.	Ob.
Very Weak	19	28.3	10	11.6	19	27.2	0
Weak	11	19.4	8	7.9	11	18.6	0
Strong	68	59.0	23	24.2	63	56.6	5
Very Strong	24	15.3	9	6.3	24	14.6	0

Very Weak Control = 0.0-0.57
Weak Control = 0.58-1.00
Strong Control = 1.01-2.38
Very Strong Control = 2.39-3.75

Table 5.21 Frequencies of observed (Ob.) vs. expected (Ex.) structures in category Use 3 in relation to control

Control	Admin.		Commercial		Industrial		Elite Dom.		Non-elite	
	Ob	Ex.	Ob.	Ex.	Ob.	Ex.	Ob.	Ex.	Ob.	Ex.
Very Weak	0	1.6	18	24.8	3	1.6	2	4.6	5	5.3
Weak	1	1.1	10	17.0	0	1.1	1	3.2	7	3.6
Strong	5	3.4	56	51.7	2	3.4	14	9.7	8	11.1
Very Strong	1	0.9	23	13.4	2	0.9	3	2.5	3	2.9

Very Weak Control = 0.0-0.57
Weak Control = 0.58-1.00
Strong Control = 1.01-2.38
Very Strong Control = 2.39-3.75

Table 5.22 Analysis of the distribution of uses of space in Neapolis and the Roman city in relation to control values

Category of Use	Chi-square	Level of Significance
Public	13.08	< 0.01
Private	1.48	not significant
Public Secular	12.27	< 0.01
Administrative	2.42	not significant
Commercial	12.29	< 0.01
Industrial	4.28	not significant
Elite Domestic	5.03	not significant
Non-Elite Domestic	3.96	not significant

Degrees of Freedom = 3

5.5.4. Minimum Street Width

There is a problem at Empúries that is common to the study of provincial urban centers around the Mediterranean but which is usually overlooked in publication. This is the problem of the minimum street width being so small that it would not have allowed access to carts and pack animals with loads. Such a restriction would have had serious consequences on how useful space along a specific street was for the production or distribution of goods. The minimum width for all of the streets analyzed is given below in table 5.23. One of the striking things about table 5.23 is the greater widths of streets in the Roman city over those in Neapolis. This probably results from the fact that the Roman city was planned while Neapolis was not. Regardless of planning, there is still a critical minimum width a street had to be in order to admit cart traffic. This minimum width was found to be consistent between the Roman city and Neapolis, as will be seen below. All the streets at Empúries are somewhat narrow in comparison to the published widths of streets in other Roman cities (table 5.24). This discrepancy may be more a result of the tendency of archaeologists to focus excavations on public buildings and surrounding primary thoroughfares rather than on private structures and more narrow side streets.

Table 5.23 Minimum widths of the streets used in the analysis in meters

Neapolis		Roman City	
street 1A	0.66	cardo A2	4.00
street 1B	2.26	cardo B	4.00
street 1C	1.80	cardo C3	2.00
street 1D	4.00	cardo D2	4.00
street 1E	2.22	decumanus B	4.00
street 1F	1.83	decumanus D	2.90
street 1G	2.70		
street 1H	1.00		
street 1I	1.36		
street 2A	2.72		
street 2B	2.86		
street 2C	1.47		
street 3	2.43		
street 4	3.20		
street 5A	1.63		
street 5B	2.10		
street 6A	1.04		
street 6B	1.57		
street 7	1.90		
street 8A	1.20		
street 8B	1.60		
street 8C	1.60		
street 9	2.63		
street 10	1.47		
street 11	2.48		
street 12	2.00		
street 13A	2.68	Sum	119.45
street 13B	3.85	Minimum	0.66
street 14	1.37	Maximum	28.00
street 15	1.00	Mean	2.91
street 16	1.35	Standard Deviation	4.15
street 17	1.40	Number of streets less	
street 18	2.17	than 2 m wide	23
Agora	28.00	Number of streets 2 m	
So. Plaza	5.00	wide or greater	18

It is obvious at Empúries that a street such as 1A with its minimum width of little more than half a meter is too small for anything but pedestrian traffic. It is a different matter for streets with a minimum width of one and a half, two, or even more meters (figs. 54 and 55). In order to determine the minimum amount of space an Emporitan cart would have needed to pass, I sought places where wheel ruts still exist around the site.

Fortunately, there is a gate in Neapolis and two in the Roman city where ruts can be seen. By measuring the space between the walls where wheel ruts are visible it was possible to settle on a fairly consistent figure of two meters as the minimum width needed for a cart to pass through ancient Empúries. This figure is quite similar to the minimum width for urban streets set by the Roman legal code, the Twelve Tables. The minimum width of a street is set at eight Roman feet on a straight street and sixteen Roman feet at a corner (vii.6, Warmington 1957). Although the text of the law does not specify that these widths are set for the benefit of cart traffic, it stands to reason that they were as a cart would need the extra room to make the turn around a corner while pedestrian traffic would have no such restrictions. The average Roman foot is equivalent to .2957 m. (Adam 1994, 41), therefore 8 Roman feet are slightly wider than 2 m.

8 Roman feet x .2957 Roman feet/meter = 2.3656 meters

away from, certain areas of the city. At Pompeii a similar phenomenon has been recorded. Residents of the city controlled wheeled traffic by the careful placement of stepping stones, curbs, and road blocks. Study of wheel-rut patterns in the streets confirms that certain streets were closed to cart traffic (Tsujimura 1990, 58-86).

The streets at Empúries were reclassified into two categories based on width in order to determine if there was any correspondence between the fact that a cart or fully loaded donkey could or could not have gone down each particular street, i.e. whether its minimum width was greater than or less than 2 m, and the use of space along that street. The degrees of freedom needed to test for the significance is of course one (two categories minus one). The results are presented in tables 5.25-5.27. The categories public and public secular proved significant, having higher than expected frequencies on streets that were wider than two meters. Commercial structures were significantly distributed, more than were expected appeared along the wider class of streets. Industrial and non-elite domestic space was also significantly distributed in higher than expected numbers along streets with the smaller width, where a donkey or cart could not have passed.

Table 5.24 Minimum width of main streets in some Roman cities (adapted from MacDonald 1986a, 41-42)

Djemila	6 m	August	14 m
Verulam um	6 m	Doclea	15 m
Apollonia (Cyrenaica)	7 m ?	Ptolemais (Cyrenaica)	15 m
Pompeii	7 m	Hierapolis (Phrygia)	16 m ?
Timgad	7 m	Bosra	19 m
Ephesus, Embolos	8 m	Side	20 m
Ostia	8 m	Rome, Via Flaminia	21 m
Ammaecara	9 m ?	Gerasa	22 m
Silchester	9 m ?	Apamea	23 m
Caerwent	11 m	Ephesus, Arkadiané	23 m
Philippoopolis	13 m	Lepcis Magna	42 m

Just as in modern times around the Mediterranean, however, carts are not the only means for transporting bulk goods; donkeys with wooden panniers are also common. In order to determine what minimum width a pack animal would have needed to navigate the streets of ancient Empúries, it was necessary to turn to an ethnographic analogy. Fortunately *burros* are still used as pack animals in L'Escala and so with the help of a local potter who transports his wares to the Sunday market on a donkey, I was able to measure the width of a fully loaded animal with her pack. The donkey, Sofía, and her panniers measured 1.7 m wide. If one allows 0.15 m per side for the swaying of the donkey, this figure rounds up to two meters for the minimum width a donkey like Sofía needs to transport goods through a town. As some streets are less than 2 m wide at their most narrow point, there is every reason to believe that the Emporitani were consciously controlling the flow of wheeled and donkey traffic to, and

Table 5.25 Frequencies of observed (Ob.) vs. expected (Ex.) structures in categories Use 1 and Use 2 in relation to minimum width

Min. Width Width	Public		Private		Public Secular		Public Religious
	Ob.	Ex.	Ob.	Ex.	Ob.	Ex.	Ob.
Less Than 2 m	8	36.0	19	14.8	8	34.6	0
Greater Than 2 m	114	85.9	31	35.2	109	82.4	5

Table 5.26 Frequencies of observed (Ob.) vs. expected (Ex.) structures in category Use 3 in relation to minimum width

Min. Width	Admin.		Comm.		Industrial		Elite Domestic		Non-elite Domestic
	Ob	Ex	Ob	Ex	Ob	Ex	Ob	Ex	Ob	Ex
Less Than 2 m	1	2.1	7	31.6	4	2.1	5	5.9	10	6.
Greater Than 2 m	6	4.9	100	75.4	3	4.9	15	14.1	13	16

low, and very low levels of social interaction. The lowest value, zero meters per door, occurring on streets where there were no doors, corresponds numerically to the category of very high levels of social interaction. But all zero results were transferred to the category of very low levels of social activity as this seemed appropriate for streets with no doors (see tables 5.29-5.31).

Table 5.27 Analysis of the distribution of uses of space in Neapolis and the Roman city in relation to minimum width of the street

Category of Use	Chi-square	Level of Significance
Public	30.98	< 0.001
Private	1.71	not significant
Public Secular	29.00	< 0.001
Administrative	0.78	not significant
Commercial	27.77	< 0.001
Industrial	2.56	< 0.11
Elite Domestic	0.20	not significant
Non-Elite Domestic	2.14	< 0.15

Degrees of freedom = 1

Table 5.28 Street length to door frequency ratio of the streets used in the analysis

Neapolis		Roman City	
street 1A	27.4	cardo A2	7.3
street 1B	8.7	cardo B	11.2
street 1C	11.5	cardo C3	34.5
street 1D	3.6	cardo D2	6.4
street 1E	4.2	decumanus B	2.6
street 1F	25.2	decumanus D	22.0
street 1G	0.0		
street 1H	0.0		
street 1I	27.0		
street 2A	4.9		
street 2B	6.6		
street 2C	4.6		
street 3	78.3		
street 4	26.7		
street 5A	35.7		
street 5B	6.0		
street 6A	0.0		
street 6B	9.1		
street 7	15.2		
street 8A	17.4		
street 8B	13.0		
street 8C	0.0		
street 9	4.5		
street 10	8.8		
street 11	19.1		
street 12	29.1		
street 13A	0.0		
street 13B	8.2		
street 14	0.0		
street 15	15.6		
street 16	0.0	Sum	542.3
street 17	12.4	Minimum	0.0
street 18	22.2	Maximum	78.3
Agora	6.5	Mean	13.
So. Plaza	6.8	Standard Deviation	14.5

5.5.5 Index of Social Interaction

Laurence, in his study of the urban layout of Pompeii, made use of a descriptive statistic derived from dividing the total length of a street in meters by the total number of doors along the street. In this way he created an index of social interaction, reasoning that the higher the frequency of doorways, the greater the amount of social interaction, while the lower frequency of doorways indicated less social interaction (Laurence 1994b, 89-96). An interesting correlate to Laurence's statistic, one that he does not consider, is that level of social interaction also indicates level of social observation. Areas with significant amounts of activity provide an audience for those who want to be noticed in some way, for instance the elite who would want to have been seen wearing fine clothes and surrounded by clients. Conversely, this same audience could have monitored the activities of deviants and visitors to the city, providing some degree of prevention of misdeeds (Jacobs 1962). The meters per door statistics for each of the streets at Empúries is given in table 5.28.

Laurence reports that the median frequency at Pompeii was 7.3 meters, compared to 3.2 meters at Ostia. He interprets this to mean that there was more intense social interaction in the streets of Ostia than at Pompeii. While he does not give the exact figures for his comparison with the streets of Rome, he does state that they were closer to the figures from Ostia than from Pompeii (Laurence 1994b, 88-96). The median for Empúries is 13.0 meters, which suggests a much less intense degree of social interaction in the streets of the provincial city.

Laurence's statistic has much interesting potential that he did not explore, especially if his numbers are broken down into categorizes for the analysis of each site. The same procedure for creating comparative categories was used for this statistic as for the others. Taking the mean as the dividing point between low levels and high levels of activity, each category was subdivided using the method described above. Summing the low and the high values for the two categories and dividing by two, creates four categories, very high, high,

At the general levels of use, there was a correspondence with public and public secular spaces and the two higher categories of social activity. Much of this correspondence is accounted for by the commercial structures, which were placed in significantly higher than expected numbers in the streets with a higher category of meters per doors. Private spaces were generally located in higher than expected numbers in streets with high amounts of social activity. The placement of structures with an industrial use was also in streets with a lower amount of social activity. Elite and non-elite domestic spaces also appeared in higher than expected proportions in the higher categories of social activity, although their significance level was rather low.

Table 5.29 Frequencies of observed (Ob.) vs. expected (Ex.) structures in categories Use 1 and Use 2 in relation to social activity

Social Activity	Public		Private		Public Secular		Public Religious
	Ob.	Ex.	Ob.	Ex.	Ob.	Ex.	Ob.
Very High	92	51.7	26	21.2	88	49.5	4
High	11	21.2	15	8.7	10	20.3	1
Low	18	31.6	9	13.0	18	30.3	0
Very Low	1	17.5	0	7.2	1	16.8	0

Very High = 2.6-7.8 m/door
High = 7.9-13.0 m/door
Low = 13.1-45.5 m/door
Very Low = 45.6-78.3 and 0 m/door

Table 5.30 Frequencies of observed (Ob.) vs. expected (Ex.) structures in category Use 3 in relation to social activity

Soc. Act.	Admin.		Commercial		Industrial		Elite Dom.		Non-elite Dom.	
	Ob.	Ex.	Ob.	Ex.	Ob.	Ex.	Ob.	Ex.	Ob	Ex.
Very High	5	3.0	82	45.3	2	3.0	12	8.5	11	9.7
High	1	1.2	9	18.6	4	1.2	5	3.5	7	4.0
Low	1	1.8	15	27.7	1	1.8	3	5.2	5	6.0
Very Low	0	1.0	1	15.3	0	1.0	0	2.9	0	3.3

Very High = 2.6-7.8 m/door
High = 7.9-13.0 m/door
Low = 13.1-45.5 m/door
Very Low = 45.6-78.3 and 0 m/door

Table 5.31 Analysis of the distribution of uses of space in Neapolis and the Roman city in relation to meters/door

Category of Use	Chi-square	Level of Significance
Public	57.87	< 0.001
Private	14.07	< 0.003
Public Secular	54.99	< 0.001
Administrative	2.81	not significant
Commercial	55.02	< 0.001
Industrial	8.05	< 0.05
Elite Domestic	5.93	< 0.11
Non-Elite Domestic	5.87	< 0.12

Degrees of Freedom = 3

5.5.6 Summary of the Analyses of the Nature of the Street at Empúries

The analyses of the correspondence between the nature of the streets and the location of certain uses of space in the city of Empúries produced some results that may seem rather obvious and others that are quite surprising. The nature of the streets on which unexpectedly high frequencies of public and public secular spaces were located is identical to the nature of the streets on which unexpectedly high frequencies of commercial space were located; commercial space makes up 88% of the spaces recorded under public and slightly more than 90% of the spaces recorded under public secular. Public, public secular, and commercial spaces were located on streets that had characteristics that made them easily accessible and central to the city. These spaces were on streets with low depths, making them easily accessible from outside the city, and on streets that were highly integrated into the urban system and which functioned to integrate the system, indicating they were also easily accessible from inside the city. The streets giving access to these spaces also had high control values, indicating that they were central to movement in the city and that anyone travelling about the city was very likely to travel along a street that contained a public structure. These streets were also wider than the streets which gave access to private structures, indicating that the transportation of heavy goods in carts and by pack animals took place on streets with public structures. This last makes sense in the case of commercial goods where it would have been possible to move large quantities of goods to and from commercial establishments. Finally, public, public secular, and commercial structures were located on streets that had a high ratio of meters per door indicating that they were positioned where there was a high degree of social interaction.

Surprisingly, there were no clear patterns for the location of administrative structures. The nature of the streets on which these structures were located have little in common. There are two possible explanations for this lack of correlation. The first is that it simply is not there, that none of the considerations raised above had any influence on where the Emporitani placed administrative structures. The second, and the more likely, is that some of the structures identified as having an administrative function did not in fact have such a function. Several structures, particularly structures 102 and 69, have only been tentatively linked to administrative functions. They may in fact have nothing to do with administration and their inclusion in this category may have clouded patterns that really do exist.

Although the examination of religious spaces was hampered by small frequency, making any statistical assessment of its importance impossible, there are still some interesting impressions worth noting. Public religious spaces were located along streets that have characteristics identical to the general public category. Public religious structures were located on streets with low depths, on streets that were highly integrated and exerted a strong control over their neighbors, were wider than two meters, and had a high ratio of meters per door. While this correlation cannot be supported statistically, it is quite interesting that it corresponds exactly to the pattern described for public space.

The patterns for private structures were not so strong. These tended to be located along streets that had a higher meters per door ratio and a depth of three. The former indicates that private structures tended to be located on streets where there was a higher degree of social interaction. The latter indicates that they were located at a medium depth, not so deep as to be difficult to reach, but not so shallow to have been easily accessible by those who had just entered the city from outside. There were no significant correlations with the other descriptive statistics, suggesting other factors played a role in their siting.

When private space is broken down into its constituent parts, the results are more interesting. Industrial establishments were located on streets that seem to have been removed from the main activity of the city. They stood on streets with a high depth, showing they were more difficult to reach from outside the city. They were placed on streets with lower ratios of meters per door, suggesting less social activity along these streets. Curiously, they were also positioned along streets that were narrower than two meters, suggesting that they could not have been reached by cart or pack animal. Perhaps the desire to hide these establishments away from general sight was more important than the convenience of easily moving bulk goods. While the frequencies are too small to test for statistical significance, it is nonetheless interesting that there does not appear to be any correlation between the location of similar types of industry. For instance, examples of the types of industry that would have produced the most smoke, metalworking and ceramics firing, can be found both in the middle of the city and at the edge, on major arteries of transport and on back streets.

The results from the residences are equally suggestive. The only correspondence between elite domestic space and the descriptive street statistics is with the higher ratios of meters per door. This suggests that the elite lived along streets where there was a higher degree of social activity. There were three statistics that corresponded to the location of non-elite domestic space. Like elite domestic space, the non-elite lived along streets that had higher meters per door ratio. They resided on streets with mid-range depths and on streets that were generally inaccessible to carts and pack animals. This last tendency must have made the streets outside their doors quieter and safer to traverse than areas along wider streets (on the dangers and annoyances caused by cart traffic in streets see Juv. iii.254-261).

5.6 Visibility

The final factor analyzed in order to determine if it has any explanatory power with regard to the location of certain uses of space in the city is visibility. GIS viewshed analyses are currently very popular in archaeology (Wheatley 1995 and 1996; Llobera 1996; Lock and Harris 1996; Gillings and Goodrick 1996; Madry and Rakos 1996) but the concept of viewshed has been profitably used by classical archaeologists before (cf. Dinsmoor 1939; Snively 1979; Buchner 1982). Archaeologists and historians have long invoked the visibility of Roman temples to help explain their positioning within the city (cf. MacDonald 1986a and 1986b; Stambaugh 1988, 215; Laurence 1994b; 20; Owens 1991,

154; Anderson 1997, 242-247). Temples were often used as landmarks in ancient texts which leads Anderson (1997) to conclude that they could be seen from afar. It has also been argued that the homes of the elite were often placed so that they had a commanding view and so that they could be seen (cf. Owens 1996, 18 and 1991; Stambaugh 1988, 169 and 190). Still, GIS has been employed only once to test what structures were visible from a given vantage point in the built environment of a classical city (Smith 1995, 239-248).

Implementing a viewshed analysis in a built landscape is similar to analyzing the view of a purely natural landscape, but it also constitutes a unique problem as buildings of varying heights can also block views. Like all viewshed analyses, the one implemented on the data from Empúries started with the creation of a Digital Elevation Model (DEM) from a digitized contour plan of the site (Wheatley 1995; Kvamme 1993). The only contour plan of Empúries published at a scale suitable for digitizing was that published by Puig i Cadafalch in 1908. This was the basis for the creation of the DEM. A height value was then assigned to every structure in the three neighborhoods of Empúries based on my field observations and published information. When the height of a building was unknown, for instance in the sections of the Roman city that have not been excavated, it was assumed there were only one-story buildings as the majority of excavated structures were of mud-brick and had too narrow a stone socle to support multiple stories. In order to give the widest possibility to the visibility of structures within the city, it was assumed that there were no trees or tall plants within the city wall capable of blocking the view. This may have been true for much of the city, structures in both Neapolis and the Roman city were built so closely together that they did not leave room for trees, however it is probably not a safe assumption for the intervening space between the cities. If this space lacked structures, as has been argued above, it could certainly have had trees growing in it. Nonetheless, as will be seen below, the assumption that the intervening area was not covered in trees had little effect on the results of the viewshed analysis.

In deciding what types of buildings to test for their visibility across the city, it was obvious that much of Empúries was crowded and that it would have been difficult to see the vast majority of structures from inside the city. There are only two long vistas punctuated by public monuments, only the Capitolium in the forum may have been seen from the south gate and part of the stoa in Neapolis was visible from one portion of street 2A. This much is evident from a glance at a plan of the site. It is equally evident from a careful study of plans and published topographic maps of the site that the only classes of structures that had a chance to be seen were elite villas and temples All other structures could not have been seen from more than few meters away in the crowded city.

No viewshed analysis was necessary to determine that the majority of the elite houses in Neapolis were also not visible from afar. They are packed in beside their neighbors and built to only one story. The best chance for seeing an elite domestic structure from afar was for the villas on the ridge in the Roman city, villas 1, 2a, and 2b. While again it is obvious these villas could not have been seen from very far away inside the Roman city, they do stand on a ridge overlooking Neapolis and so may have been visible form there. Just villa 2b was tested as the results would have been essentially the same for the other two villas. In order to provide as generous parameters as possible, the computer analyzed from which areas the top portion of the back wall of the villa could have been seen, assuming the wall stood 3 m high. Viewer height was also not taken into account, again to allow for as liberal parameters as possible, so that the computer tested the viewshed for even the shortest of viewers The resulting viewshed is presented in figure 56. Areas hatched could have been seen from the villa and, presumably, anyone standing in those areas could have seen the villa. The view point is circled.

The surprising result of this analysis is the invisibility of the villas in the Roman city. Much of the area from which the villas would have been visible is in fact the roofs of buildings in Neapolis, not the public streets and plazas. Thus one would only have caught an occasional glimpse of the villas as one moved about Neapolis.

The results from this viewshed test for one of the temples proves it was likewise invisible from most parts of Neapolis. By studying the plans of the Roman city and Neapolis, it is easy to realize that most of the temples were not visible from the streets. The Serapeum and the temples in the forum were completely enclosed by porticoes of equal height to the temple. The only group of temples that may have had the possibility of being seen from afar were those in the Asklepieion. The central temple in the Asklepieion was selected for the viewshed analysis. The temple is represented by a circled dot on figure 57. Like the analysis of the villas, the viewshed analysis proves the temple would have been virtually invisible from the streets of Neapolis because of the crowded nature of the structures in the city. The builders at Empúries must have realized that the buildings they were creating could not be seen from far off inside the city. To make up for this, they made certain that there was an open plaza in front of the public architecture so that viewers could take several steps back and actually see the entire façade of the building. All the temples have space in front of them, as does the stoa in the Neapolis agora and the monumental entrance to the amphitheater, just outside of the Roman city, ensuring the façade could be seen as a whole.

One of the interesting things revealed by the viewshed analysis, however, is the fact that both the villa and the temple had views of the sea and, therefore, could have been seen from the sea. While the reason for this may have been the desire of the villa owner for a view of the sea and the ritual needs of the worshippers of Asklepios for a view of the horizon or perhaps the rising sun, the only way to have seen and appreciated the city must have been from the sea. The cityscape must have made a strong impression on a person arriving by sea. Unfortunately, while there are not enough data available to determine what was visible in Palaiapolis, it is still safe to assume that the Temple of Artemis was visible from the sea as the church of Sant Martí, which probably stands on the site of the temple, stands on a bluff facing the sea..

5.7 Summary of the Use of Space in the Imperial Period at Empúries

Raper argued that the use of space at Pompeii had few patterns. He found some public structures clustered together and tabernae lining important streets, but in the end he decided that the use of space was mixed in a random pattern around the city. The present analysis calls this finding into question. While there are certainly mixtures in the use of space at Empúries, these mixtures do not appear to be random at all; they were highly structured. There seem to have been very specific rules or social norms about where structures with specific functions could be placed and what types of use of space could, or could not, be placed beside one another.

The strongest and most consistent patterns in the use of space detected in the descriptive statistics above were in Use 1: public, Use 2: public secular, and Use 3: commercial space. It is quite interesting that these patterns confirmed those detected by Raper at Pompeii. At Empúries, public, public secular, and commercial structures were clustered together in the same parts of the city and often in the same blocks. These structures were located on streets that facilitated movement around the city and along streets where there was much social activity. Public, public secular, and commercial spaces were not particularly visible across the city. When visibility was important for a public structure, the Emporitani usually built an open plaza in front of the structure so a viewer could have a clear line of sight from far enough away to be able to see most of the structure.

The descriptive statistics used above were of little value in identifying patterns in the location of space devoted to administrative, educational, and entertainment functions. The problem in the first case is almost certainly a problem with identifying the use of space in the archaeological record. In the latter cases the problems arise from the very simple reason that the amphitheater and palaestra were situated outside the city's gates, thus rendering the statistics useless. Nonetheless, the one interesting factor they have in common is their visibility. In the forum and the agora the administrative buildings were built on the edge of open space, rendering them highly visible. Perhaps it is this visibility that helps to explain why the majority of statuary and inscriptions were found associated with administrative spaces. The same is true for the amphitheater and the palaestra outside the city walls.

The description of the location of religious space also presented problems from the small number of areas available for sampling; certain patterns, nonetheless, still appeared. The entrances to religious spaces were located along important thoroughfares where there must have been much activity. The temples were not particularly visible from outside their precincts, although they dominated the space within their grounds. Finally, religious space appears to have been exclusive space divided from other uses. While the temples in the Roman forum shared the space with buildings of an administrative nature and those in the Asklepieion and Serapeum with structures for defensive purposes, all other uses of space were excluded from the blocks where the temples stood.

While there were patterns in the distribution of private space, these patterns were fewer and much more difficult to detect than the patterns observed for public space. Private spaces had a tendency to be clustered together on the same blocks and were not particularly visible from afar. Non-elite domestic structures were built side by side while elite domestic structures were limited to one per block. Private domestic spaces appeared on streets with higher amounts of social activity while private industrial spaces had the opposite distribution, being located on streets with lower amounts of social activities. Both non-elite domestic and industrial structures were located along streets that were quieter, usually barring wheeled traffic and standing farther from the gates.

This chapter has focused on the identification and description of patterns for the use of space at Empúries during the second half of the first century A.D. The number of patterns found indicates that the use of space in the city was highly structured by social norms. The following chapter offers an explanation of the observed patterns and the implied social norms. The explanation places the observations made in this chapter into the context of Roman urban society and focuses on the people who lived and worked in the city of Empúries.

6

CONCLUSION: THE URBAN DIALOGUE

Abstulerat totam temerarius institor urbem
            inque suo nullum limine limen erat.
iussisti tenuis, Germanice, crescere vicos,
            et modo quae fuerat semita, facta via est.
nulla catenatis pila est praecincta lagonis
            nec praetor medio cogitur ire luto,
stringitur in densa nec caeca novacula turba,
            occupat aut totas nigra popina vias.
tonsor, copo, cocus, lainus sua limina servant.
            nunc Roma est, nuper magna taberna fuit.

Those impetuous shopkeepers had stolen the entire city,
            their shops' thresholds spilled into the streets themselves.
Now you, Germanicus, have ordered narrow alleys to grow wide
            and what was recently a footpath is now a true city street.
No column is chained with a wine shop's flagon anymore.
            No praetor is forced from the sidewalk to walk in the muddy road.
The barber's razor is not wielded blindly in tangled crowds.
            Nor does a grimy cook shop occupy every street.
Barber, wine seller, cook and butcher are kept in their places.
            And Rome is a city again, while recently it was merely one giant shop.

Martial, *Epigrammata* 7.61

6.1. Introduction

In the above epigram, Martial praises an edict by Domitian, referred to as Germanicus by the poet, issued in A.D. 92 that ordered the widening of Rome's streets and banned the extension of shops beyond their buildings' thresholds. Superficially, this epigram can be read as an indication of the power of one of the Roman elite in shaping the form of urban space. This power cannot be denied and there are numerous examples of elites placing monuments within the urban framework or reorganizing urban space in order to remake the city to fit their vision of what a city should be (Anderson 1997, 227-230 and 242-247; Zanker 1988).

Despite claims to the contrary, admitting that the elite could assert their power and augment their status through the modification of urban space does not mean that they were solely responsible for the organization of cities. The urban form does not represent a monologue on the part of the elite. A more subtle reading of Martial's epigram suggests a dialogue between elite and non-elite over the use of space provided by the street. The elite, in this case the emperor and praetors, saw the city street as a vehicle for movement. They wanted travelers along the streets to be able to reach their destinations rapidly and not be distracted by the neighborhoods through which they had to pass. The elite wanted the visitors to these streets to be isolated from the residents of the streets. The non-elite, on the other hand, appear to have wanted to include the visitors in their neighborhoods. By slowing the visitors' progress through numerous obstacles in the street, the non-elite opened their neighborhoods to visitors, encouraging them to linger and shop or to take advantage of the services that the people of the neighborhood had to offer.

The epigram implies that the form of the city as a whole represents a dialogue rather than a monologue. The different constituents of the city generated the social norms that determined the placement of specific uses of space within the city as each sought to meet their own needs for the use of urban space. Martial states that there was a stark difference between the appearance of the streets of Rome before and after Domitian's edict. No doubt this is hyperbole intended to flatter the emperor. Domitian was not the first, nor the last, emperor to take such measures, which suggests that the imperial edicts were, at best, respected temporarily before shop owners began to exploit the city streets for their own purposes again. The real situation probably did not change significantly after the edict was issued. The non-elite must have agreed to leave part of the street open to allow for the rapid passage of traffic while the elite must have allowed the shop-keepers to use parts of the streets and sidewalks to advertise their wares and supply their services. Such a compromise would have given the travelers along the street the option of lingering or rapidly passing through as they desired.

As was demonstrated above in chapter 5, the arrangement of space in the Roman city of Empúries was highly structured. The commonalities in the arrangement of space at Empúries suggest social norms about how certain space could be used and where certain uses of space could be placed. These social norms were the result of a dialogue among all of the city's constituents, with the intention of meeting everyone's needs for the use of space. These urban constituents can be divided into a number of categories although, unfortunately, only the broadest social categories can be recognized in the archaeological record at Empúries. These constituents include resident elite, resident non-elite, non-resident visitors, and the supernatural. Each of these groups had specific needs for the use of space within the city and the final form of the city represents the contribution of each to the dialogue over how space should be used. These needs were conditioned by the role of each group in society and their uses of space can only be understood in the specific context of Roman culture. The uses of space by each group are each examined individually below.

First, however, it is important to remind the reader that at Empúries the majority of the evidence dates to the latter half of the first century A.D. The dialogue among the urban constituents was certainly in a constant state of flux as the needs of each group changed over time. Thus Imperial Empúries had a very different appearance from the Republican or Late Antique Empúries. The analysis of the data presented here is applicable mainly to the Imperial period at the site. At the end of this chapter, however, a different set of constituents is considered for an earlier point in time. Although the evidence is limited, there is still enough to consider how the use of space at the site was used to define ethnic boundaries during the Republican period.

6.2. The Elite

Although all male citizens had the right to participate in the political life of the city, it was only those citizens who had the resources to spend time in the town, free from other duties, who dominated the political scene (Reynolds 1988, 15-51). In order to gain ever-higher public offices, elites volunteered to use the excess resources produced on their private rural estates for the improvement of urban centers. This was probably the mechanism that led to the building of the amphitheater and forum at Empúries. Their munificence was acknowledged by an elite's peers, i.e., the other town magistrates, through the authorization of the setting up of statues and inscriptions in the forum and other public places around the city recognizing the magistrate's contribution to the city (Mackie 1990, 179-192). Elite status was also determined by the number of clients who were bound to the elite in a patron-client relationship (Falla 1980). The client owed the patron for the favors and benefactions he received and the patron could call upon his clients to return the favors whenever he needed them (Stambaugh 1988, 92-93). This was a formal relationship demonstrated and strengthened in Rome by a morning visit, or *salutatio*, by the clients to their patrons' homes to pay their respects, to make requests, and to receive small gifts (Juv. 184-189; Mart. x.74; Sen. *Ep.* xlvii.18; Sall. *Cat.* xxviii.1).

The patron-client system was certainly employed at Empúries as the city was thoroughly Romanized. The majority of the citizens of the Roman city were immigrants from Italy (Livy xxxiv.9.3) and many of the Greek citizens of Neapolis seem to have adopted Roman customs (see section 6.6 below). The forms of architecture in both Neapolis and the Roman city and the urban layout of the Roman city are identical to structures and urban layouts in the Roman cities of the Italian peninsula, demonstrating the strong cultural ties between Empúries and Rome. Finally, the villas of Empúries contain the requisite architectural features for the visit of a client to his patron, the atrium and the peristyle.

The role of the elite was, to a degree, created and reinforced by the arrangement of space at Empúries. In public space, the elite made certain that their presence was felt through statues and inscriptions, although the spaces with these embellishments appear to have been few. All 221 fragments of statuary found in public contexts at Empúries were discovered only in the religious precincts, the forum, and the agora. The distribution of the 44 fragments of inscriptions found in the city is similarly restricted. These distributions are typical of Roman cities. What is interesting, however, is the absence of statues and inscriptions along streets or in plazas other than the forum, the agora, and the religious precincts. It seems that the elite limited the erection of statues and inscriptions to certain nodes within the city that were separated, to some degree, from the bustle and distractions of the rest of public space. The exclusion of commercial activity and wheeled traffic from the Imperial-period forum must have made this space a relatively calm place from which to escape the noise of the markets directly north and south of the forum. The portico around the plaza containing the Serapeum and the walls around the Asklepieion must have had a similar effect, shutting out the distractions from the shops and traffic in the southern plaza. The same was probably not true of the agora, which remained an important node in the street network connecting the southern and northern ends of Neapolis. The agora maintained its Hellenistic layout, however, and was not adapted to new cultural ideas after the two cities were joined. Another node in Neapolis where the elite created architectural settings where statues and inscriptions may have stood include the small stoa (structure 103). Similar settings in the Roman city may be found at the amphitheater and palaestra just outside the Roman city gates, and possibly the large unexcavated structure in the Roman city along cardo C (see section 4.4.3.2). Thus the presence of the elite did not dominate the city. The elite did not place statues or inscriptions along every city street; instead they selected certain points where they could create an entire architectural setting and decorate it as they chose to remind people of their role in urban and provincial life.

W. MacDonald has argued for a similar arrangement of space in Roman cities in general. He pointed out that streets in Roman cities had the purpose of conducting traffic at a fairly rapid pace. The flow of traffic was slowed at certain nodal points where the traveler was encouraged to linger to rest, fetch water, or attend to some other business. MacDonald argued there was no point in having elaborate architecture and decoration along streets, as the purpose of the street was to facilitate movement and such things would only slow movement down as people lingered to look at the monuments. Fine architecture and other embellishments were reserved for nodal points in the street network where traffic was meant to be diverted in conjunction with some other function of urban space, such as the plazas in front of temples or by fora (MacDonald 1986, 32-33 and 62-63).

With the arrangement of the visibility of their private space, it appears that the elite had no intention of building their homes in such a way that all residents of, and visitors to, the city were constantly reminded of their presence. Their houses were not particularly visible from the outside. Even when it would have been possible to build a structure that could have dominated all views from the public portions of the city, something which would have been easy for the owners of villas 1, 2a, and 2b to have done, they chose not to. Instead they built low structures with gardens toward the crest of the hill that served to screen their residences from viewers in the city.

The elite living in Neapolis also appear to have wanted their homes to be separated from one another. There is only one elite house per insula in Neapolis. Robinson found a similar distribution of elite domestic structures at Pompeii and interpreted it to mean that the elite were surrounded by a neighborhood they controlled, owning and renting out many of the properties attached to, or located near, their villas. He also argued that the separation of the elite allowed them to avoid direct competition for the loyalties and attentions of the people living in their neighborhoods (Robinson 1997). Both of these are possible explanations for the distribution of elite housing in Neapolis. A third possible explanation for the dispersion of elite residences is that the elite simply wanted to be able to expand their villas if the opportunity arose. The structural evidence from several villas at Empúries indicates that their owners acquired neighboring properties at some point and either incorporated the existing structures into their villas or tore them down and built new additions. Such a construction tactic is known to us from ancient literature as well (Sall. *Iug.* xli.8-9). It would have been easier for an elite villa owner to absorb a neighboring non-elite or industrial structure than to fight with another villa owner for the chance to expand. It must be noted, however, that the separation of elite homes occurred only in Neapolis. In the Roman city four villas were originally built next to each other, two each on two adjoining blocks. Two of these villa owners seem to have had no problem acquiring portions of their neighbor's properties in order to expand their own villas.

The elite also lived on streets that had a high degree of social activity. This may be related to the element of appearance so important in Roman society. In order to maintain their status, the patricians had to be seen wearing good dress and surrounded by clients as they walked about the city. Emerging from their house on to a street where there were lots of people engaged in diverse errands and business would have increased that visibility. Also, people seeing a line of clients outside the doors of an elite house waiting to perform the morning *salutatio* must also have increased the patron's status.

To some extent the large number of doorways, and therefore the large amount of social activity, located along the streets where the elite lived was a pre-existing condition of the street and may have helped the elite decide to locate there. There can be no doubt, however, that the elite increased the number of doorways and the amount of social activity. Several of the elite structures at Empúries had associated tabernae built into their façades. Such arrangements are common at Pompeii and other Roman urban sites and are frequently assumed to have a financial explanation, namely that the elite rented out these tabernae for extra income. It is also possible, however, that this was a calculated feature of the Roman elite that allowed them to live on streets where there was much social activity, thus increasing the elites' visibility.

It is difficult to say who was involved in much of the

manufacturing that went on at Empúries and whether their status was that of an elite or non-elite. There are simply no clues to who was utilizing the bloomeries on the coast or extracting the stone from the quarries, or even of the date of these activities. The kilns, both of which stand immediately outside and inside the city walls, also rarely have an associated structure to indicate the status of the person or persons who used them. Nonetheless, we can be sure that some elite did engage in some sorts of industrial activity. The fact that the majority of the Dressel 8 Ampuritana amphoras and amphoras stamped "ANTH" have been found in villa 1 indicates that the owner of the property engaged in manufacturing amphoras, probably for wine. Whether this production was for profit, or simply for home use and distribution among clients and friends in order to increase social status is impossible to say. More interesting is the case of structure 57, whose owner installed metal production equipment in the middle of his peristyle, possibly indicating that he had fallen on tough financial times. This suggestion of a haphazard entrance into manufacturing may explain why there were so few patterns in the locations of industrial activities. The elite may not have acquired property with the intention of engaging in industrial activity; they may have taken up production of goods where they could when the need arose.

6.3. The Non-Elite

In literature, the Romans idealized those who made their livelihood on their own land (Cic. *Off.* i.42; Columella *Rust.* i). Those who sold their labor or goods in order to earn their bread were considered to have a lower status. The non-elite of Empúries certainly included people in both of these categories. Those who owned and cultivated small plots of land around the city, producing enough to survive and perhaps a bit more, lived within the city's walls. In addition, people who manufactured goods as well as those who traded Mediterranean imports for food and other resources from the countryside also lived in the city. It was this class of people who sought the favors of the elite and thus became their clients.

These farmers, manufacturers, and merchants played an important role not only in the economy of the city, but in the economy of the region as well. Empúries was a center for redistribution of goods from the local countryside to the wider Mediterranean world and from the Mediterranean to the local countryside. As discussed in chapter 2, Empúries was located at the end of several routes of communication that lead from the interior to the coast. These routes allowed for the transport of cereals, grapes or wine, and metals from the countryside to the city. Many of the raw products produced in the countryside were processed at the city of Empúries. Several of the structures discussed in chapter 4 had industrial features used for converting raw ores to refined metals. The owner of villa 1 may have been producing amphoras to be filled with wine made from grapes grown outside the city. Strabo also claimed that the Emporitani were known for their skill at working flax, a raw material that was grown outside the city (iii.4.9). The ships that took these products away from Empúries also brought products to the city. The large amount of imported ceramics discovered at the site is some indication of the types of products that were distributed to the countryside from Empúries. The role of Empúries as a redistribution node is also indicated by the discovery of southern Gaulish ceramics and Baetican oil amphoras found on the shipwreck Cala Culip IV, which sank near Empúries in the first century A.D. (Nieto et al. 1989; Wiseman 1996, 10-13; Millett 1993, 415-419).

The few industrial establishments associated with the non-elite have little in common, suggesting that there were few social norms or municipal laws referring to the placement of industries. In general, they seem to have been tucked away in areas with low levels of social activities. Non-elite industrial establishments were difficult to reach. The Emporitani seem to have wanted to isolate industrial structures, perhaps to separate the noises, smells, smoke, and sights associated with manufacturing from the rest of the town. The frequent placement of industrial establishments on streets too narrow for carts or pack animals also confirms that considerations other than functional ones played an important role in their placement, as the narrow nature of the streets would have made it difficult to transport raw materials or the resultant products. The manufacturers of goods probably did not invite the public directly into their workshops to display and sell their goods, as these locations would have been difficult to find, rather they probably brought the finished products to shops in more prominent locations.

Included among the non-elite are the proprietors and, presumably, the residents of the tabernae. The locations of the tabernae were carefully calculated to take advantage of areas where there were the greatest numbers of people passing by. Tabernae were nearly always placed together, so that each shop would benefit from the other's customers. This clustering resulted in a low meters-per-door ratio since the structures were often small, consisting of one or two cells. This small size allowed for more doorways to be placed on streets where there were tabernae and insuring that the streets on which they were placed would have a high degree of social interaction. Tabernae owners or renters exploited streets that served to tie the city together, i.e. the main arteries and the streets easily accessible from the city gates. This way they could gain the attention both of residents and visitors to the town. Their placement along the wider streets also guaranteed the easy transportation of products to and from their shops. The non-elite seem to have controlled the appearance of these main streets; the elite did not attempt to compete by placing statues and inscriptions along them.

The non-elite who lived in houses rather than tabernae had their houses beside one another, unlike the elite. They had little opportunity to separate themselves from other non-elite for the simple functional reason of limited space. There were more non-elite domestic structures than there were elite domestic structures at Empúries, making it unlikely for any block containing housing not to have a non-elite house. The non-elite lived in areas that must have had a distinct neighborhood feel to them. Their houses were located in areas that were moderately difficult to reach from the city's gates, insuring that it would be slightly difficult for strangers

to the city to wander into the streets where their houses stood. In addition, these streets had a great deal of social activity, which would have ensured that enough residents were around to monitor and police what happened in their neighborhood. The neighborhood feel must have been reinforced by the exclusion of pack animals and carts making the area quiet and safe.

6.4. The Non-Residents

Non-residents were just as important to the social life of Empúries as were the residents of the city. Non-residents were attracted to the city for a number of reasons. They took advantage of the services the city provided to have tools repaired, to be entertained, and to engage in business. The religious services offered by the city were certainly important to the non-residents, and the temple of Asklepios must have attracted pilgrims from all over the territory around Empúries seeking cures for physical ailments. Administrative services provided by the city played an important part for non-residents. Taxes were collected and justice was dispensed through cities, so Empúries must have been an important regional administrative center and the city's elite must also have played the role of a regional elite. The city also provided non-residents with the opportunity to purchase goods produced in the city or its immediate vicinity, or imported from all over the Mediterranean. In exchange for these goods and services, the non-residents brought produce and raw materials from the countryside that were vital to the survival of the city as Empúries was certainly incapable of supporting itself from the farmland available in the immediate vicinity of the city (see chapter 3, section 3.2). The lively trade in goods between the coast and the interior must have provided the basis for much wealth, as is indicated by the Alexandrian merchant who funded the construction of a temple and precinct to his native gods (see chapter 4, section 4.5.2).

Although non-residents did not have a voice in deciding how space should be arranged, they were still constituents of the ancient city. The Emporitani must have taken the needs of non-residents into consideration when deciding how they wanted to interact with outsiders, and they arranged space in their city accordingly. Public spaces, the spaces non-residents would use, were positioned to allow easy access to visitors. They were grouped together along streets with low depths, thus making them easily accessible from the gates of the city. Public spaces were located along the main arteries of the city. These streets facilitated movement through the city as they allowed for quick and easy movement to other streets and other areas of the city. These factors would have made it possible for non-residents visiting Empúries for the first time to find their way with relative ease to the goods or services they were seeking. Public spaces were also located on wider streets, which were thus important for the movement of bulk goods from the port through the city to the countryside and from the countryside to the port. The spaces providing religious and administrative services were easy to find as well and were segregated from the rest of the city by porticoes and walls. These features made the forum and temple precincts much quieter and more solemnly monumental for both the non-resident visitor and the resident.

While all of these features indicate that the Emporitani made an effort to integrate non-residents into the fabric of their city, it still appears that the residents of the city harbored a desire to keep non-residents separate and controlled to some degree. The most obvious indication of this is the existence of the city wall. The Emporitani do not appear to have hesitated to dismantle parts of their city wall when they wanted to eliminate the barriers separating the Roman city from Neapolis. Yet they chose to maintain their city walls even during the time of peace following the accession of Augustus. Besides serving an obvious defensive function, the system of walls and gates allowed the Emporitani to monitor non-residents entering the city and perhaps to exact customs duties. The gates also directed the progress of the non-resident into the city along specific, streets.

A similar desire to separate resident and non-resident can be seen in the placement of the non-elite domestic spaces. The fact that these were often located along streets that were too narrow for cart or pack-animal traffic ensured that non-residents bringing produce and raw materials to the city would be incapable of passing through their neighborhoods. Where they did allow non-residents into their town, the Emporitani seem to have taken the precaution of locating the places non-residents would have wanted to visit in areas with high degrees of social activity. The degree of social activity was equally high for locations of private homes of the elite, places where many non-residents must have gone to seek favors or loans from prominent Emporitani. Directing non-residents to streets with high social activity insured that there would be resident Emporitani present to monitor the activities of the strangers.

The only exception to this rule of selective integration is to be found in the location of industrial establishments. It would have been very difficult for a non-resident to find a producer of ceramics or iron goods within the city, although these would certainly have been important to a person from a part of the countryside that could not afford to keep an iron worker or ceramist in business. The hidden nature of industrial establishments is emphasized for comic effect in Terence's, *Adelphoe* (570-590). In the scene a conniving slave sends his master's brother to find a furniture shop knowing he will become lost, thus giving the slave plenty of time to perform evil deeds at home. It is possible that the manufacturers of goods at Empúries did not actually interact with customers at the site of their workshops. They may have brought their finished products to a separate location in the agora or forum or to one of the tabernae lining the streets of Neapolis and the Roman city. While such a hypothesis is impossible to prove, it is supported by sculptural evidence from reliefs discovered in Italy (Frank 1940, 187-188 and 262). In addition, the discovery of two ceramic molds in separate locations, both of which were clearly commercial in nature and far from any indication of ceramic kilns, also lend credence to the idea that workshops and commercial shops worked together in separate locations. One mold was discovered in a taberna on the agora in Neapolis and the other, depicting a scene of the death of Adonis, was discovered in the shops excavated in villa 3 (Mar and Ruiz 1993, 426; Almagro 1962, Lam. 2).

6.5. The Supernatural

A final class of constituents of the city to consider is the supernatural, i.e. the gods and the dead. The supernatural had an important role in civic life; they were thought to make important contributions to the wellbeing of individuals and to the city as a whole. Like the non-residents, the supernatural did not make decisions about how space should be arranged. The Emporitani made these decisions and attempted to accommodate what they perceived to be the needs of the supernatural and to direct their interactions with mortals.

It is quite interesting that the functions associated with these constituents were exclusive. There was little mixing of religious and funerary activities with other uses of space. This is a bit peculiar because small street-side shrines were common in Roman cities. Their absence in the Roman city may be a result of the lack of excavation, only 10% of the site has been excavated, while their absence from Neapolis may have something to do with the conversion of the area into a Christian cemetery. The evidence for temples, on the other hand, is much more complete. The areas containing the Serapeum and the Asklepieion have no other uses, with the exception of defense, the city wall forming part of their precincts. Otherwise, residences, shops, and all other types of structures were kept away from the temples. In the forum, administrative and religious functions appear in the same space, although the religious functions were clearly separated from the administrative by the line of the decumanus, which would have separated the two halves of the forum. All other types of structures were separated from forum temples by the porticos lining the forum on all sides. As is commonly seen at other Roman urban sites, the dead were also relegated to exclusive zones, not to be mixed with other functions. The only possible exception is the necropolis at Les Coves where evidence for metal working and quarrying was also found (see chapter 4, section 4.6.1.4). The industrial functions, however, seem to have been limited to the very edge of the promontory, adjacent to the sea, while the burials were located further inland, thus suggesting spatial segregation.

The religious precincts were placed in areas that were easy to reach from both inside and outside the city, standing along the important arteries of communication near the city gate. This would have facilitated visits from non-residents and, in the case of the Asklepieion, would have eased the rapid removal of those who died while seeking cures for their ailments. The precincts of Asklepios in Corinth, Delos, and Pergamon are similarly placed on the edges, or outside, of the cities (Edelstein and Edelstein 1988, 735-822). The religious precincts of Empúries were not visible from most parts of the city and the walls separated the temple precincts from the rest of the city. The purpose of this separation may have been to give worshippers a quieter area from which to make their sacrifices and prayers, undisturbed by the noise and confusion of the streets directly outside the precinct walls. Such quiet may have been particularly important to the worshippers of Asklepios who were required to sleep in order to have a vision of the god.

The placement of temples behind precinct walls is typical in the Roman world, allowing for a physical barrier to separate sacred and profane spaces. Precinct walls were also required around sanctuaries of the mystery cults because the uninitiated were not allowed to see the rites. Hiding the precincts behind walls may also have had the calculated effect of providing an experience of epiphany as the house and the image of the god were suddenly and dramatically revealed once the worshipper entered the temple grounds. Such an effect would have been important in the rites of the mystery cults of Serapis and Isis. The effect would also have been important for the worshipper of Asklepios who would have mounted a broad, high stairway to enter the precinct. Quite literally rising above the noise, crowds, and distractions of the southern plaza, the worshipper would have entered a quiet and serene space dominated by the temple of the god. This arrangement is identical to the layout of the precincts of Asklepios at Kos, although the Kos precinct was built on a much grander scale than the one at Empúries. The visitor to the precinct at Kos would ascend through stages from the abaton to reach the altar and temple.

The placement of the Asklepieion on the edge of the city may have had advantages other than simply allowing visitors easy access. There also seems to have been a desire to keep the sanctuaries of Asklepios in areas that were set away from much of the population of the city. This is seen not just at the sites where the Asklepieion is placed near or outside the city walls; at Rome the god's sanctuary was placed on an island in the Tibur, while at Carthage and Athens the temples were placed on the acropoleis (Walton 1979, 36). At Empúries the Asklepieion was similarly located in an area with a low population density, between the city wall and the acropolis.

Placement of space for the dead was equally important. The bodies of the dead had to be placed outside the city walls and the magical protective boundary of the pomerium, as spirits of the dead could be malevolent and dead human bodies were considered to be ritually impure (Plaut. *Cas.* 353). Laws were passed requiring burial of the dead outside the city walls (Cic. *Leg.* ii.58). Yet the dead could not be forgotten. For this reason, sepulchre monuments were built. The issue of access to the monuments was of little importance. There is no indication that the Emporitani made any attempt to direct traffic through the cemeteries of the town. The cemeteries lined public roads leading to the city gates (Juv. i.170-171). People were free to leave the road and wander about and inspect monuments as they saw fit. The more important principle of spatial organization in the Roman cemeteries was visibility. Some sepulchre monuments were placed just outside the gates of Neapolis and the Roman city so that residents and visitors would see them as they passed in and out of the city. Others were placed on hills near the city. Only one of these funerary monuments survives today above ground, but even in its ruined state it can be seen for miles in all directions.

6.6. Iberians, Greeks, and Romans

The constituents of the city can also be divided into categories based on their ethnic affiliations. Unfortunately, the remains of the ethnic component of the urban dialogue has not left as strong traces as the other components described above. Nonetheless, it is possible to assemble some of the fragmentary data in order to examine ethnicity and the use of space in the city at an earlier time than the rest of this study, in the Republican period.

The three ethnic groups at Empúries were Iberians, Greeks, and Romans. Written sources suggest tension between Greeks and Iberians, probably reflecting the situation during the Iberian Revolt of 197-195 B.C. Livy and Strabo state that there was a general assimilation of Greeks and Iberians by the Romans in the late Republican period (Livy xxxiv.9; Strabo iii.4.8; Almagro 1951b; Sanmartí 1993a; Sanmartí 1993b). As discussed in chapter 3 (section 3.5), the written sources claim that prior to the end of the third century B.C. and the arrival of the Romans, the Greeks and Iberians lived in spatially segregated sections of the same settlement. No evidence for an Iberian neighborhood or town has been discovered at the site, despite excavations on all landward sides of Neapolis. Clearly both Livy and Strabo were reporting a confused account of the exact physical relationship between the settlements. Nonetheless, an Iberian settlement, Indika, did exist near or in Neapolis. This is proved by the coins issued in the name of the Iberian town (Villaronga 1977; Almagro 1955, 55-62) and the existence in the Flavian period of a group referred to as the *Indicetani* at Empúries (see chapter 3, section 3.5) (Fabré et al. 1991).

Despite their confusion, there are enough clues within Livy's and Strabo's descriptions to offer an alternative to the literal reading of the texts. They give four characteristics of the location and layout of Indika. The first, that Indika adjoined Neapolis, has been proven false by excavation. Livy and Strabo maintained further that Indika lay inland from the Greek city (meaning either west or south of Neapolis), that it was much larger than Neapolis, and that only one gate led from the Greek to the Iberian sector. If one substitutes the Roman city for Indika in this description, it begins to make more sense. The Roman city did lie inland from, and was much larger than, Neapolis. In addition, the Roman city was a double city, with adjoining neighborhoods separated by a wall, the transverse wall, apparently linked by only one gate. It could be that the mistake of Livy and Strabo was chronological, rather than physical. They may have been mixing accounts of M. Porcius Cato from the time of the Iberian revolt with other sources that discussed Empúries at the time Livy and Strabo were writing.

In this alternative reading of the sources, Indika stood west of Neapolis on a small, easily defensible plateau above Neapolis. The Romans recognized the strategic importance of the plateau when they arrived, and built their first military camp on the plateau south of Indika and west of Neapolis. Livy suggests that the Indicetani were granted a legal status uniting them with the citizens of the Roman city before the Greeks were given the same privilege. The numismatic record confirms the close tie between the Romans and Indicetani in the Republican period, a tie that excluded the Greeks. Issues of coins with Greek legends ceased at the time of the Roman arrival and were substituted for coins with Iberian legends spelling out the Iberian name for Indika, *Untikesken*. The Romans were certainly responsible for this change, since the new issues fit the Roman metrological system and there was a mixture of Roman and Iberian names among the magistrates named on the coins (Villaronga 1977,

17-21).

Eventually the Roman fort was rebuilt as a true Roman city. At that time, the ties between the Indicetani and the Romans may have been manifested in the incorporation of Indika into the new urban layout of the Roman city. Although there were ties, there also appear to have been barriers between Romans and Indicetani. The fact that legal advocates in the Flavian period could represent a group of Indicetani in a case so serious that it involved arbiters appointed by the emperor (Fabré et al. 1991, nos. 172, 173, 174) suggests that the Indicetani had their own legal status. This legal status must have separated them from the other citizens of the Roman city. If the Indicetani had been completely assimilated into the Roman city, use of the term Indicetani would have been an anachronism. This legal differentiation in status may have had a physical manifestation in the form of the transverse wall that separated the northern and southern halves of the Roman city. It is possible that the people living in the southern half of the Roman city had full Roman citizenship while the Iberians living in the northern half had an affiliated status. This type of physical manifestation of differing legal statuses is known from other Roman cities (Knapp 1983, 13-14; Jobst 1983, 124 ff.).

Ethnic and legal relations between Romans and Greeks also had a spatial component at Empúries. The most obvious evidence is the fact that Romans and Greeks had separate walled cities standing quite near one another. It is possible, however, to see a much more subtle relationship between Greeks and Romans by examining the reaction of the Greeks to the arrival of the Romans in the Republican period through a study of the changes in the Greek use of space at that time.

The Roman presence must have caused massive changes and disruptions in Neapolis, whether or not the Romans intended this. The revocation of the right to mint coins must have been very disruptive to the Greeks. In addition, the amount of Campanian pottery excavated in levels of Neapolis that dates to after the Roman arrival is quite large, contrasting with the small amount of pottery from Campania excavated in pre-Roman levels (Sanmartí 1978). The increase in the amount of Campanian imports suggests changes in the focus of trade, and possibly in who was conducting that trade. Finally, some time during the first half of the second century B.C., the Romans built a large public structure immediately outside the southern gate of Neapolis. This structure utilized a construction technique common in Campania at the beginning of the second century B.C. known as *opus africanum* (Sanmartí et al. 1983-1984, 110-153; Adam 1984, 120-121). It is impossible to know to what use the structure was put because so little of it has been excavated. Nonetheless, the structure seems to have had a public function since it was very large and finely constructed. The Romans located the new building on a Greek necropolis, which appears to have been used until immediately before the Roman building was constructed. Thus the Romans built a public structure on top of a Greek cemetery that had been used within living memory. One can only imagine how distressing the construction of this building was to the Greeks in Neapolis.

Although much of Neapolis has not been excavated to the Greek levels, the areas that have been excavated indicate that the first half of the second century B.C. was a period during which there were several large construction projects in Neapolis. All of these construction projects are discussed in detail in chapter 4. One of the projects involved the extension of the southern city walls so as to include the Asklepieion. Once included inside the city, the sanctuary was completely rebuilt to give it a monumental appearance. Simultaneously, a block of housing in the center of Neapolis was leveled so that the agora could be extended. As part of the reforms to the agora, a large two-story stoa was built to line its northern end. None of these construction projects can be dated with great precision, but all can be generally placed within first half of the second century B.C.

We cannot know the relative sequence of construction for any of the projects mentioned above, but I suggest that the Greek projects were an attempt to resist the colonization of the Romans. Ostensibly, the Romans did not come to Empúries to take over the Greek city. The Greeks and Romans were allies in the Second Punic War and during the Iberian Revolt. Their alliance probably explains why the Romans respected the boundaries of Neapolis and built their military camp away from the Greek city. Still, the Roman arrival was an act of colonization. The troops who arrived at Empúries for the first time were launching the conquest of the entire Iberian peninsula. The needs of the military and civil settlements of the Romans at Empúries put severe pressures on the Greeks. These pressures appear in the numismatic and archaeological records in the transfer of the authority to mint coins, the import of massive amounts of goods from Campania, and the construction of the Roman public building over Greek graves.

The first Greek reaction to these pressures may not have been acquiescence. During the first generation after the arrival of the Romans, the Greeks may have resisted Roman attempts, intentional or otherwise, at colonization by trying to assert their own ethnic identity. Neapolis, at the time Roman forces landed there for the first time, did not appear to be very similar to other contemporary Greek cities. As far as we can tell, there were no temples in the city, a very small agora, and no significant public architecture. All of this quickly changed during the first half of the second century B.C. The Greeks extended the southern wall to include the Asklepieion, thus claiming the sanctuary for Neapolis, forcing worshippers to pass through the Neapolis gate and enter the city to seek a cure from the god. They may have rebuilt the sanctuary along lines current at other Hellenistic sanctuaries of Asklepios in order to display their Greek heritage. At the same time they enlarged the agora, the symbol of political independence in the Greek world, embellishing it with a purely Greek form of architecture, the monumental stoa. In reaction to Roman colonial pressures, the Greeks of Neapolis may have been asserting their ethnic identity in an act of cultural resistance to Romanization.

Over the course of the next 200 years, the Greeks in Neapolis apparently continued to emphasize their Greek identity, although their motivation for doing so may have changed. The union of the Greek and Roman cities in the Augustan period clearly indicates that the Greeks in Neapolis saw their best chance for political gain was by assimilating their political institutions to those of the Romans. Lomas has argued that populations in the Greek cities of southern Italy consciously displayed their Greek origins by using Hellenic terminology for their political offices, despite the fact that these offices had been thoroughly Romanized, in an attempt to gain favor with a philhellenic Roman elite (Lomas 1995, 107-120). The very same may well have been taking place at Empúries during the first century B.C. Some time after 150 B.C., the Temple of Asklepios was decorated with what would have been an antique statue of the god made in Greece. In the first century B.C., Greek inscriptions written in mosaic tiles appeared in private dining rooms. Also in the first century B.C. Numa, chose to commemorate his generosity in building the Temple of Serapis in a bilingual Greek-Latin inscription. All of these acts may have been attempts by the population of Neapolis to remind the Romans of their Greek roots at a time when they were maneuvering for political gain, which was eventually manifest in the union of the two cities. In the case of Neapolis, Greek ethnic symbols would not only appeal to philhellenic attitudes among the elite of the Roman city, but also to their patriotism. These symbols could easily have been used to remind the Romans that the Greeks had helped them during two serious political crises, the Second Punic War and the Iberian Revolt.

The population of Neapolis seems to have consciously asserted a Greek identity from the moment the Romans arrived through the Augustan era. In the beginning they may have been resisting Roman acculturation in an attempt to maintain their cultural identity in the face of a massive Roman cultural invasion. By the time of Augustus the residents of Neapolis may have been appealing to Roman interest in Greek culture as they moved ever closer to assimilating their political institutions.

6.7. Implications for the Study of Roman Urbanism

This study has demonstrated that the organization of space in the Roman city of Empúries was highly structured. The evidence presented challenges the work of Raper and calls into question his conclusion about the lack of patterns in the use of space at Pompeii. The definition of new patterns in the use of space at Empúries suggests that Raper's conclusion resulted from an inappropriate execution of his methods of analysis. I argue instead that a refined version of his method, quadrat analysis, along with other methods of spatial analysis developed at other sites and in other disciplines, provide the tools necessary for recognizing patterns in the use of space. These patterns do exist in Empúries and, I believe, at other Roman urban sites as well.

Empúries is a good place to conduct a study of the use of Roman urban space for several reasons. With large portions of the city excavated, enough of the urban layout is understood to make it possible to study the city as a whole. As a result of the conservation ethic of excavation directors over the last 90 years, the ruins as they stand today represent, for the most part, a picture of the city at the end of the first or beginning of the second century A.D. Through a combination of first-hand inspection of these ruins and a careful reading of available excavation reports it was possible to produce maps of the site that recorded the use of every space inside and immediately outside the city.

Using quadrat analysis, tests that defined the nature of the street on which specific buildings were located, and a test for the visibility of locations, patterns in the arrangement of space in the city emerged. These patterns have been interpreted as representing the social norms of the constituents of the city. Residents of Empúries translated these social norms literally into stone so that the urban architecture could both reproduce their social system as well as reinforce it. The social norms that were translated into physical form, however, were the result of a dialogue between the elite, the non-elite, the non-residents, and the supernatural constituents who used the city. The patterns in the use of space emphasize the roles of each group in, and their contributions to, the urban society of Roman Empúries. The elite used the arrangement of space to highlight their roles as benefactors of the city by creating relatively quiet locations where statues and inscriptions recording their accomplishments could be contemplated. They also placed their homes in locations where they could gain the most attention as they came and went followed by their clients. The non-elite engaged in business placed their commercial structures in areas with the most amount of traffic in the town, no doubt to increase the volume of their business. Non-elite homes were located in quieter neighborhoods that had plenty of residents around to monitor activity and prevent deviant behavior. The Emporitani gave non-residents a certain amount of access to parts of the city, facilitating their visits to public religious and secular buildings. At the same time, they maintained a certain amount of distance between themselves and strangers, giving outsiders easy access to areas that were well monitored. Finally, the Emporitani ensured that the gods had appropriate spaces for their sanctuaries, separated from the mundane and low activities of city life in quiet and serene environments that would impress the worshipper who came to pay respects and seek blessings. They also made certain that the dead had proper spaces where they would be safely outside the sacred boundary of the city but not so far away and not so out of sight that they could be forgotten.

Finally, in this study the use of space was examined to define ethnicity during the Republican period. The data are not robust enough to sustain statistical analyses, but they suggest, nonetheless, that space was used to define ethnic identity. In the Roman city there appear to have been separate neighborhoods for Iberians and Romans. This physical and ethnic separation may have been reinforced by a legal differentiation in the status of the citizens of each community. At the time of the Roman conquest, the Greeks in Neapolis also seem to have used space to reinforce their ethnic identity. By claiming the Asklepieion, rebuilding it in a monumental Hellenistic fashion, as well as by reconstructing the agora with a monumental Hellenistic stoa, the Greeks appear to have been resisting Roman attempts at colonization.

The use of space at the Roman urban site of Empúries was highly structured. Such a conclusion raises the question of whether or not the same is true at Pompeii or at other sites across the Roman world and at different periods in time.

Indeed, there are indications that space at Pompeii was more structured than has been acknowledged in the past. Raper assumed that the mixture of uses that he identified at Pompeii could be equated with the random use of space. The patterns emerging at Pompeii, however, are proving to be much more complex than his methods were capable of identifying. As at Empúries, much of the space at Pompeii appears to have been organized in terms of lines of communication, not simply in terms of clustering. Wallace-Hadrill noted that structures devoted to gambling and prostitution were nearly always placed along narrow side streets to separate deviant pursuits from more proper ones (Wallace-Hadrill 1995, 39-62). Robinson argued elite houses were separated from one another, perhaps indicating that the elite house owners controlled the neighborhoods directly surrounding their homes (Robinson 1997). Laurence identified the organization of Pompeii into neighborhoods through an examination of the distribution of street shrines and public fountains (Laurence 1994b). Tsujimura pointed out that traffic patterns were carefully controlled with some streets being closed to cart traffic (Tsujimura 1990, 58-86).

Surely Empúries is not the only site at which an urban dialogue can be detected, yet that dialogue must take on different shades and hues as different constituents play different roles in other urban centers and at other times. The techniques used here have great potential for examining the use of space at other urban sites. These techniques are open to refinement and development. Their poorer performance in identifying patterns in the distribution of private space at Empúries suggests that other factors were at play, factors that it may be possible to identify through other quantifiable techniques. Nonetheless, the analytical methods developed from the structuralist assumption that architecture serves to include certain social groups and exclude others have immense power for identifying the social texture of a Roman urban center.

GLOSSARY OF LATIN AND GREEK ARCHITECTURAL TERMS USED IN THE TEXT

abaton a room in a sanctuary of Asklepios where the sick slept in order to obtain a vision in which they would learn how to cure their illness

acropolis the inner fort of a city, the most easily defended part of the city

agora a plaza in center of a Greek city that served as the political, economic, and social hub of the city

ala a room that usually occurs in pairs flanking an entryway to a house, possibly used for storage or the location of a porter

alveum a small wading pool in a bath complex

ambulacrum a covered walkway

apodyterium a dressing room in a bath complex

atrium a forecourt of a Roman house, a place to greet strangers

basilica a rectangular building, usually separated into a nave and aisles, used for law courts, official meetings, and as an indoor market

calidarium a portion of a bath with hot water

cardo an archaeological term for a street in an orthogonally planned Roman town, running north to south

cardo maximus an archaeological term for the central north-south street in a Roman town

cartilabrum a table placed in the tablinum for the house owner to receive or distribute small gifts

cavea the seating area in a theater or amphitheater

cella the interior room of a temple that contained the image of the deity

chora the countryside surrounding a city

collegium a meeting place for group of associates usually united in commercial business

cryptoporticus a covered, vaulted gallery usually used as a platform for another structure

cubiculum a room for sleeping in a house

curia a building for the meeting of municipal government

decumanus an archaeological term for a street in an orthogonally planned Roman town running east to west

decumanus maximus an archaeologial term for the central east-west street in a Roman town

diaconion a room in a church for the storage of sacred vessels

fauces a hallway leading from the street to the interior of a house

forum a plaza in center of a Roman city that served as the political, economic, and social center of the city

hortus a garden

impluvium an opening in roof of the atrium that allowed light and rain water to enter, the latter being stored in a cistern below

insula 1) a city block 2) a large, multistory apartment building

labrum a basin or tub in a bath

mola asinaria a grinding stone powered by a harnessed donkey

nave the central portion of a basilica, usually flanked by aisles

nympheum a fountain or cistern to supply public with water

opus africanum a construction technique in which rectangular blocks are used as a frame to hold unshaped blocks

opus caementicum construction in cement

opus certum wall construction with regularly cut blocks set in cement

opus incertum wall construction with irregularly cut blocks set in cement

opus reticulatum wall construction with small blocks cut in a diamond shape set in cement

opus signinum a pavement made of crushed pottery into which is set small square pieces of white and black stone arranged in a geometric pattern or spelling out a word or phrase

opus tesellatum a pavement of regularly cut stone pieces in a variety of colors arranged in geometric designs

opus vittatum wall construction with small blocks cut in a diamond shape set in cement

palaestra an exercise ground

peristylium a courtyard surrounded by a colonnade

pistrinum a bakery

pomerium the ritual boundary defining the city, usually corresponding to the course of the city walls

porticus a colonnade, a covered walkway

praefurnim the furnace room in a bath complex

praesidium the headquarters building in a military camp

pronaos the front porch of a temple

proteichisma a defensive screening wall built outside of a city wall

stoa a rectangular structure with a roof stretching from a back wall to front row of columns

taberna a one or two room space primarily used as a shop, but also used for industrial production and residence by the shopkeeper as well as for storage

tablinum a room of the atrium in a house often containing a table on which gifts were placed for the house owner

tegula a roof tile

temenos a wall defining a sacred precinct

tepidarium a portion of a bathing complex with warm water

tesserce small cut stones arranged in patterns to decorate mosaic pavements

territorim the countryside surrounding a city

thermae public baths

thermopolium a shop for the selling of warm food

triclinium a dining room in a house

villa an elite house usually containing an atrium and a peristyle

APPENDIX A
CONCORDANCE OF STRUCTURE LABELS IN NEAPOLIS

Name Used in Text	Mar and Ruiz 1993	Other Names
Walls		
South Wall		
West Wall		
Watchtower	Torre Atalaya	
Street Network	**Red de calles**	
Street 1A	Calle 1	
Street 1B	Calle 1	
Street 1C	Calle 1	
Street 1D	Calle 1	
Street 1E	Calle 1	
Street 1F	Calle 1	
Street 1G	Calle 1	
Street 2Aa	Calle 2	
Street 2B	Calle 2	
Street 2C	Calle 2	
Street 2D	Calle 2	
Street 2E	Calle 2	
Street 3	Calle 3	
Street 4	Calle 4	
Street 5A	Calle 5	
Street 5B	Calle 5	
Street 6	Calle 6	
Street 7	Calle 7	Gandía: Calle F
Street 8A	Calle 8	
Street 8B	Calle 8	
Street 8C	Calle 8	
Street 9A	Calle 9	
Street 9B	Calle 9	
Street 10	Calle 10	
Street 11	Calle 11	
Street 12	Calle 12	
Street 13A	Calle 13	
Street 13B	Calle 13	
Street 14	Calle 14	
Street 15	Calle 15	
Street 16	Calle 16	
Street 17		
Street 18		
Structures	**Conjunts**	
Structure 1	Conjunt 1	Domus de las inscripciones
Structure 2	Conjunt 2	
Structure 3	Conjunt 3	
Structure 4	Conjunt 4	
Structure 5	Conjunt 5	Puig i Cadafalch: Casa G
Structure 6	Conjunt 6	
Structure 7	Conjunt 7	Puig i Cadafalch: Domus H
Structure 8	Conjunt 8	
Structure 9	Conjunt 9	Casa de la escalera
Structure 10	Conjunt 10	Casa de los cuatro departamentos
Structure 11	Conjunt 11	
Structure 12	Conjunt 12	
Structure 13	Conjunt 13	
Structure 14	Conjunt 14	
Structure 15	Conjunt 15	
Structure 16	Conjunt 16	
Structure 17	Conjunt 17	

Name Used in Text	Mar and Ruiz 1993	Other Names
Structure 18	Conjunt 18	Gandía: Casa H
Structure 19	Conjunt 19	
Structure 20	Conjunt 20	Casa del ángulo
Structure 21	Conjunt 21	
Structure 22	Conjunt 22	
Structure 23	Conjunt 23	
Structure 24	Conjunt 24	
Structure 25	Conjunt 25	
Structure 26	Conjunt 26	
Structure 27	Conjunt 27	
Structure 28	Conjunt 28	Casa de la herrería
Structure 29	Conjunt 29	Herrería
Structure 30	Conjunt 30	
Structure 31	Conjunt 31	Factoría de salazones
Structure 32	Conjunt 32	
Structure 33	Conjunt 33	
Structure 34	Conjunt 34	Domus del atrio tetrástilo
Structure 35	Conjunt 35	
Structure 36	Conjunt 36	
Structure 37	Conjunt 37	
Structure 38	Conjunt 38	
Structure 39	Conjunt 39	
Structure 40	Conjunt 40	
Structure 41	Conjunt 41	Casa de la puerta geminada
Structure 42	Conjunt 42	Casa de la conducción de ánforas
Structure 43	Conjunt 43	Casa de la esquina del ágora
Structure 44	Conjunt 44	
Structure 45	Conjunt 45	
Structure 46	Conjunt 46	
Structure 47	Conjunt 47	
Structure 48	Conjunt 48	
Structure 50	Conjunt 50	
Structure 51	Conjunt 51	
Structure 52	Conjunt 52	Casa del mosaico con inscripción Hedykoitos
Structure 53	Conjunt 53	
Structure 54	Conjunt 54	
Structure 55	Conjunt 55	Casa sobre el depósito de espadas
Structure 56	Conjunt 56	Casa sobre el horno griego
Structure 57	Conjunt 57	Casa de horno
Structure 58	Conjunt 58	
Structure 59	Conjunt 59	
Structure 60	Conjunt 60	
Structure 61	Conjunt 61	
Structure 62	Conjunt 62	
Structure 63	Conjunt 63	
Structure 64	Conjunt 64	
Structure 65	Conjunt 65	
Structure 66	Conjunt 66	
Structure 67	Conjunt 67	
Structure 68	Conjunt 68	
Structure 69	Conjunt 69	Edifico del prótiro
Structure 70	Conjunt 70	
Structure 71	Conjunt 71	
Structure 72	Conjunt 72	
Structure 73	Conjunt 73	
Structure 74	Conjunt 74	
Structure 75	Conjunt 75	Casa de la cistern en L
Structure 76	Conjunt 76	Casa de la ciserna ermitorio
Structure 77	Conjunt 77	
Structure 78	Conjunt 78	
Structure 79	Conjunt 79	

Appendix A

Name Used in Text	Mar and Ruiz 1993	Other Names
Structure 80	Conjunt 80	Casa del mosaico con inscripción Xaire Agathos Daimon
Structure 81	Conjunt 81	
Structure 82	Conjunt 82	
Structure 83	Conjunt 83	Casa de los silos de ladrillo
Structure 84	Conjunt 84	
Structure 85	Conjunt 85	Gandía: Domus del clypeus
Structure 86	Conjunt 86	
Structure 87	Conjunt 87	Gandía: Casa N
Structure 88	Conjunt 88	
Structure 89	Conjunt 89	
Structure 90	Conjunt 90	
Structure 93	Conjunt 93	
Structure 94	Conjunt 94	
Structure 95	Conjunt 95	
Structure 96	Conjunt 96	
Structure 97	Conjunt 97	
Structure 98	Conjunt 98	
Structure 99	Conjunt 99	
Structure 100	Conjunt 100	
Structure 101	Conjunt 101	Casa del peristilo
Structure 102	Conjunt 102	
Structure 103	Conjunt 103	Stoa del Basamento
Structure 104	Conjunt 104	
Structure 105	Conjunt 105	
Structure 106	Conjunt 106	
Structure 107	Conjunt 107	
Agora	Ágora	
Baths / Funerary Basilica	Conjunt 91	Termas de la basílica cristiana
Asklepieion	Asklepieion	Puig i Cadafalch: cel-la C, cel-la M, and cel-la P
Ceramics Kilns	Hornos cerámicos	
Furnace in Insula S	Hornos de la insula S	
Macellum	Conjunt 49	Mercado de la cisterna pública
Serapeum	Serapeum	
Southern Plaza	Plaza del sur	
Stoa	Conjunt 92	

APPENDIX B
CONCORDANCE OF STRUCTURE LABELS IN THE ROMAN CITY AT EMPÚRIES

Name Used in Text	Mar and Ruiz 1993	Other Names
Walls		
East Wall	Muralla Roura and Muralla Rubert	
South Wall	Muralla sur	
Transverse Wall	Muralla transversal	
Connecting Walls		
Streets		
Cardo A1	Cardo A	Castanyer: Kardo A
		Lamboglia and Almagro: Decumanus A
Cardo A2	Cardo A	Castanyer: Kardo A
		Lamboglia and Almagro: Decumanus A
Cardo B	Cardo B	Castanyer: Kardo B
		Ripoll: Decumanus B
Cardo C1	Cardo C	Almagro: Decumanus Maximus
		Puig i Cadafalch: Cardo Maximus
Cardo C2	Cardo C	Almagro: Decumanus Maximus
		Puig i Cadafalch: Cardo Maximus
Cardo C3	Cardo C	Almagro: Decumanus Maximus
		Puig i Cadafalch: Cardo Maximus
Cardo D1	Cardo D	
Cardo D2	Cardo D	
Cardo E1	Cardo E	
Cardo E2	Cardo E	
Cardo F1	Cardo F	
Cardo F2	Cardo F	
Decumanus A	Decumanus A	
Decumanus B	Decumanus B	
Decumanus C1	Decumanus C	Pena: Decumanus Maximus
Decumanus C2	Decumanus C	Pena: Decumanus Maximus
Decumanus D	Decumanus D	
Decumanus E	Decumanus E	
Decumanus F1	Decumanus F	
Decumanus F2	Decumanus F	
Decumanus G	Decumanus G	
Decumanus H	Decumanus H	
Decumanus I	Decumanus I	
Structures		
Amphitheater	Anfiteatro	
Basilica (forum)		
Villa 1	Casa Romana 1	
Villa 2a	Casa Romana 2a	Casa Romana 2b
Villa 2b	Casa Romana 2b	Casa Romana 2a
Villa 3	Casa Romana 3	
Collegium		
Curia		
Forum		
Macellum	Macellum de les cisternes públiques	
Palestra		
Bakery	Pistrinum	
Port		
Thermopolium		
Unexcavated Public Structure		

APPENDIX C
CONCORDANCE OF AREA LABELS IN THE EXTRAMURAL SECTORS OF EMPÚRIES

Name Used in Text	Mar and Ruiz 1993	Other Names
Church of Sant Martí	Iglesia de Sant Martí	Temple of Artemis of Ephesus
Mole	Muella	
Cemeteries		Almagro: Necropolis Ballesta
		Almagro: Necropolis Bonjoan
		Almagro: Necropolis Castellet
		Almagro: Necropolis Las Corts
		Almagro: Necropolis Les Coves
		Almagro: Necropolis Estruch
		Almagro: Necropolis Granada
		Almagro: Necropolis Martí
		Almagro: Necropolis Mateu
		Almagro: Necropolis Mitjavila
		Almagro: Necropolis Nofre
		Almagro: Necropolis Parralli
		Almagro: Necropolis Patel
		Almagro: Necropolis Pí
		Almagro: Necropolis Portichol
		Almagro: Necropolis Rubert
		Almagro: Necropolis Sabadí
		Almagro: Necropolis Torres
		Almagro: Necropolis Viñals
Kiln?		Nolla: Deposito del agua
Parking Lot		Sanmartí: Àrea del pàrking
Open Area		Almagro: Macellum

NUMBER OF OBSERVED (OB.) VS. EXPECTED (EX.)STRUCTUES ON THE STREETS OF NEAPOLIS AND ROMAN CITY

Street	Public		Private		Public Secular		Public Religious	Administrative		Commercial		Industrial		Elite Domestic		Non-Elite Domestic	
	Ob.	Ex.	Ob.	Ex.	Ob.	Ex.	Ob.	Ob.	Ex.	Ob.	Ex.	Ob.	Ex.	Ob.	Ex..	Ob.	Ex.
1A	0	2.2	0	0.9	0	2.1	0	0	0.1	0	1.9	0	0.1	0	0.4	0	0.4
1B	0	0.7	1	0.3	0	0.7	0	0	0.0	0	0.6	0	0.0	0	0.1	1	0.1
1C	1	1.9	1	0.8	1	1.8	0	0	0.1	1	1.6	1	0.1	0	0.3	0	0.3
1D	0	0.9	2	0.4	0	0.8	0	0	0.1	0	0.8	0	0.1	0	0.1	2	0.2
1E	7	6.6	4	2.7	7	6.3	0	0	0.4	7	5.8	0	0.4	3	1.1	1	1.2
1F	0	2.0	1	0.8	0	1.9	0	0	0.1	0	1.8	0	0.1	0	0.3	1	0.4
1G	0	0.6	0	0.2	0	0.5	0	0	0.0	0	0.5	0	0.0	0	0.1	0	0.1
1H	0	1.3	0	0.5	0	1.2	0	0	0.1	0	1.1	0	0.1	0	0.2	0	0.2
1I	0	2.2	1	0.9	0	2.1	0	0	0.1	0	1.9	0	0.1	0	0.4	1	0.4
2A	17	8.7	5	3.6	17	8.3	0	1	0.5	16	7.6	2	0.5	0	1.4	2	1.6
2B	6	4.3	2	1.7	6	4.1	0	1	0.2	5	3.7	0	0.2	1	0.7	1	0.8
2C	4	2.2	2	0.9	4	2.1	0	0	0.1	4	1.9	0	0.1	0	0.4	2	0.4
3	1	6.3	0	2.6	1	6.0	0	0	0.4	1	5.5	0	0.4	0	1.0	0	1.2
4	0	4.3	2	1.8	0	4.1	0	0	0.2	0	3.8	0	0.2	1	0.7	1	0.8
5A	0	2.9	1	1.2	0	2.7	0	0	0.2	0	2.5	0	0.2	0	0.5	1	0.5
5B	4	1.9	0	0.8	4	1.8	0	0	0.1	4	1.7	0	0.1	0	0.3	0	0.4
6A	0	1.3	0	0.5	0	1.2	0	0	0.1	0	1.1	0	0.1	0	0.2	0	0.2
6B	0	1.5	2	0.6	0	1.4	0	0	0.1	0	1.3	0	0.1	1	0.2	1	0.3
7	1	2.4	1	1.0	1	2.3	0	1	0.1	0	2.1	0	0.1	1	0.4	0	0.5
8A	0	1.4	0	0.6	0	1.3	0	0	0.1	0	1.2	0	0.1	0	0.2	0	0.3
8B	1	1.0	0	0.4	1	1.0	0	0	0.1	1	0.9	0	0.1	0	0.2	0	0.2
8C	0	1.3	0	0.5	0	1.2	0	0	0.1	0	1.1	0	0.1	0	0.2	0	0.2
9	6	4.0	5	1.6	6	3.9	0	0	0.2	6	3.5	0	0.2	4	0.7	1	0.8
10	0	5.0	7	2.0	0	4.8	0	0	0.3	0	4.4	0	0.3	3	0.8	4	0.9
11	1	3.1	1	1.3	1	3.0	0	0	0.2	1	2.7	0	0.2	1	0.5	0	0.6
12	1	2.3	1	1.0	1	2.2	0	0	0.1	0	2.0	0	0.1	0	0.4	1	0.4
13A	0	3.7	0	1.5	0	3.6	0	0	0.2	0	3.3	0	0.2	0	0.6	0	0.7
13B	1	2.0	2	0.8	1	1.9	0	0	0.1	1	1.7	0	0.1	1	0.3	1	0.4
14	0	1.3	0	0.5	0	1.3	0	0	0.1	0	1.2	0	0.1	0	0.2	0	0.2
15	1	2.5	1	1.0	1	2.4	0	0	0.1	1	2.2	1	0.1	0	0.4	0	0.5
16	0	1.7	0	0.7	0	1.7	0	0	0.1	0	1.5	0	0.1	0	0.3	0	0.3
17	0	2.0	2	0.8	0	1.9	0	0	0.1	0	1.7	2	0.1	0	0.3	0	0.4
18	1	1.8	0	0.7	1	1.7	0	0	0.1	0	1.6	0	0.1	0	0.3	0	0.3
Agora	6	4.7	2	1.9	6	4.5	0	1	0.3	5	4.1	0	0.3	0	0.8	2	0.9
So. Plaza	5	2.7	0	1.1	3	2.6	2	0	0.2	3	2.4	0	0.2	0	0.4	0	0.5
Cardo A2	6	5.9	4	2.4	6	5.7	0	0	0.3	5	5.2	0	0.3	4	1.0	0	1.1
Cardo B	8	7.2	0	2.9	7	6.9	1	1	0.4	6	6.3	1	0.4	0	1.2	0	1.4
Cardo C2	12	2.8	0	1.1	12	2.7	0	0	0.2	12	2.4	0	0.2	0	0.5	0	0.5
Cardo D1	13	6.2	0	2.5	12	5.9	1	1	0.4	11	5.4	0	0.4	0	1.0	0	1.2
Dec. B	18	3.6	0	1.5	17	3.4	1	1	0.2	16	3.1	0	0.2	0	0.6	0	0.7
Dec. D	1	1.8	0	0.7	1	1.7	0	0	0.1	1	1.5	0	0.1	0	0.3	0	0.3

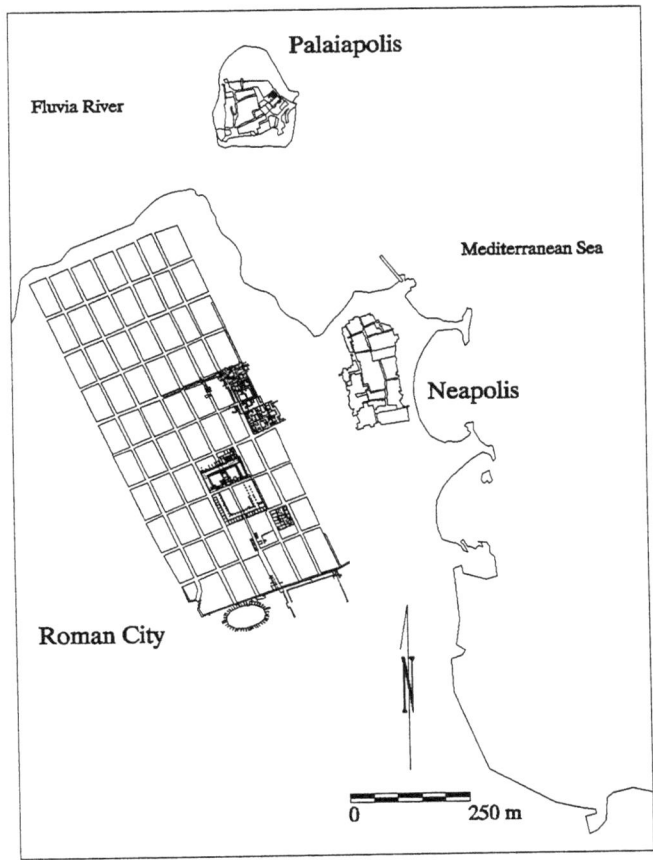

Fig. 1: General plan of Empúries with the ancient coastline.

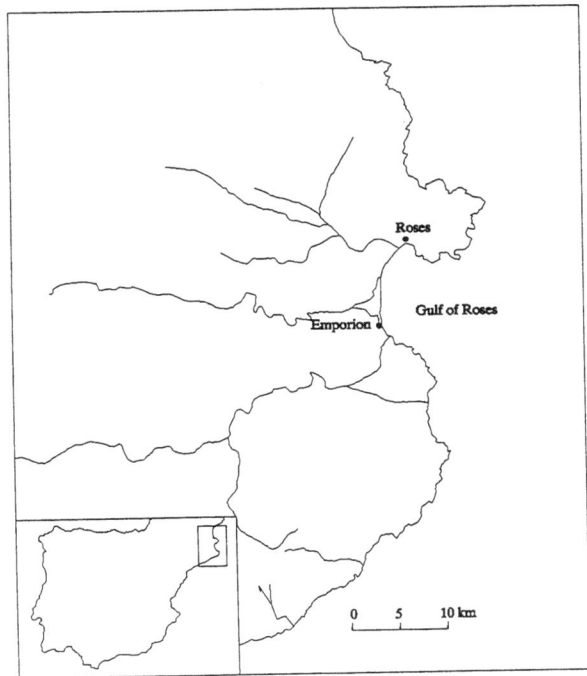

Fig. 2: Location of Empúries in the Empordà.

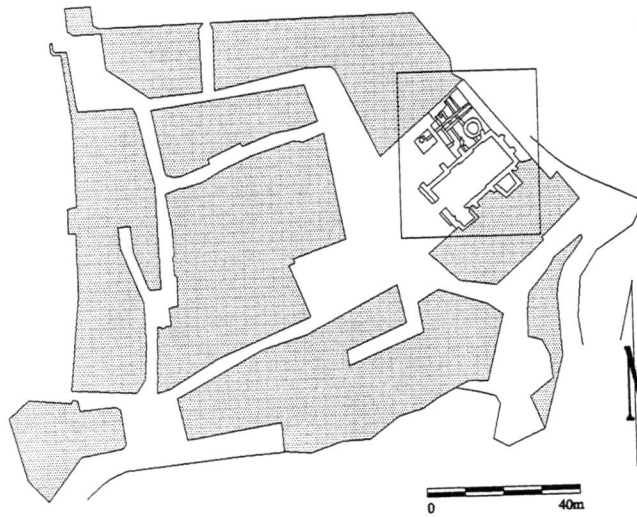

Fig. 3: Sant Martí.

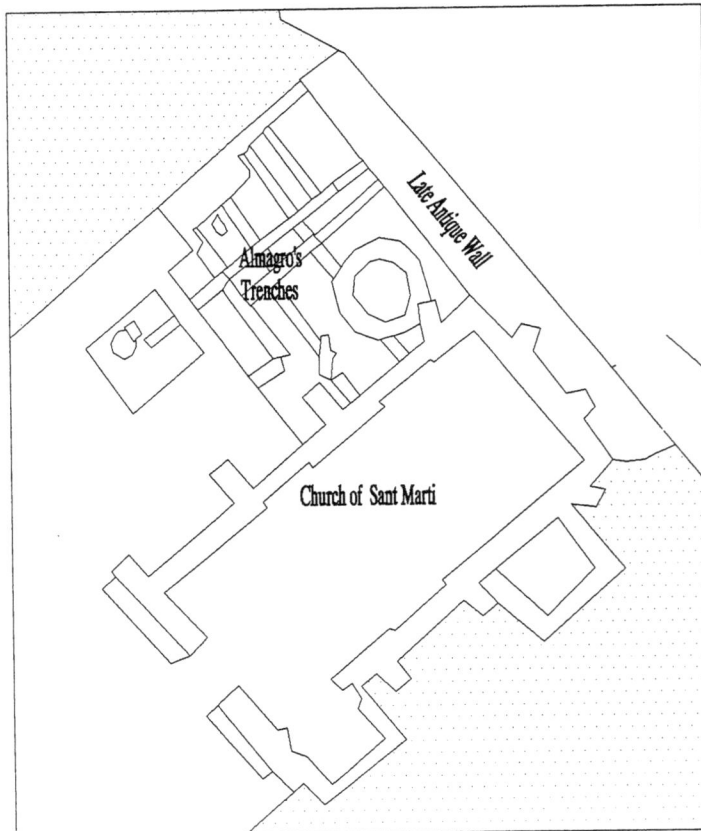

Fig. 4: Church of Sant Martí and its environs.

Fig. 5: Map of the excavated ruins of Neapolis.

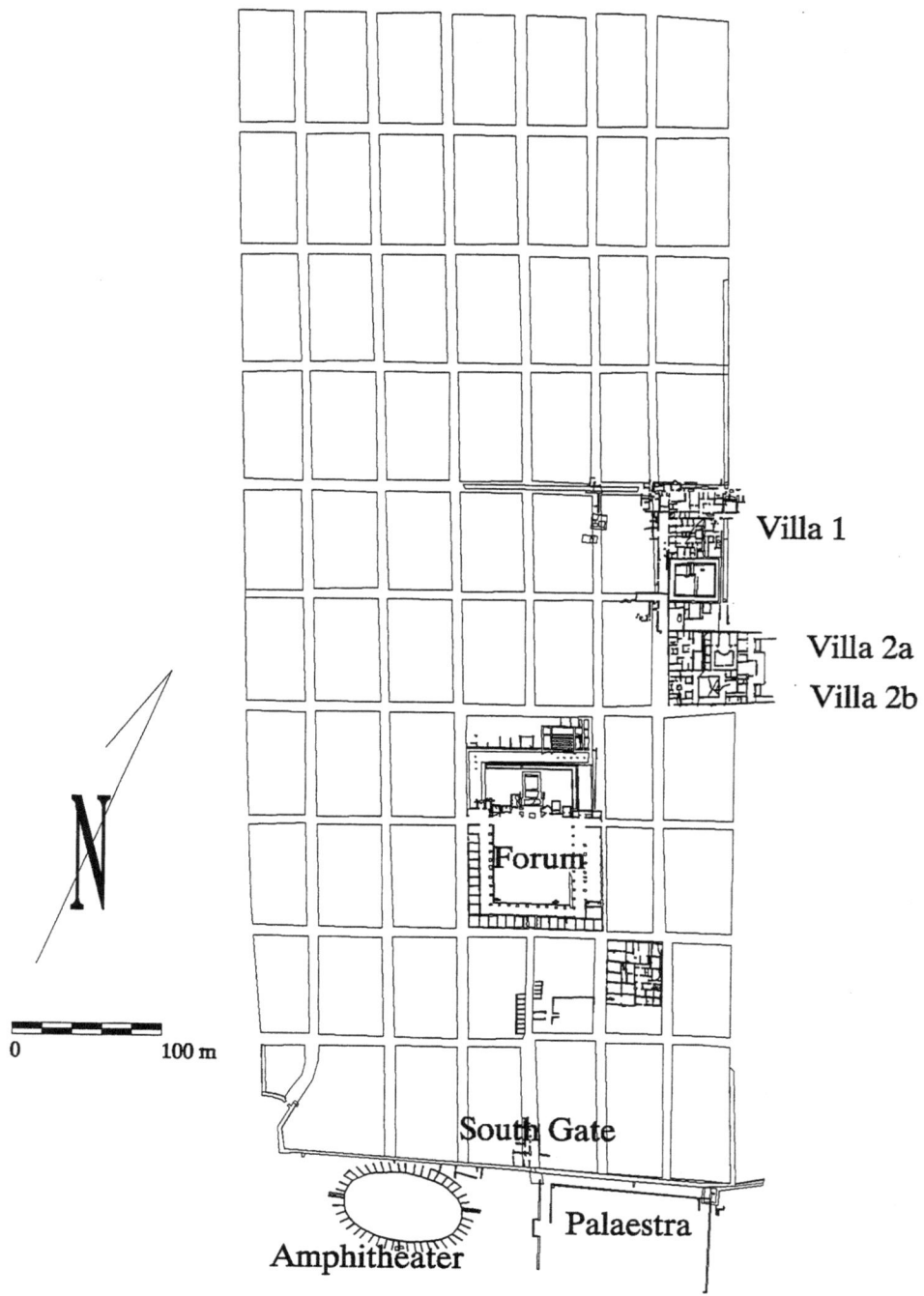

Fig. 6: Map of the excavated remains of the Roman city and the street network as it is known from aerial photographs.

Watch Tower

Conjunt 17

Conjunt 16

Proteichisma

Military Storehouses
(tabernae)

6-5th Century B.C. Walls

4th Century B.C. Walls

First half of the 2nd Century B.C. Walls

N

0   25m

Fig. 7: Defensive features of southern Neapolis.

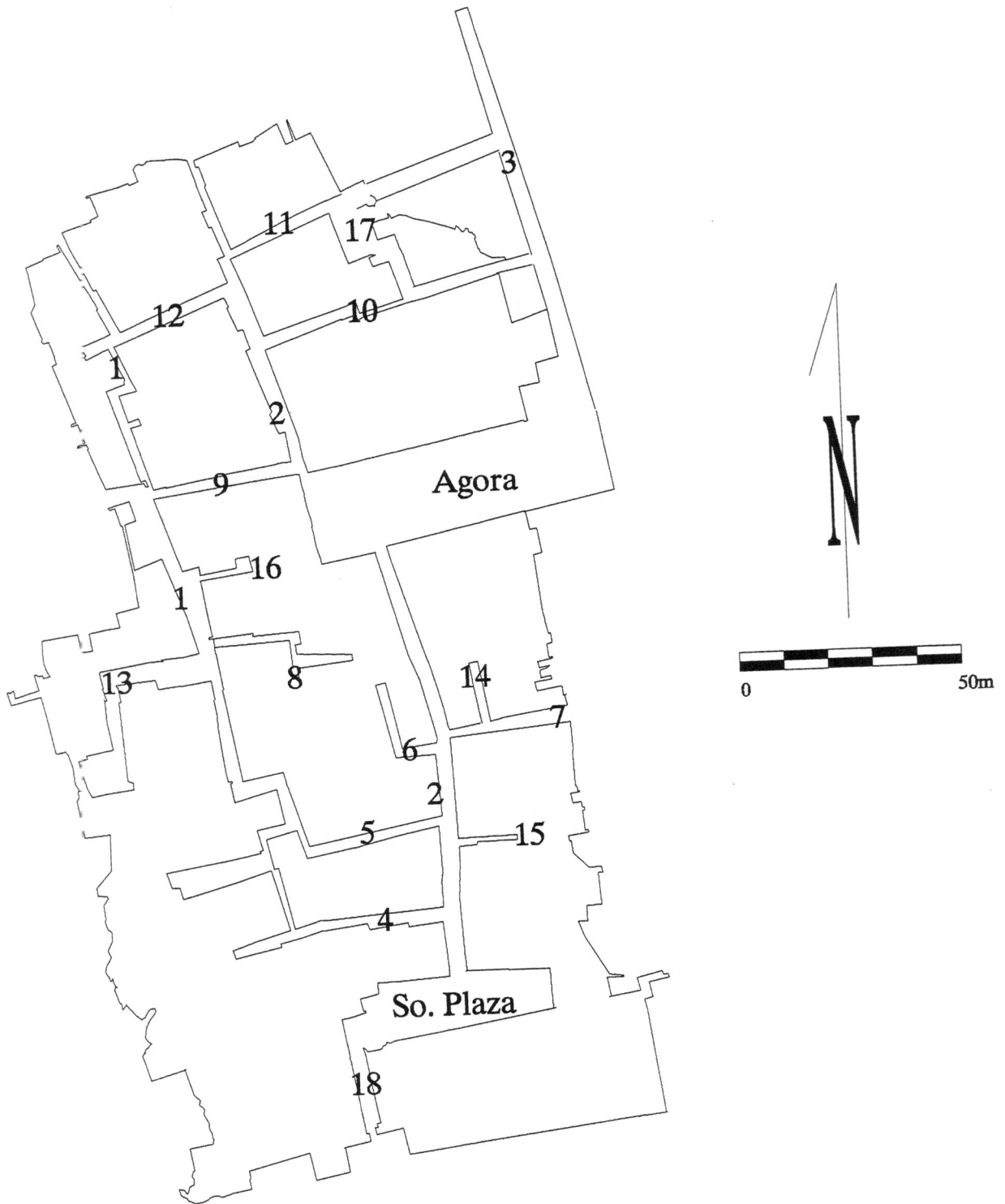

Fig. 8: Street plan of Neapolis.

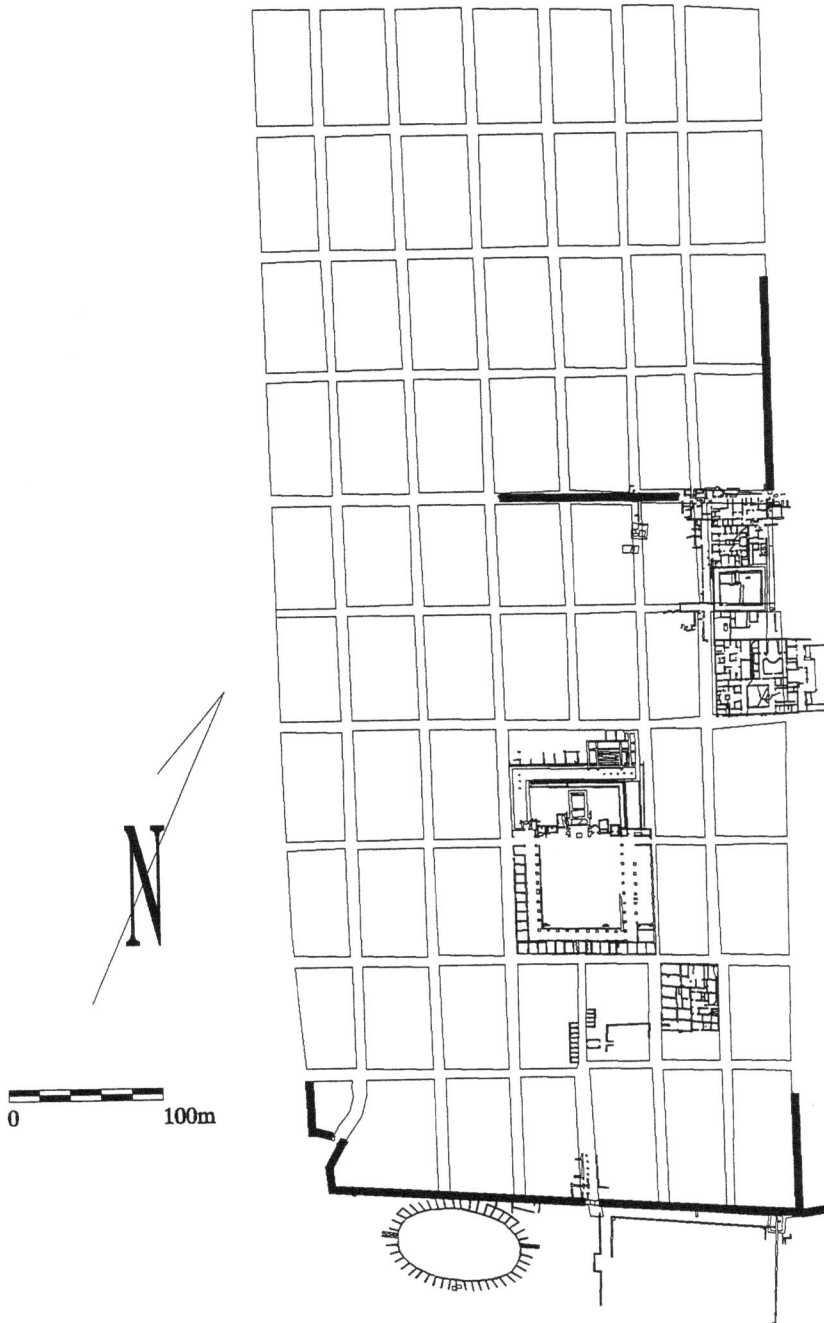

Fig. 9: Defensive features of the Roman city.

Cardines

F E D C B A

Decumani

I

H

G

F

E

D

C

B

A

N

0   100 m

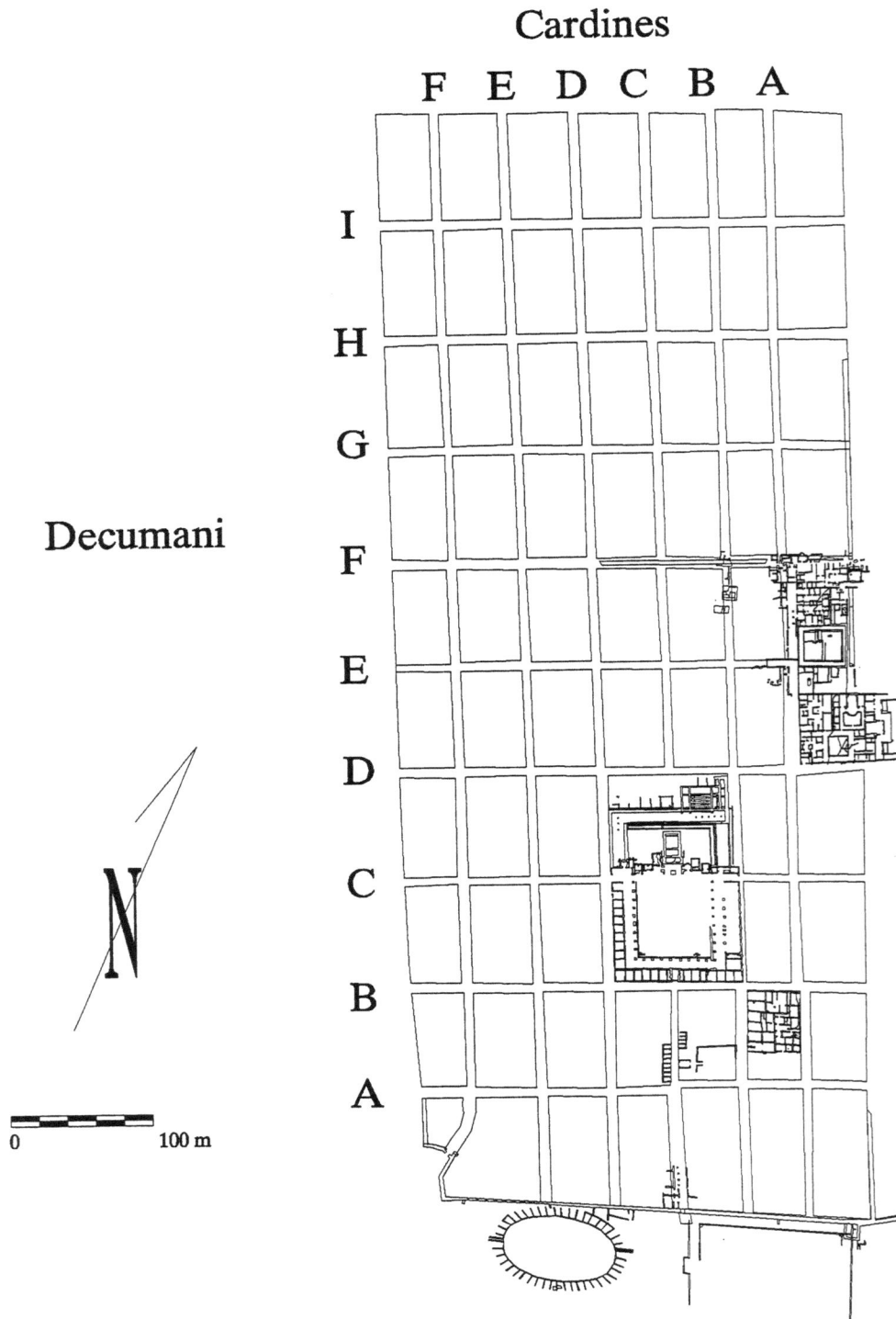

Fig. 10: Street plan of the Roman City.

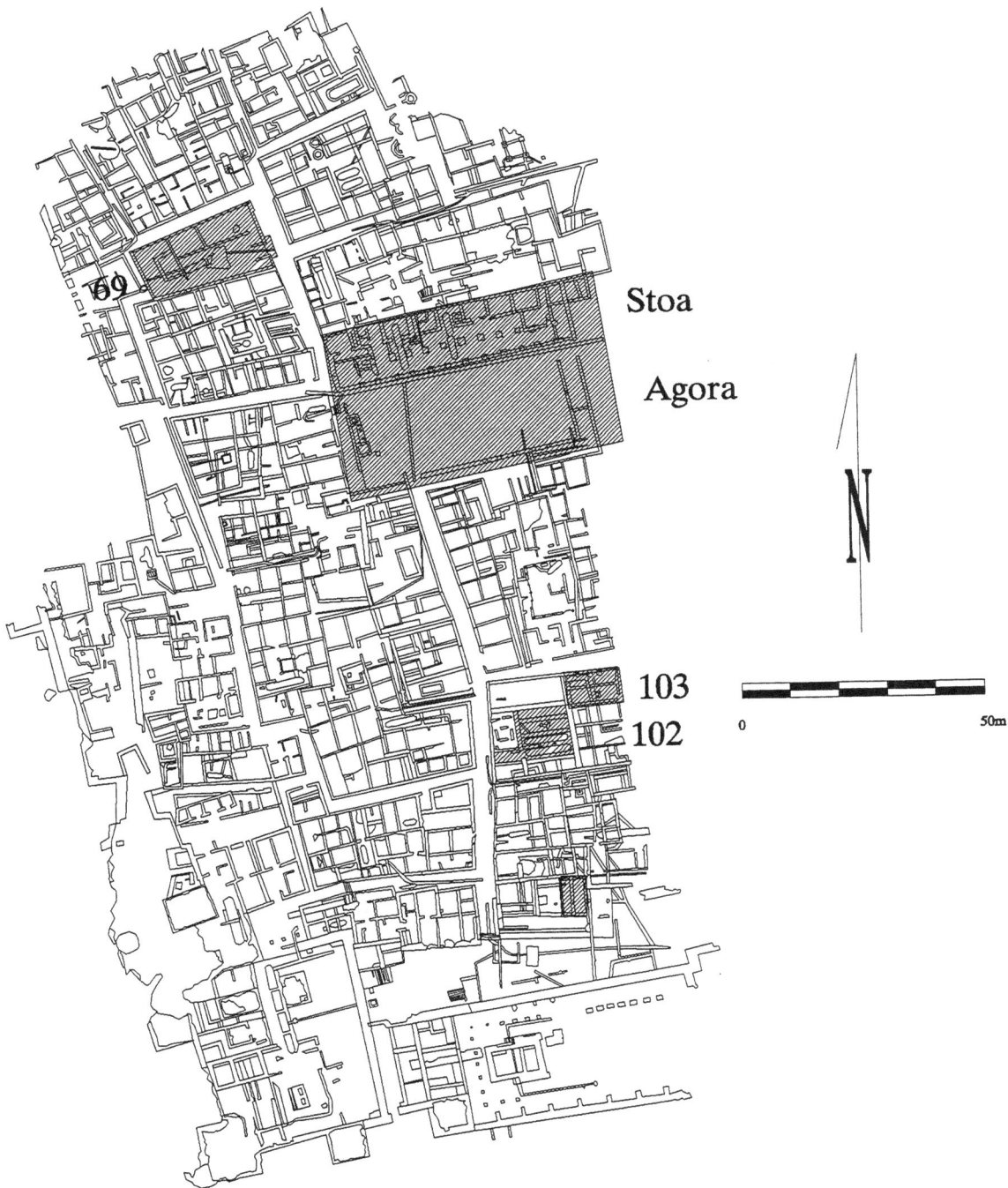

Fig. 11: Distribution of administrative space in Neapolis.

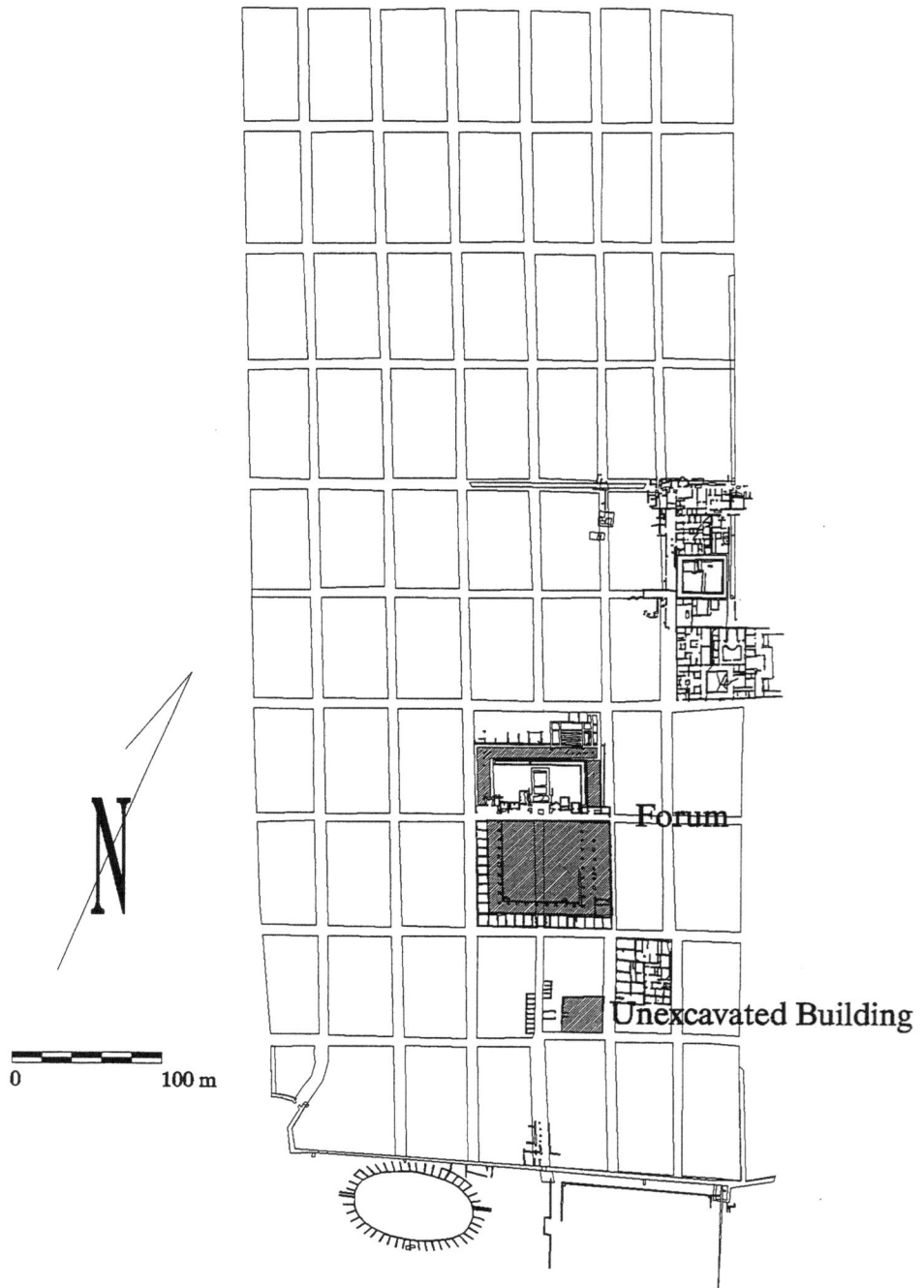

Fig. 12: Distribution of administrative space in the Roman city.

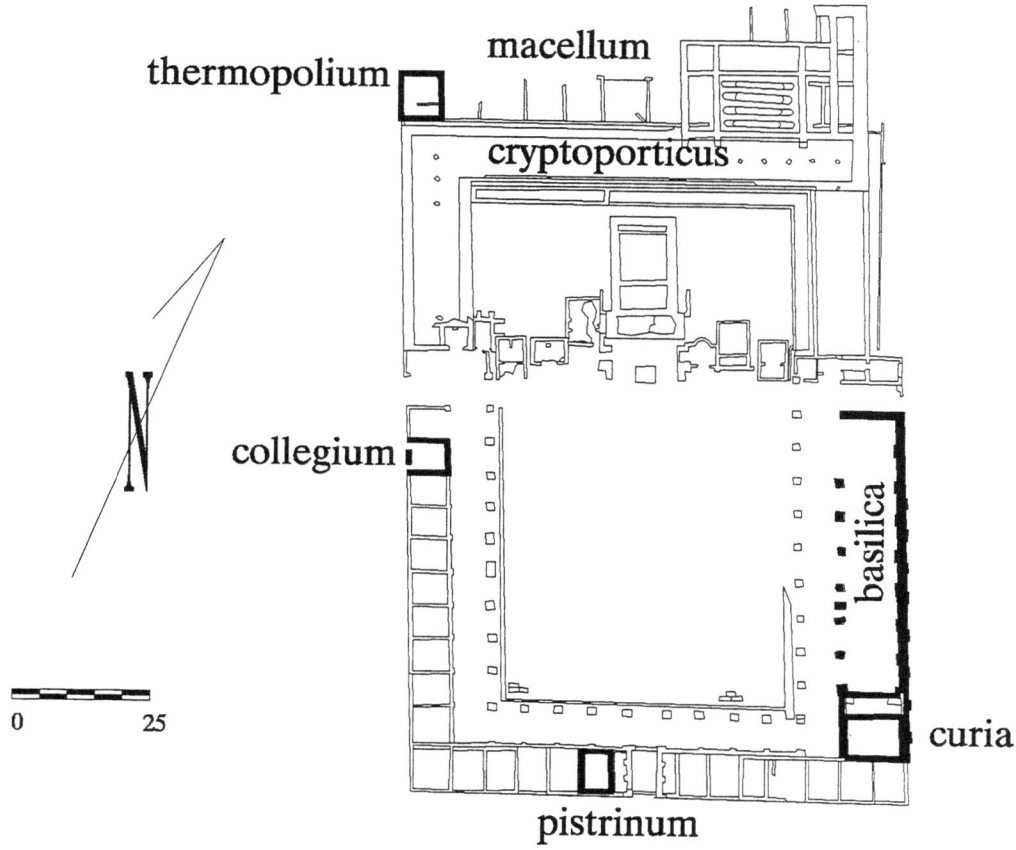

thermopolium

macellum

cryptoporticus

collegium

N

basilica

curia

0   25

pistrinum

Fig. 13: Forum of the Roman city.

Fig. 14: Distribution of commercial space in Neapolis

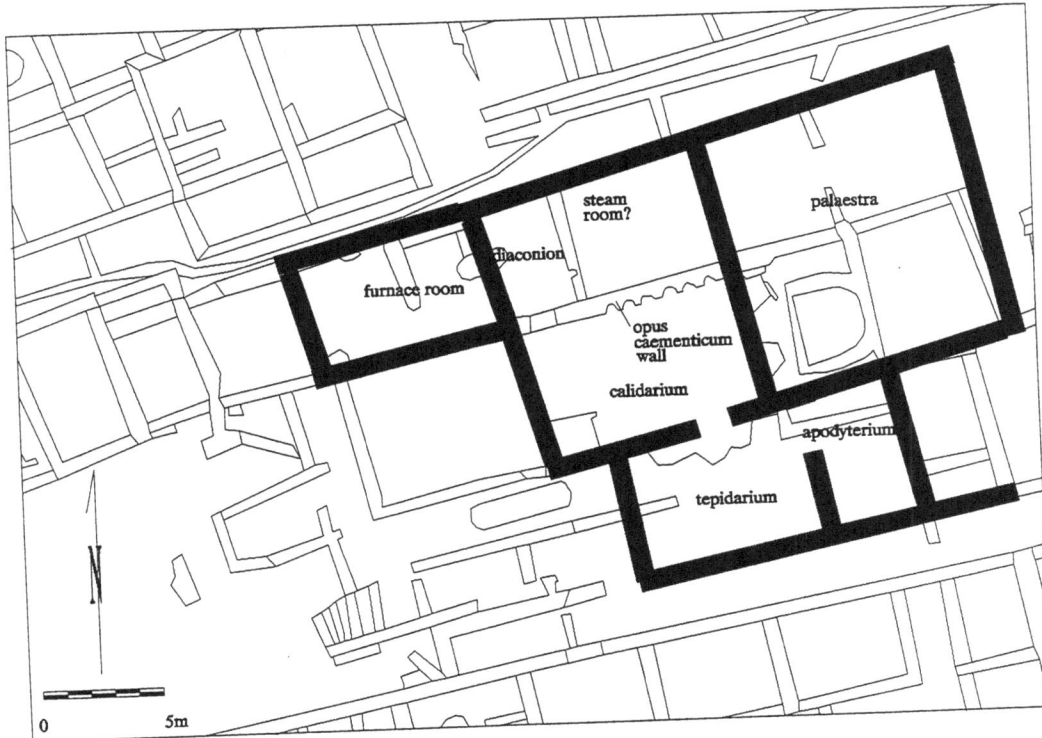

Fig. 15: Neapolis baths.

Fig. 16: North wall of Neapolis baths.

Fig. 17: Wall of the Roman city.

Fig. 18: Base of the north wall of the caldarium in the Neapolis baths.

Fig. 19: Niche in the caldarium of the Roman bath in Neapolis.

Fig. 20: Niche in the *diaconion* of the Christian funerary basilica built in the Neapolis baths.

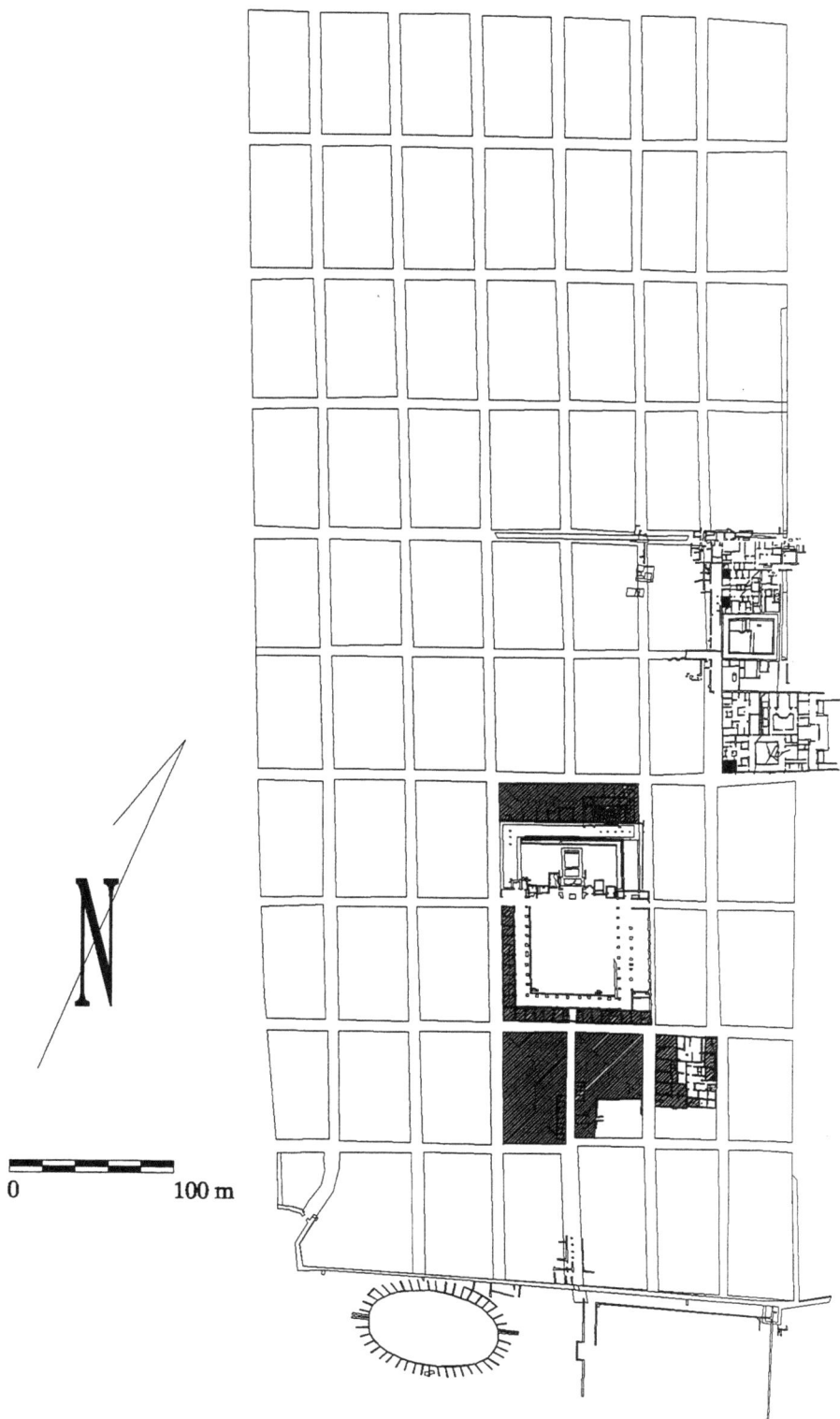

Fig. 21: Distribution of commercial space in the Roman city.

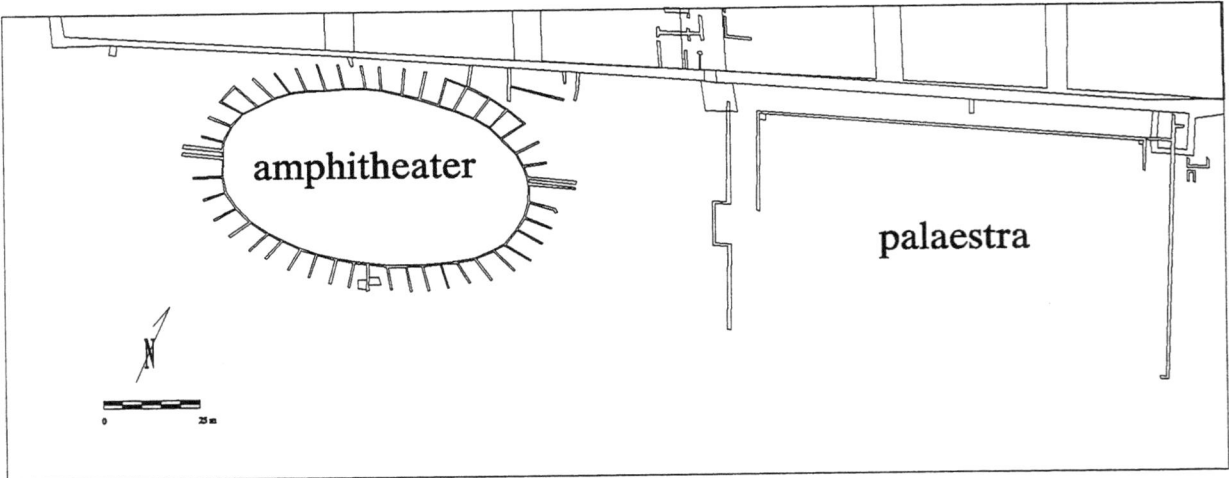

Fig. 22: Distribution of entertainment and educational space at Empúries.

Fig. 23: Distribution of public religious space in Neapolis.

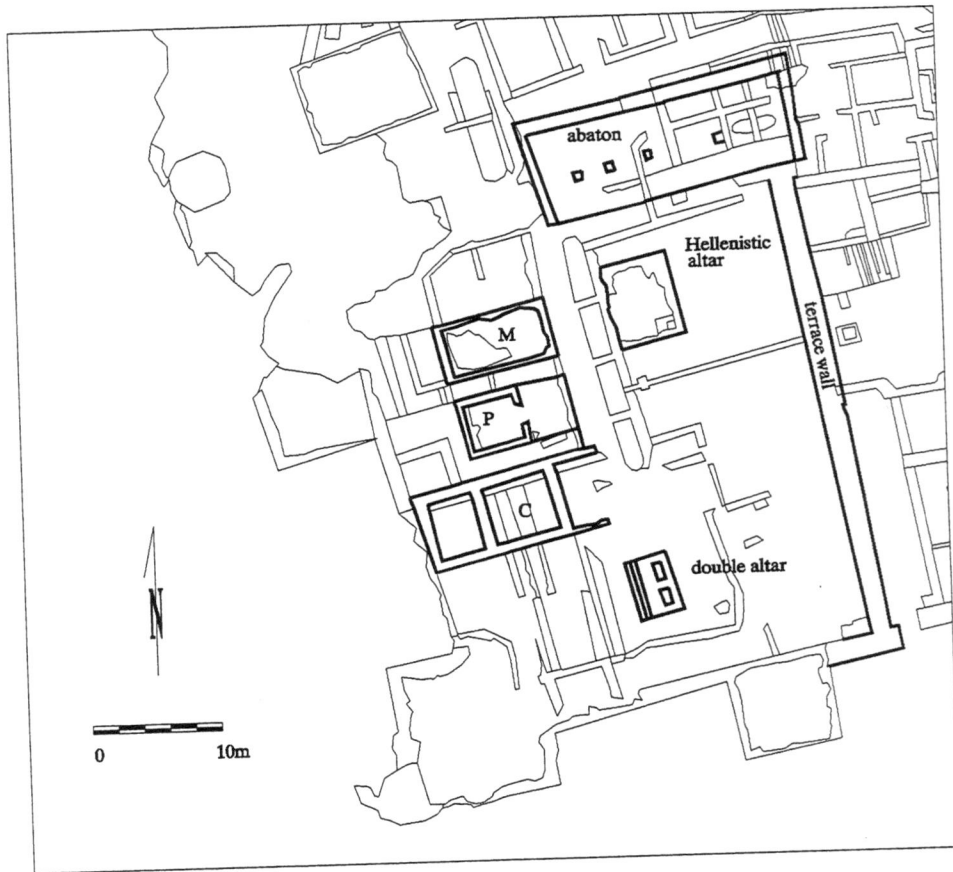

Fig. 24: Asklepieion.

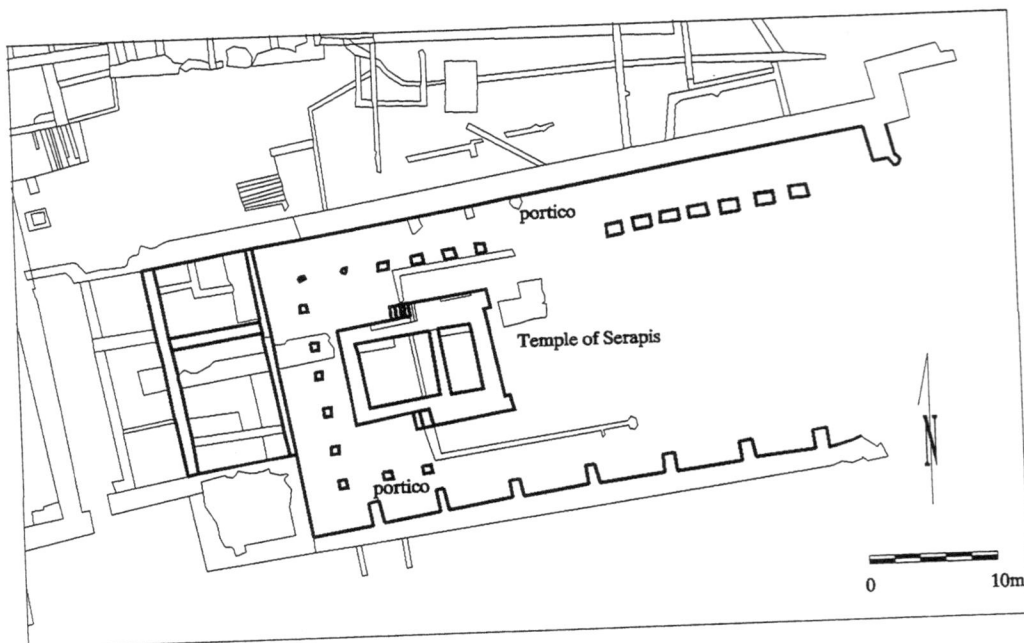

Fig. 25: Serapeum.

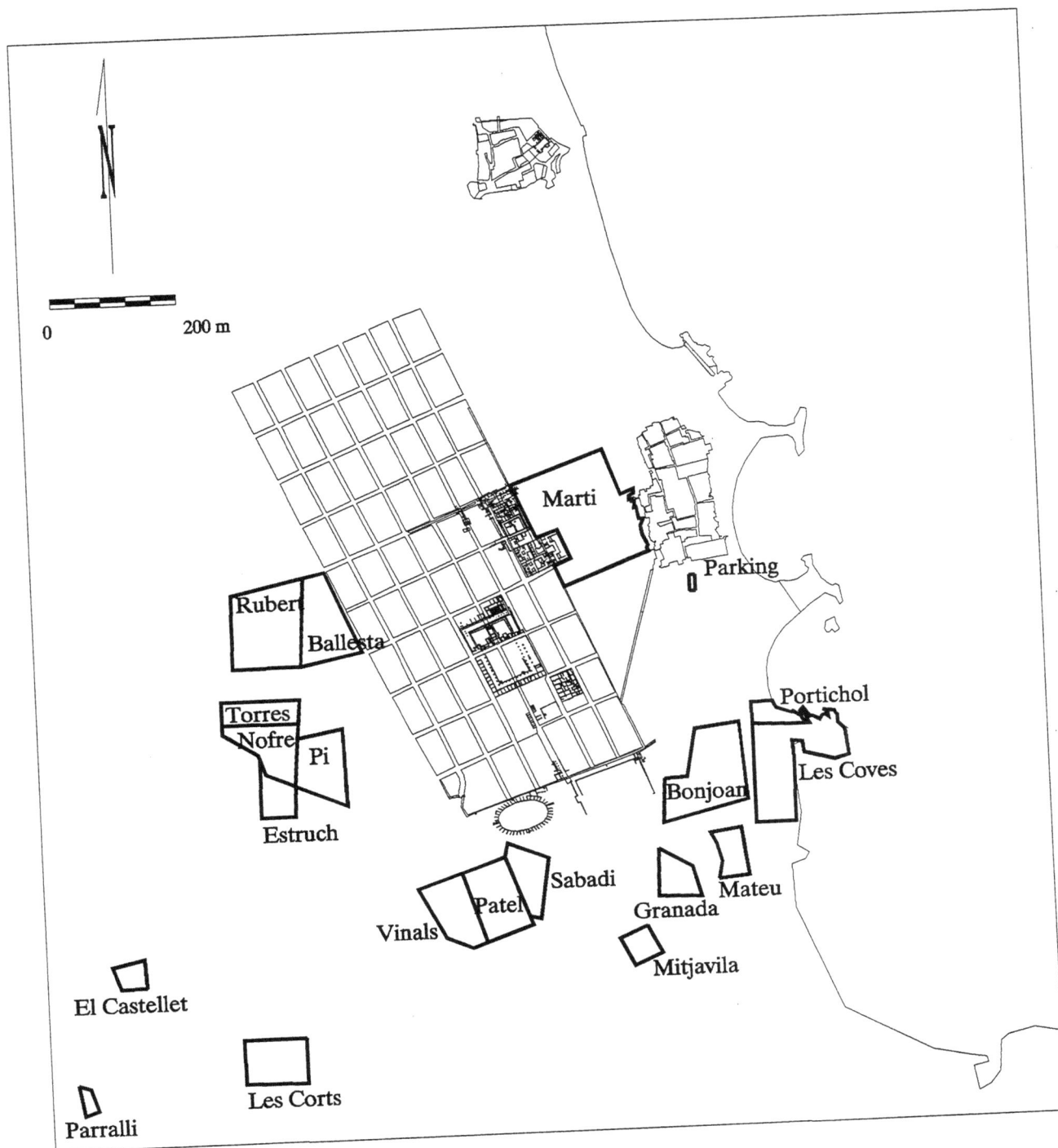

Fig. 26: Location of cemeteries around Empúries shown with the modern coastline.

16th cent.
kilns

double chambered furnaces

54

57

1st cent. BC
kilns

29

31

107

taberna

N

0   50m

Fig. 27: Distribution of industrial space in Neapolis.

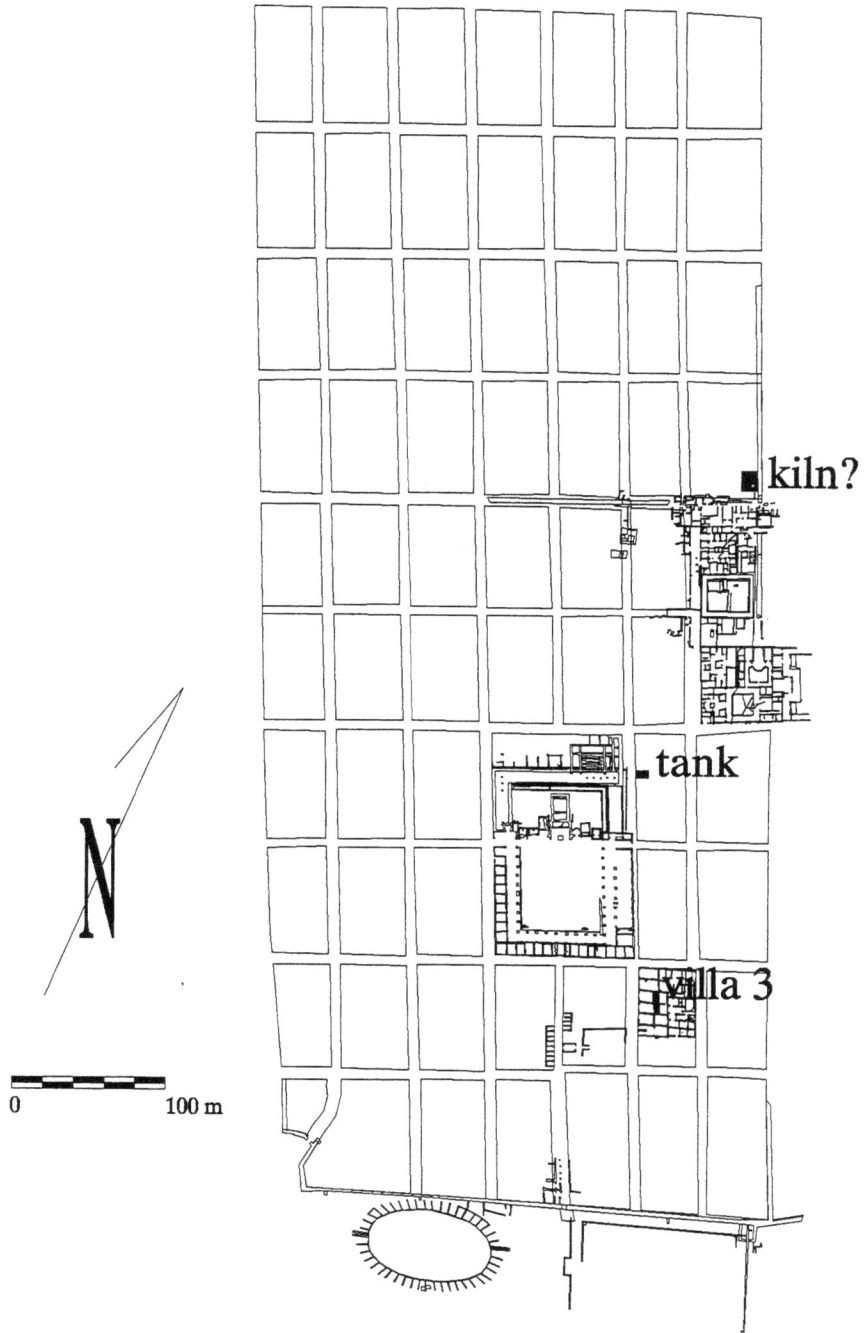

Fig. 28: Distribution of industrial space in the Roman city.

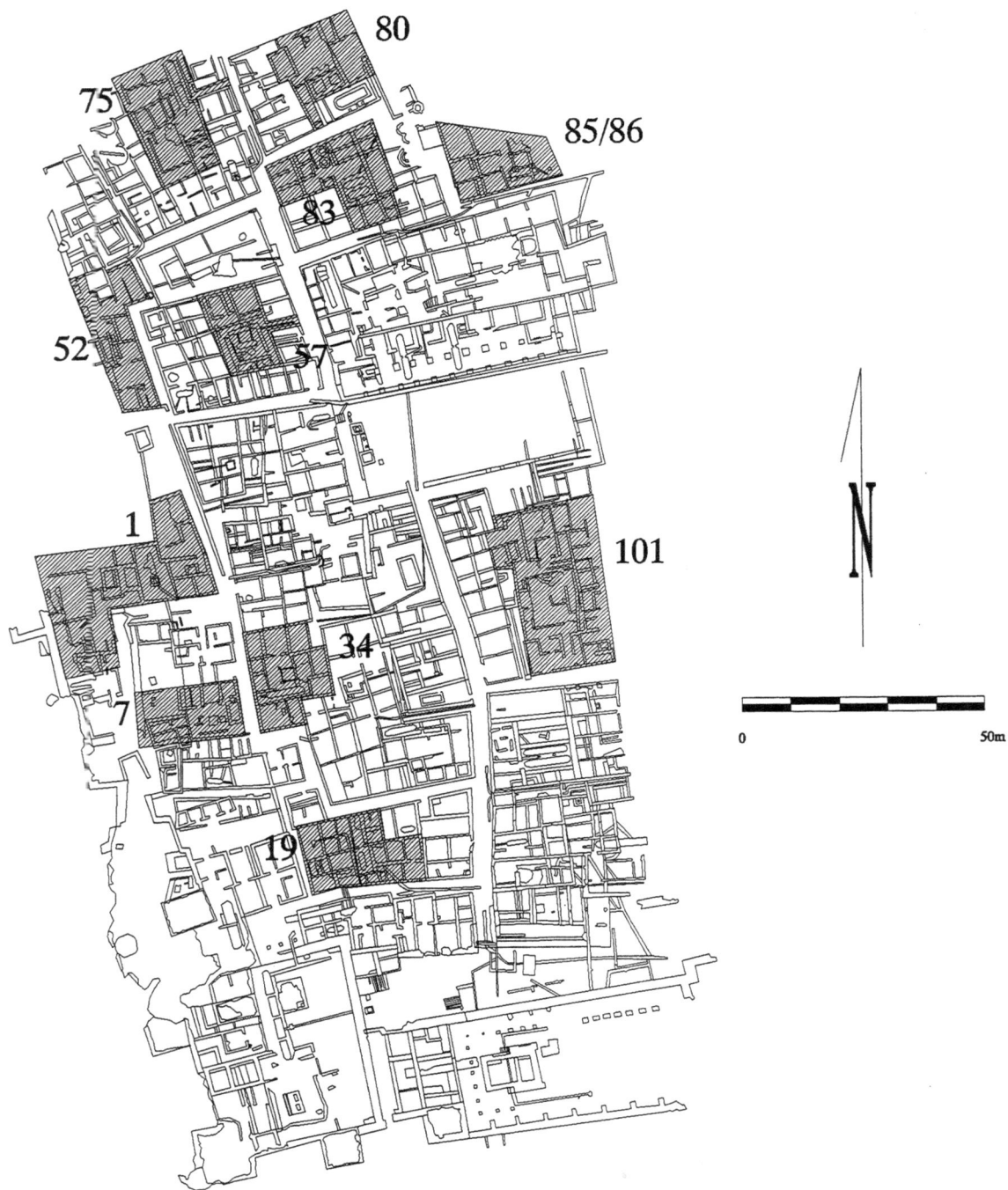

Fig. 29: Distribution of elite domestic space in Neapolis.

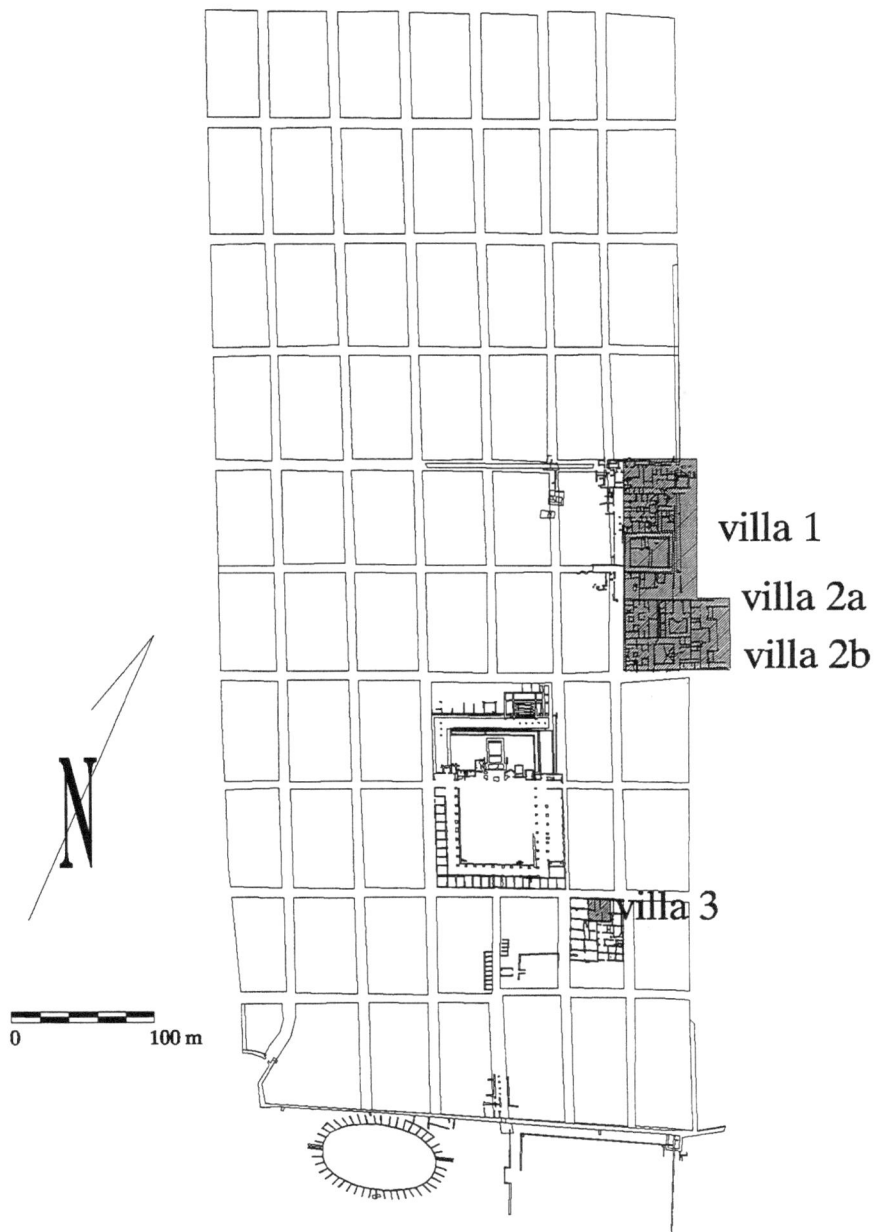

villa 1

villa 2a

villa 2b

villa 3

N

0   100 m

Fig. 30: Distribution of elite domestic space in the Roman City.

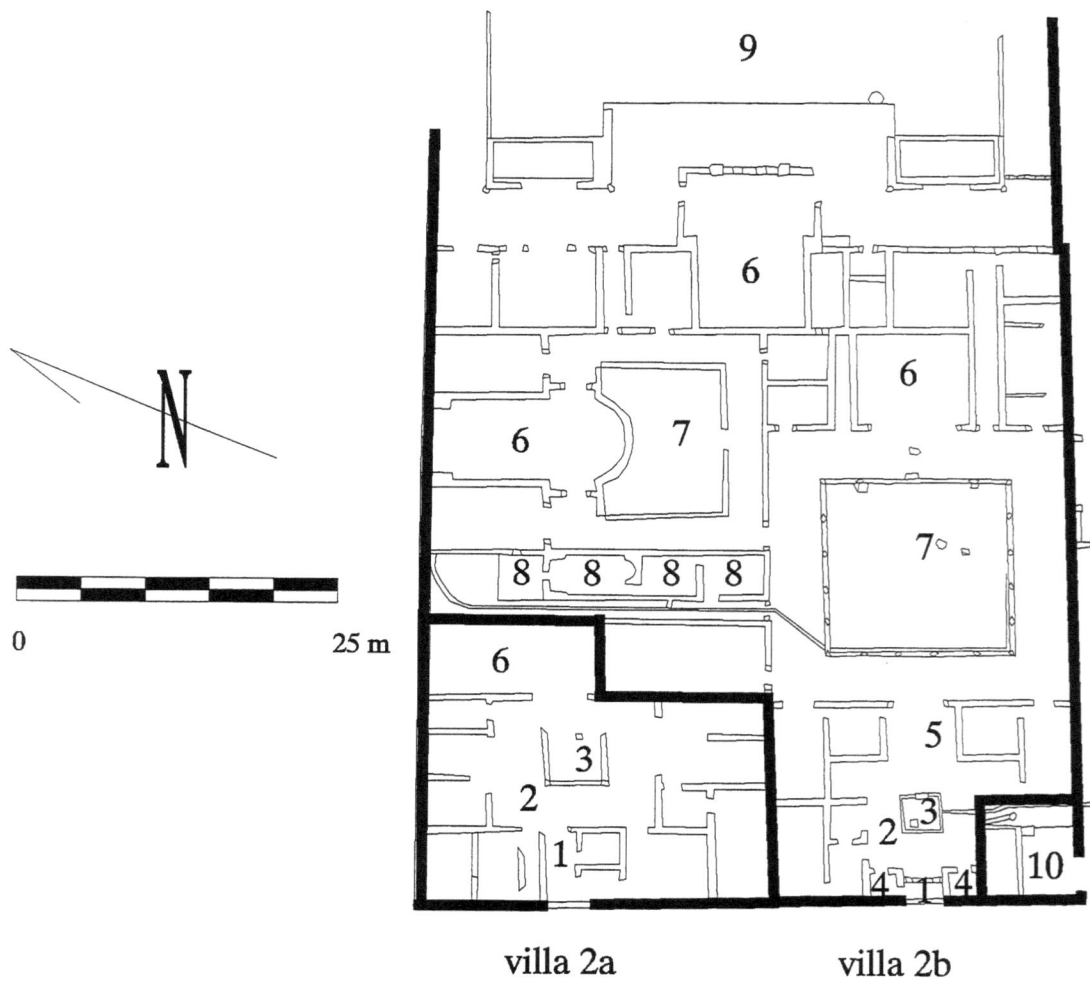

Fig. 31: Villas 2a and 2b in their final form (1=fauces; 2=atrium; 3=impluvium; 4=ala; 5=tablinum; 6=triclinum; 7=peristyle; 8=bath; 7=garden).

Fig. 32: Distribution of non-elite domestic space in Neapolis.

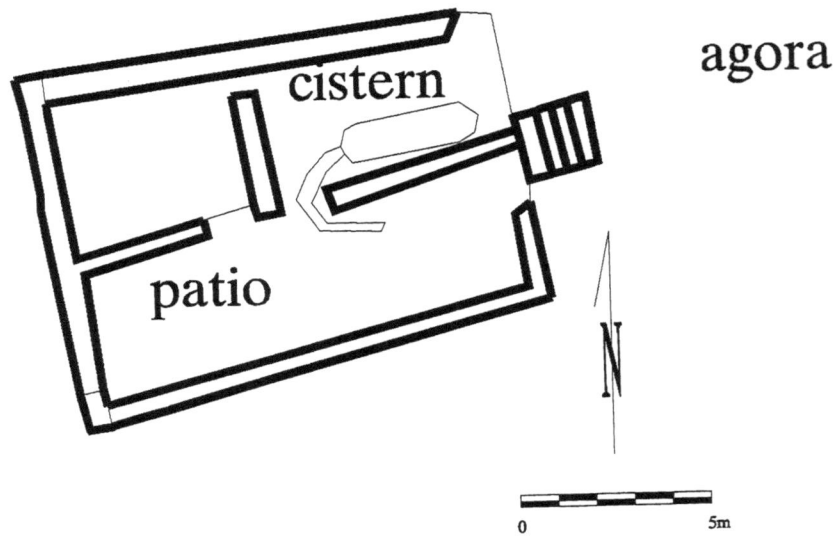

Fig. 33: Structure 43 in Neapolis, a lateral patio house.

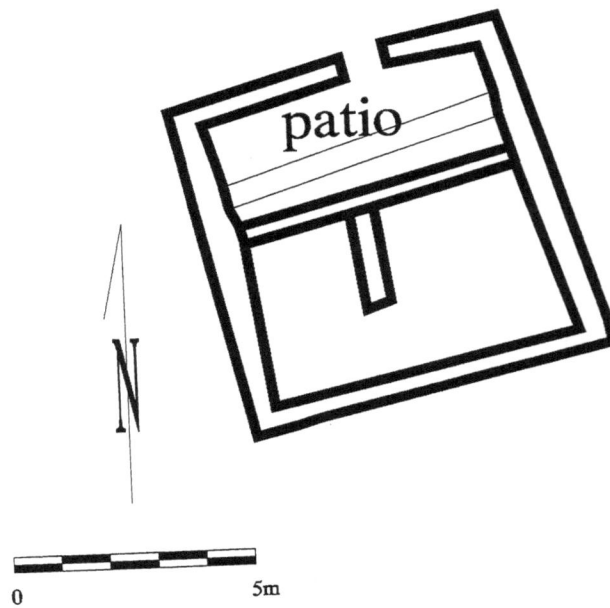

Fig. 34: Structure 18 in Neapolis, a lateral patio house.

Fig. 35: Plan of the street network of Neapolis laid over 1m contour plan.

Fig. 36: Digitized points at the center of elite domestic structures in Neapolis.

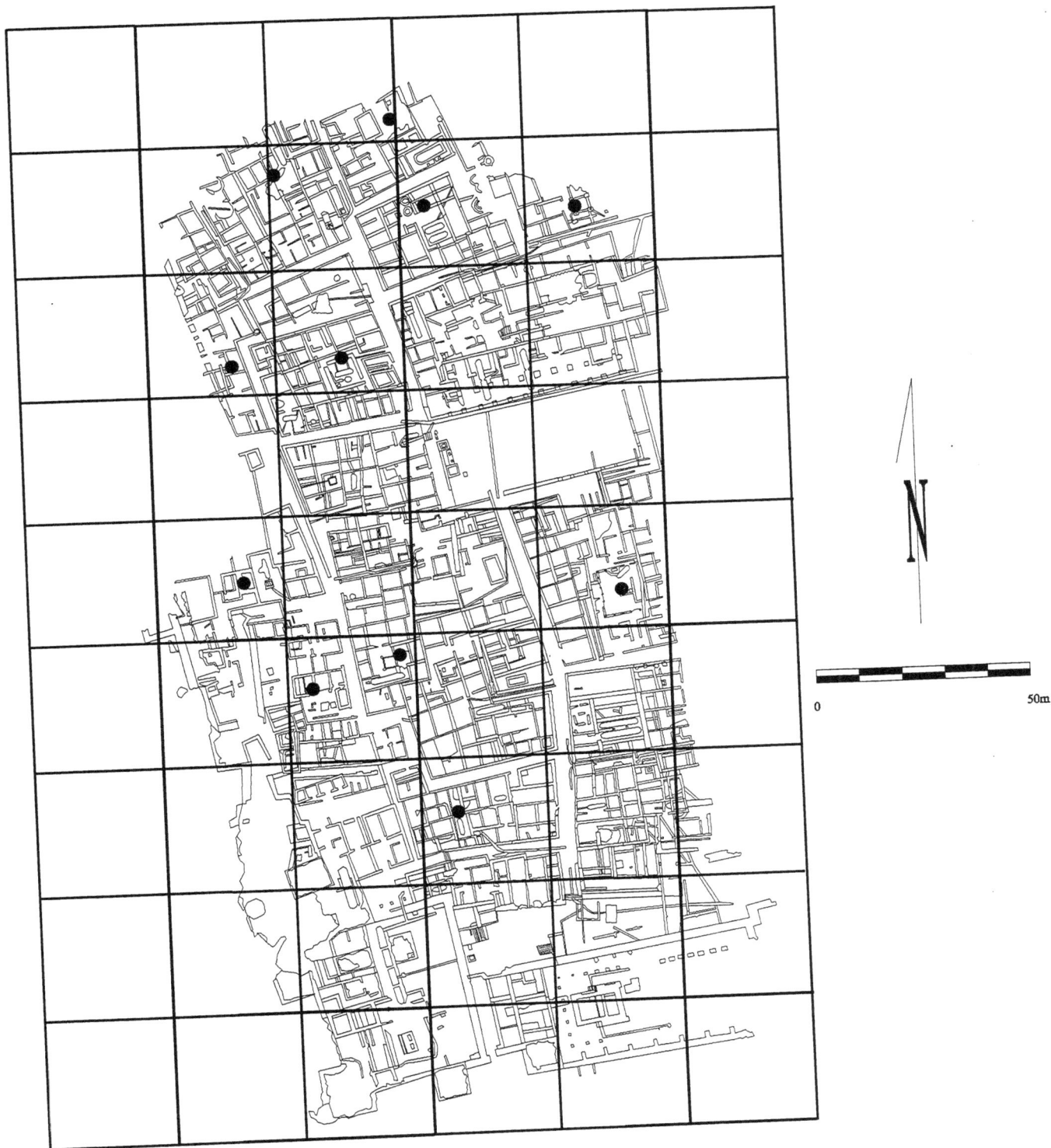

Fig. 37: Points representing elite structures in Neapolis with grid overlay.

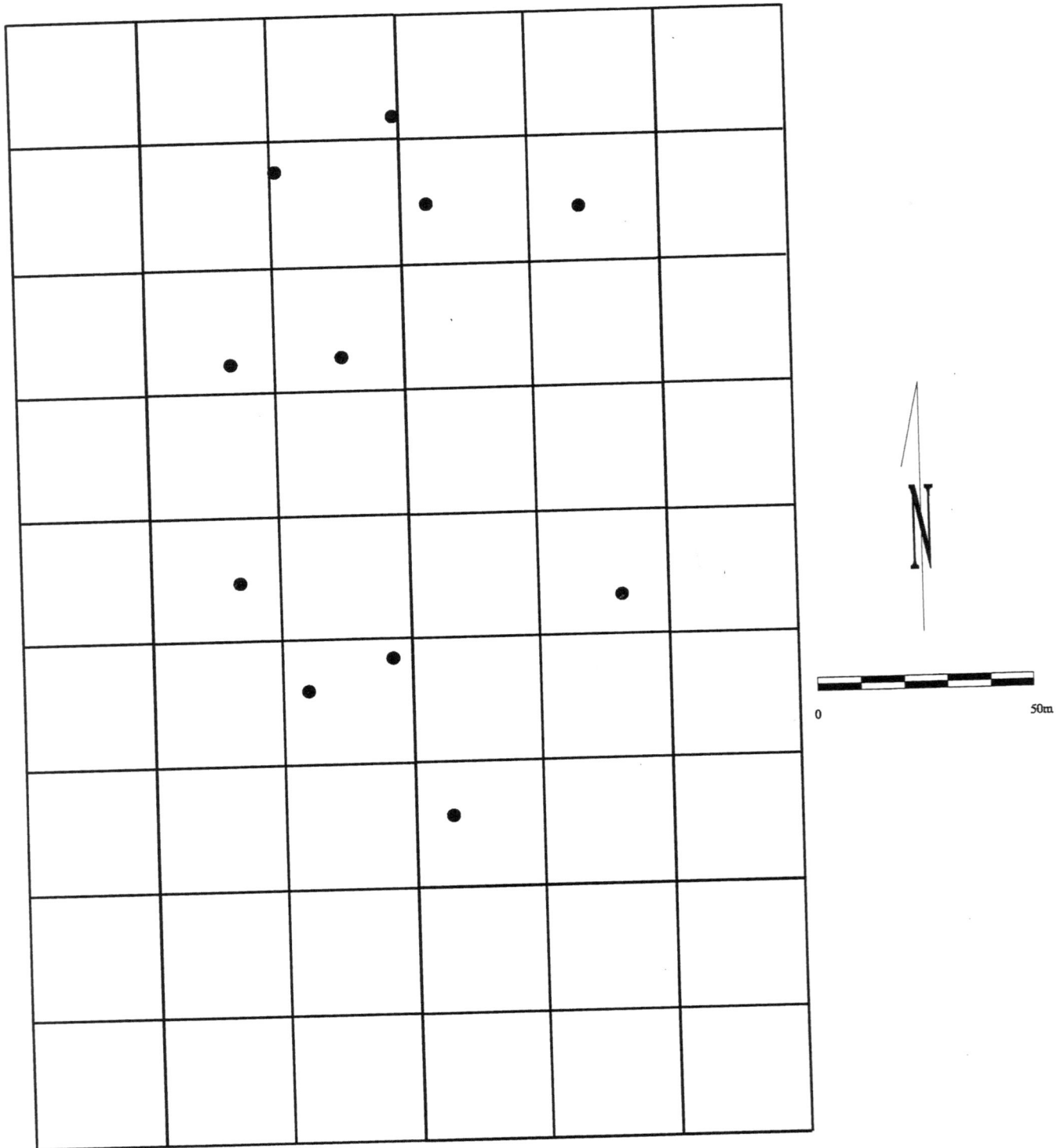

Fig. 38: Grid laid over digitized points at the center of elite domestic structures in Neapolis.

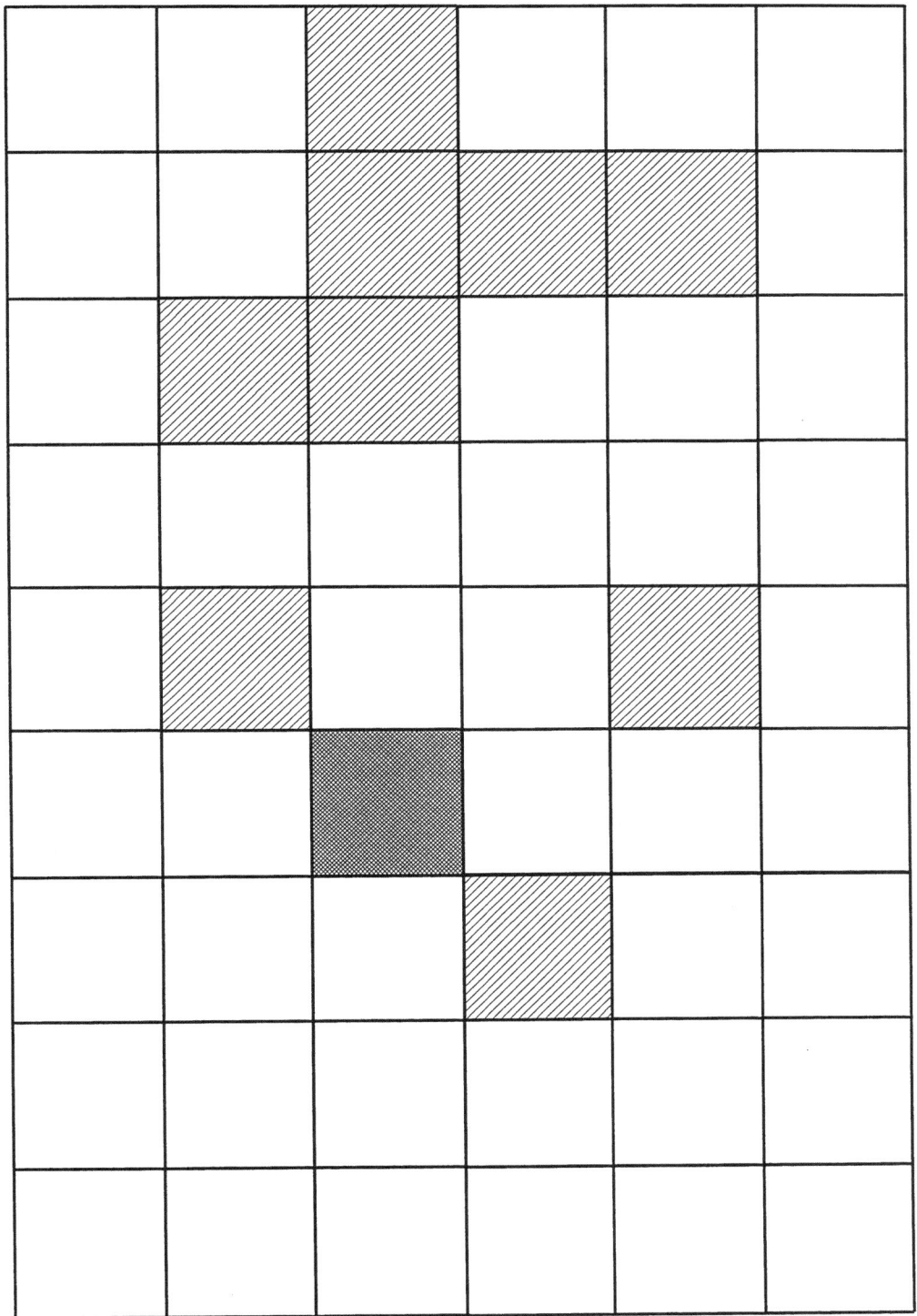

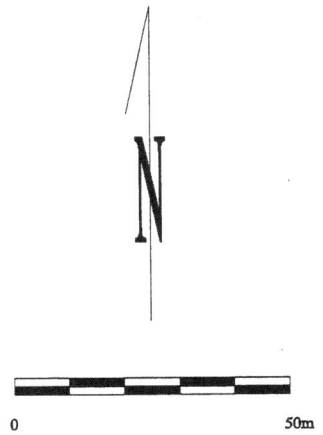

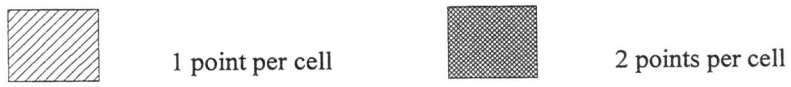

Fig. 39: Counts of points representing elite structures in Neapolis within each grid cell.

Fig. 40: Distribution of public structures in Neapolis.

Fig. 41: Distribution of private structures in Neapolis.

Fig. 42: Distribution of public secular space in Neapolis.

Port

2C

1I

11

17

3

12

10

1H

1G

2B

1F

9

Agora

16

1E

8A

13B

8C

8B

14

6B

7

6A

13A

1D

2A

1C

1B

5A

15

5B

1A

4

So. Plaza

18

N

0   50m

Fig. 43: Relabeled street plan of Neapolis

113

Cardines

F1 E1 D1 C1 B A1

Decumani

I

H

G

F

F2 E2 D2 C2 A2

E

D

C1 C2

B

C3

A

N

0 100 m

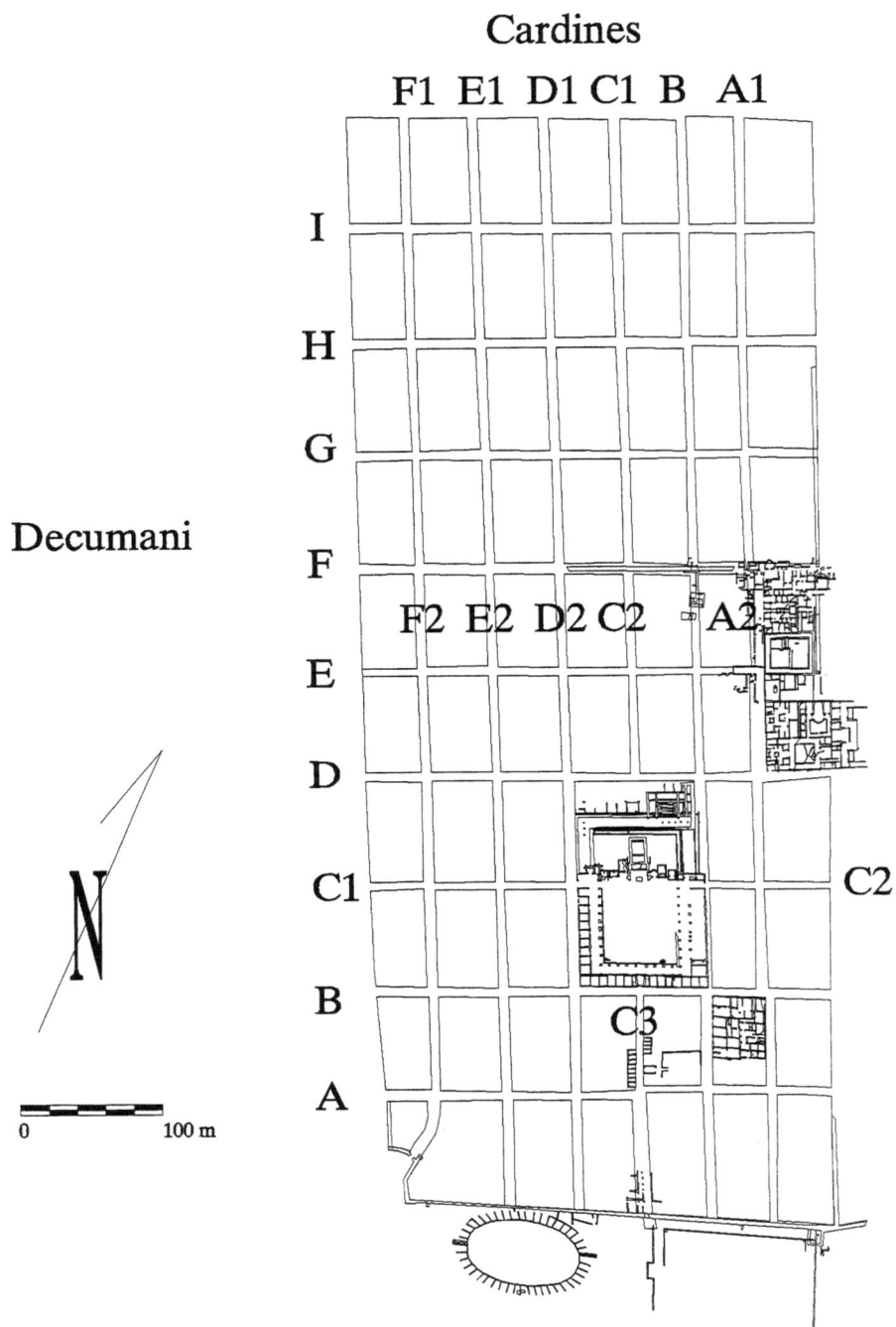

Fig. 44: Relabeled street plan of the Roman city.

114

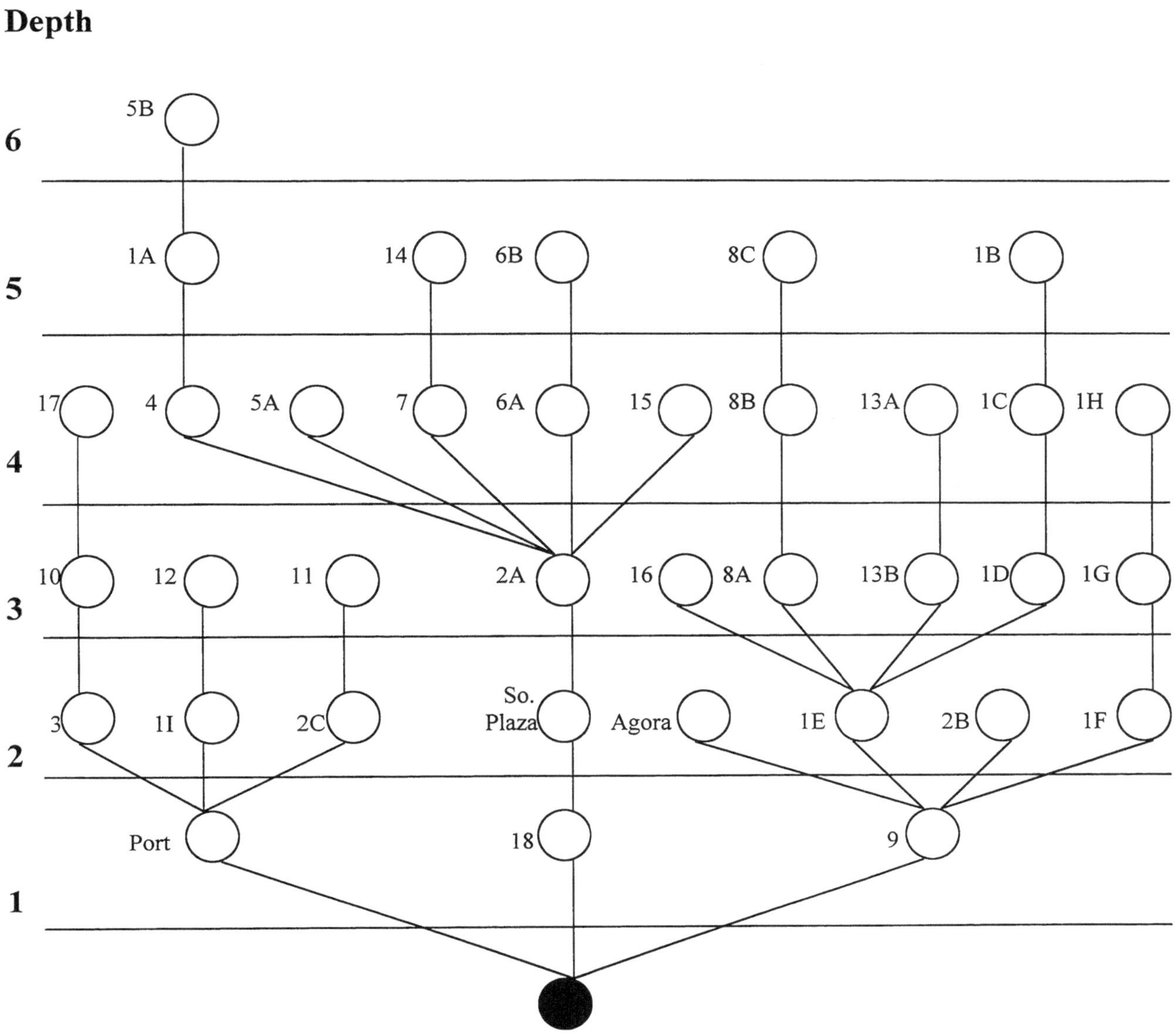

Depth

Fig. 45: Justified map of Neapolis.

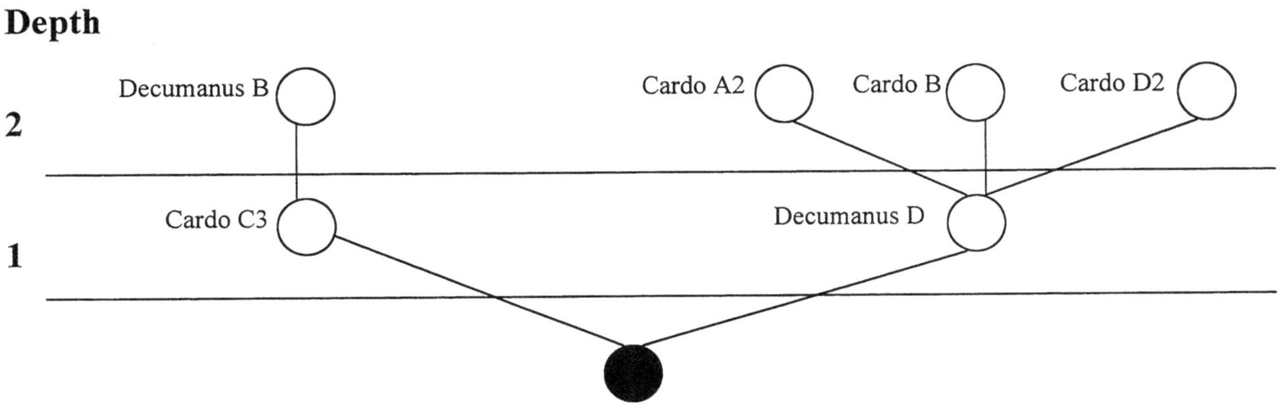

Depth

Fig. 46: Justified map of the excavated streets in the Roman city.

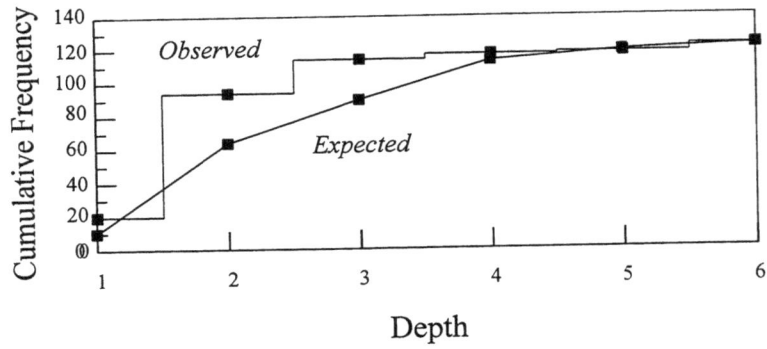

Fig. 47: Distribution of public spaces in relation to depth.

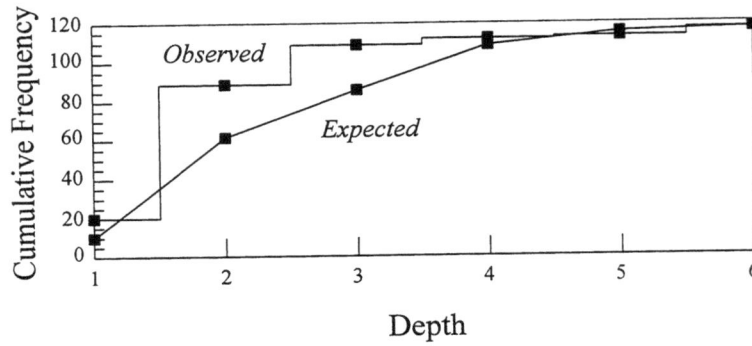

Fig. 48: Distribution of public secular spaces in relation to depth.

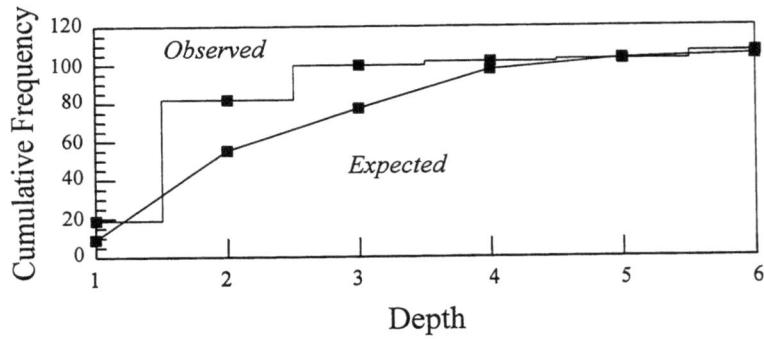

Fig. 49: Distribution of commercial spaces in relation to depth.

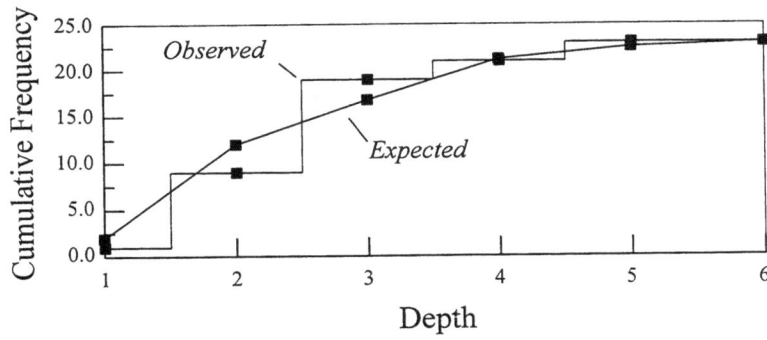

Fig. 50: Distribution of non-elite spaces in relation to depth.

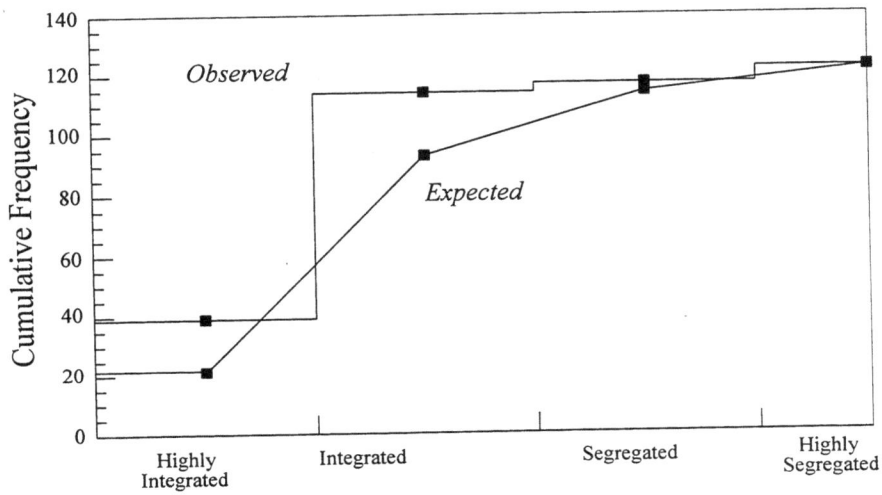

Fig. 51: Distribution of public spaces in relation to RRA.

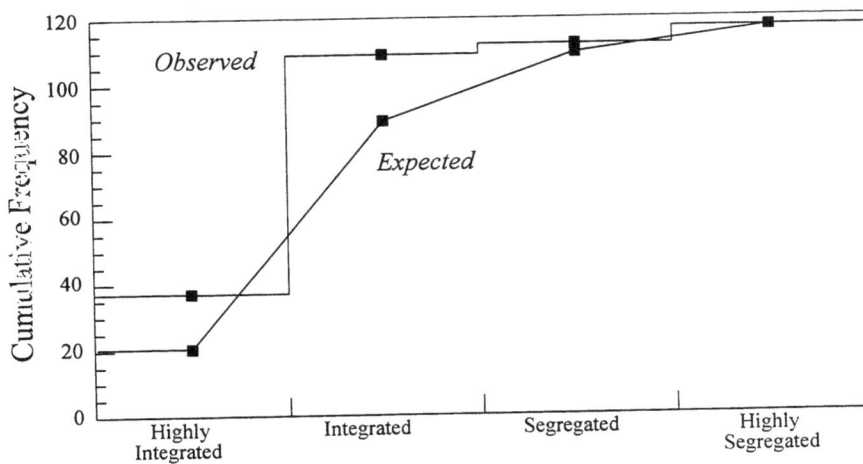

Fig. 52: Distribution of public secular spaces in relation to RRA.

117

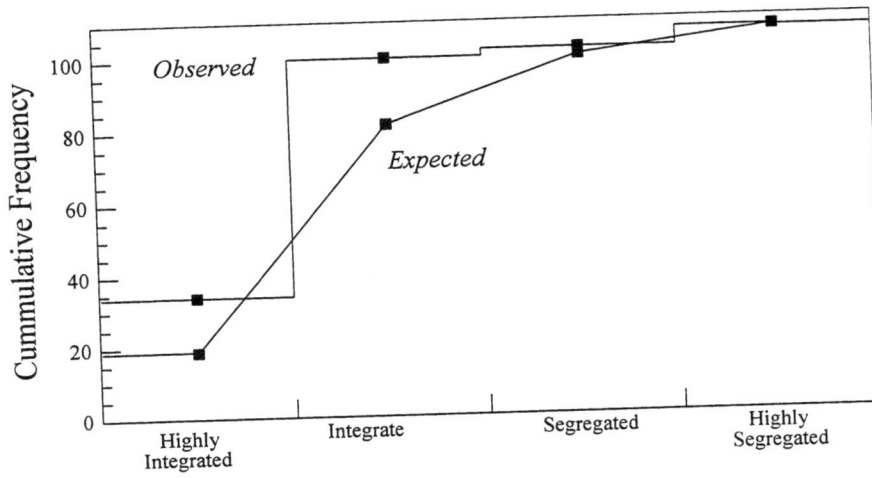

Fig. 53: Distribution of commercial spaces in relation to RRA.

Fig. 54: Street 2B, one of the wide streets in Neapolis at 2.72 m.

Fig. 55: Street 1A, the most narrow street in Neapolis. The scale represents 20 cm.

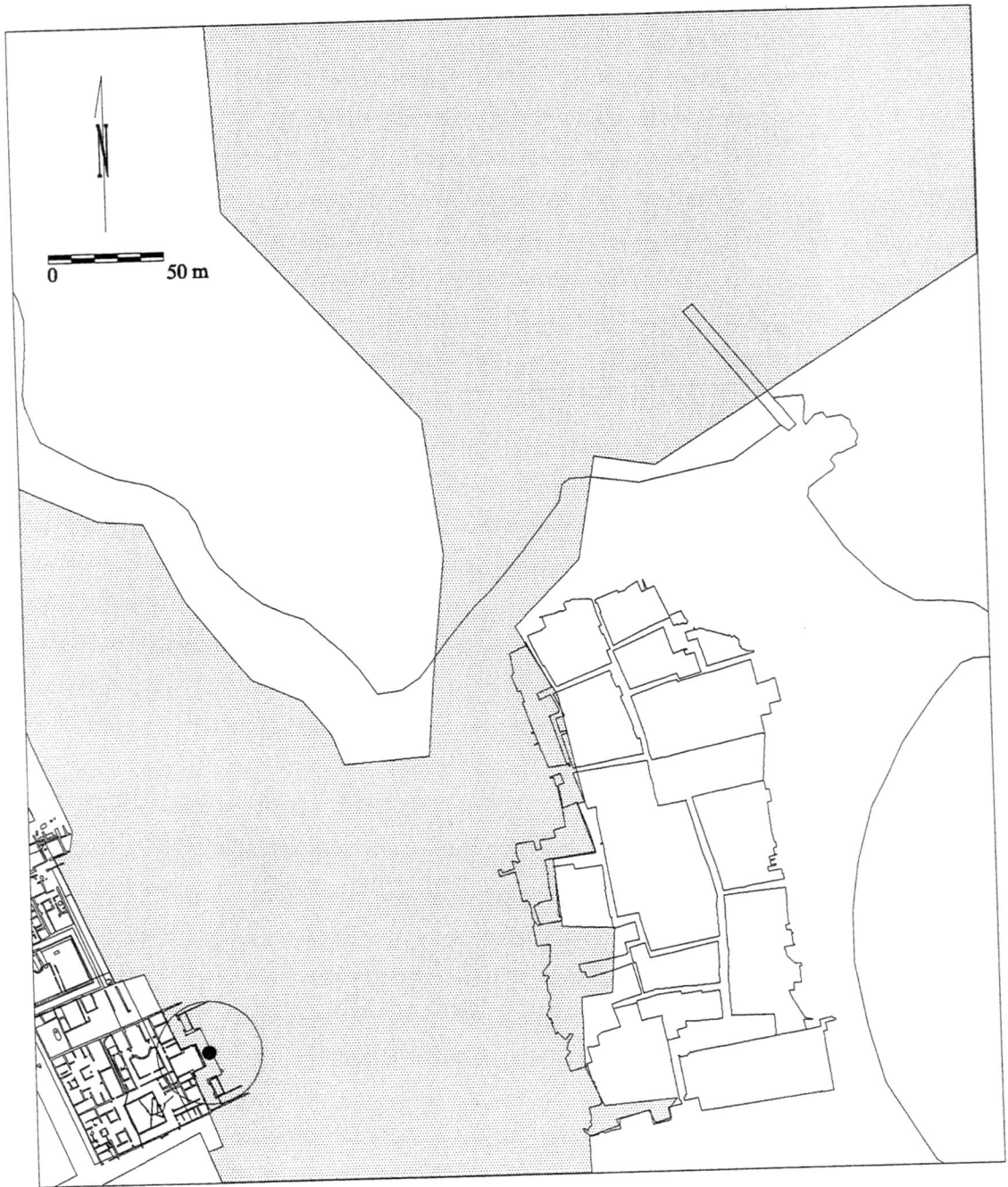

Fig. 5ϵ: Viewshed from villa 2B.

Fig. 57: Viewshed of the Temple of Asklepios in the Neapolis.

121

ABBREVIATIONS

AEA   *Archivo Español de Arqueología.*

AIEC   *Anuari de l'Insitut d'estudis Catalans.*

AJA   *American Journal of Archaeology.*

CIL   *Corups Inscriptionum Latinorum.*

EAE   *Excavaciones Arqueologicas en España.*

JFA   *Journal of Field Archaeology.*

BIBLIOGRPHY

Adam, J. P. 1984 *La construction romaine* (Paris).

Ager, D.V. 1980 *Geology of Europe* (New York).

Alarcão, J. and Etienne, R. 1977 *Fouilles de Conimbriga 1. L'Architecture* (Paris).

Albertini, E. 1911–1912 "Sculptures du Antiques du Conventus Tarraconensis," *AIEC* 4 323–474.

Alcock, S. E., Cherry, J. F., and Davis, J. L. 1994 "Intensive Survey, Agricultural Practice and the Classical Landscape of Greece," in I. Morris ed., *Classical Greece: Ancient Histories and Modern Archaeologies* (Cambridge) 137–170.

Allen, K. M. C. 1996 "Iroquoian Landscapes: People, Environments and the G.I.S. Context," in H. D. G. Maschner ed., *New Methods, Old Problems: Geographic Information Systems in Modern Archaeological Research* (Carbondale) 198–222.

Allison, P. M. 1997 "Roman Households: an Archaeological Perspective," in H. Parkins ed., *Roman Urbanism. Beyond the Consumer City* (New York) 111–146.

Almagro Basch, M. 1940 "Las excavaciones de Ampurias," *Ampurias* 2 171–173.

_____ 1941 "Los trabajos de consolidación y excavación en las ruinas de Ampurias," *AEA* 14 449–451.

_____ 1942 "Nuevas excavaciones en la colonia grecorromana de Ampurias," *Investigación y Progreso* 13 129-134.

_____ 1945 "Excavaciones de Ampurias. Últimos hallazgos y resultados," *AEA* 18 99–75.

_____ 1947a "Estratigrafía de la ciudad helenístico-romana de Ampurias," *AEA* 20 177–199.

_____ 1947b "Dos cortes estratifgráficos con cerámica ibérica en Ampurias," *Crónica del III congreso arqueológico del sudeste España* 137–146.

_____ 1951 *Ampurias. Historia de la ciudad y guía de las excavaciones* (Barcelona).

_____ 1951 *Las fuentes escritas referentes a Ampurias* (Barcelona).

_____ 1952 *Inscripciones ampuritanas griegas, ibéricas y latinas. Monografías Ampuritanas* 2 (Barcelona).

_____ 1953 *Las Necrópolis de Ampurias*, 1. Monografías Ampuritanas 3 (Barcelona).

_____ 1955 *Las Necrópolis de Ampurias*, 2. Monografías Ampuritanas 4. (Barcelona).

_____ 1955–1956 "El anfiteatro y la palestra de Ampurias," *Ampurias* 17–18 1–26.

_____ 1962 *Ampurias, las excavaciones de 1957 a 1961*, EAE 9 (Madrid).

_____ 1964 *Excavaciones en la palaiapolis de Ampurias*, EAE 27 (Madrid).

Almagro Basch, M. and Lamboglia, N. 1959 "La estratigrafía del Decumano A de Ampurias," *Ampurias* 21 1–26.

Almagro Basch, M. and de Palol, P. 1962 "Los restos arqueológicos paleocristianos y altomedievales de Ampurias," *Revista de Girona* 20 27–41.

Álvarez i Pérezi, A. and de Bru de Sala, E. 1983 "Materials locals utilitzats a Empúries en època greco-romana," *Informació Arqueològica* 41 158–162.

_____ 1983–1984 "Els marbres de Paros i Naxos. La selva utilització a Empúries," *Empúries* 45–46 294–301.

Anderson, J. C. 1997 *Roman Architecture and Society* (Baltimore).

Aquilué i Abadías, X. 1998 *Sant Martí d'Empúries. Una illla en el temps* (Tarragona).

Aquilué i Abadías, X., Burés, L., Castanyer i Masoliver, P., Santos Retolaza, M., and Tremoleda i Trilla, J. 1996 "Excavacions Arqueològiques a Sant Martí d'Empúries (L'Escala, Alt Empordà)," in *III Jornades d'Arqueologia de les Comarques de Girona* (Santa Coloma de Farners) 52–64.

Aquilué i Abadías, X., Mar Medina, R., Nolla i Brufau, J. M., Ruiz de Arbulo Bayona, J., and Sanmartí i Grego, E. 1984 *El fòrum romà d'Empúres, Excavacions de l'any 1982. Un aproximació arqueològica al procés històric de la romanizació al nord-est de la peninsula ibèrica*. Monografies emporitanes 6 (Barcelona).

Aquilué, J., Mar, J. R., and Ruiz de Arbulo, J. 1983 "Arquitectura de la Neápolis ampuritana. Espacio y función hacia el cambio de Era," *Información Arqueològica* 40 127–137.

Aquilué, J., Nolla, J. M., and Sanmartí, E. 1986 "Das römische Forum von Ampurias (L'Escala, Alt Empordà, Prov. Gerona)," *Mitteilungen des Deutschen Archäologischen Instituts, Abteilung Madrid* 27 225–234.

Aranegui, C. 1987 "Evolución del área cívica saguntina," *Journal of Roman Archaeology* 5 56–68.

Bibliography

Arxé i Gálvez, J. 1982 *Les llànties tardo-republicanes d'Empúries* (Barcelona).

Balil, A 1955 "Ampurias: Ultimos hallazgos y excavaciones," *Estudios Clásicos* 2, 13 387–389.

_____ 1970 "Casa y urbanism en la España antigua, I," *Boletín del Seminario de Arte y Arqueología de la Universidad de Valladolid* 36 289–334.

_____ 1972 "Casa y urbanism en la España antigua, II," *Boletín del Seminario de Arte y Arqueología de la Universidad de Valladolid* 38 55–131.

Barbarà : Farràs, J. and Morral, E. 1982 "La porta sud de la muralla de la ciutat romana d'Empúries (Campaynes 1972–1975)," *Ampurias* 44 133–145.

Barker, G. 1995 *A Mediterranean Valley. Landscape Archaeology and Annales History in the Biferno Valley* (London).

Barral i Altet, X. 1986–1989 "La història moderna del mosaic del sacrifici d'Ifigènia d'Empúries," *Empúries* 48–50, 1 94–99.

Bates, W. 1983 "A Spatial Analysis of Roman Silchester," *Scottish Archaeological Review* 2, 2 134–143

Blasco Baena, J. C. and Recuero, V. 1995 "The Spatial Analysis of Bell Beaker Sites in the Madrid Region of Spain," in G. Lock and Z. Stancic, eds., *Archaeology and Geographical Information Systems: A European Perspective* (London) 101–117.

Bonneville, J. N. 1986 "Les patrons du municipe d'Emporiae (Ampurias, Espagne)," *Revue des Études Anciennes* 88 181–200.

Borao Mateo, J. E. 1987 "Las possibles centuraciones ampuritanas," *Annals de l'Institut d'Estudis Empordanesos* 20 279–326.

Bosch Gimpera, P. 1913–1914 "La catapulta d'Empúries," *AIEC* 5 105–110.

Brugière de Grogot, A. 1918 *Dans les ruines d'Ampurias, Sonnets* (Paris).

Buchner, E. 1982 *Die Sonnenuhr des Augustus: Nachdruck aus RM 1976 und 1980 und Nachtrag über die Ausgrabung 1980/1981* (Mainz am Rhein).

Burnham, B. C. 1979 "Pre-Roman and Romano-British Urbanism? Problems and Possibilities," in B. C. Burnham and H. B. Johnson eds., *Invasion and Response. The Case of Roman Britain*, B.A.R. British Series 73 (Oxford) 255–272.

Burnham, B. C. and Wacher J. 1990 *The 'Small Towns' of Roman Britain* (London).

Cahill, N. 1991 *Olynthus: Social and Spatial Planning in Greek City.* Doctoral Dissertation (Ann Arbor).

Camp, J. M. 1986 *The Athenian Agora. Excavations in the Heart of Classical Athens* (London).

Campo, M., Ruiz de Arbulo Bayona, J. 1986–1989 "Conjuntos de abandono y circulación monetaria en la Neápolis Emporitana," *Empúries* 48–50, 1 152–163.

Campo M. and Sanmartí i Grego, E. 1991 "Nuevos datos para la cronología de las monedas fraccionarias de Emporion (revisión del tesoro Neápolis—1926)," *Huelva Arqueologica* 13, 2 153–172.

Carrión Masgrau, I. and Santos Retolaza, M. 1993 "Etude préliminaire de la maison 2b d'Emporiae: programmes décoratifs et phases constructives," in E. M. Moormann, ed., *Functional and Spatial Analysis of Wall Painting, Proceedings of the Fifth International Congress on Ancient Wall Painting. Amsterdam 9–12 September 1992* (Leiden) 103–110.

Casanovas i Romeu, A. and Rovira i Port, J. 1994 "Las Naves Grabadas de Ampurias. Un testimonio excepcional de embarcaciones romanas en aguas ampuritanas," *AEA* 67 103–113.

Casellas, R. 1911 "Les troballes esculptòriques a les excavacions d'Empúries," *AIEC* 3 281–295.

Castagnoli, F. 1971 *Orthogonal Town Planning in Antiquity* (Cambridge, Mass.).

Castanyer i Masoliver, P., Sanmartí i Grego, E., Santos Retolaza, M., Tremoleda i Trilla, J., Benet, C., Carrete, J. M., Fabrega, X., Remola, J. A., and Rocas, X. 1993 "L'excavació del Kardo B. Noves aportacions sobre l'abandonnament de la ciutat romana d'Empúries," *Cypsela* 10 159–194.

Cazurro, M. 1908a "Fragments de vasos ibèrics d'Ampuries," *AIEC* 2 551–555.

_____ 1908b "Adquisicions del Museo de Girona," *AIEC* 2 563–568.

_____ 1912 "Crònica de les excavacions d'Empúries. Estratificació," *AIEC* 4 672.

_____ 1912 "Adquisicions del Museu de Girona en els anys 1911–1912," *AIEC* 4 706–709.

Cazurro, M. and Gandía, E. 1914 "La estratificación de la cerámica en Ampurias y la época de sus restos," *AIEC* 5 658–686.

Chapman, J. 1991 "The Creation of Social Arenas in the Neolithic and Copper Ages in S.E. Europe: The Case of Varna," in P. Garwood, D. Jennings, R. Skeates, and J. Toms eds., *Sacred and Profane:*

Proceedings of a Conference on Archaeology, Ritual and Religion (Oxford).

Crawford, M. 1974 *Roman Republican Coinage* (London).

Crook, J. 1967 *Law and Life of Rome* (London).

Day, J. 1932 "Agriculture in the Life of Pompeii," *Yale Classical Studies* 3 167–208.

Dearden, B. 1984 "The Ancient Communications System of the Ampurdan, Province of Gerona, Spain: A Preliminary Note," in T. F. C. Blagg, R. F. J. Jones and S. J. Keay eds., *Papers in Iberian Archaeology*, B.A.R. International Series 193 (Oxford) 466–473.

Delorme, J. 1960 *Gymnasion; étude sur les monuments consacres à l'éducation en Grèce (des origines à l'Empire Romain)* (Paris).

de Palol, P. 1967 *Arqueología Cristiana de la Hipania Romana (Siglos IV–VI)* (Madrid).

de Ruyt, C. 1983 *Macellum. Marché alimentaree de Romains* (Louvain-la-Neuve, Belgium).

Dinsmoor, W. B. 1939 "Archaeology and Astronomy," *Proceedings of the American Philosophical Society* 80 95–173.

Diputació de Barcelona 1993 *Imatges d'Empúries* (Barcelona).

d'Olwer, L. N. 1912 "Crònica de les excavacions d'Empúries. Inscripcions," *AIEC* 4 675–676.

_____ 1914 "Inscripcions," *AIEC* 5 110–111.

d'Ors, A. 1967 "Una nueva inscripción ampuritana," *Ampurias* 29 293–295.

Drees, L. 1967 *Olympia. Gods, Artists and Athletes* (New York).

Dupré i Raventós, X. 1995 "New Evidence for the Study of the Urbanism of Tarraco," in B. Cunliffe and S. J. Keay eds., *Social Complexity and the Development of Towns in Iberia From the Copper Age to the Second Century A.D.* (Oxford) 355–369.

Edelstein, E. J. and Edelstein, L. 1988 *Asklepius. A Collection and Interpretation of Testimonies* (Salem, N. H.).

Engels, D. 1990 *Roman Corinth. An Alternative Model for the Classical City* (Chicago).

Eschebach, H. 1970 *Die städtebauliche Entwicklung des antiken Pompeji, mit einem plan 1:1000* (Heidelberg).

Fabré, G., Mayer, M., Rodà, I. 1991 *Inscriptions romaines de Catalogne, Vol. 3, Gérone,* (Paris).

Fairclough, G. 1992 "Meaningful Constructions—Spatial and Functional Analysis of Medieval Buildings," *Antiquity* 66 348–366

Fear, A. T. 1996 *Rome and Baetica. Urbanization in Southern Spain c. 50 B.C. – A.D. 150* (Oxford).

Ferguson, T. J. 1996 *Historic Zuni Architecture and Society: An Archaeological Application of Space Syntax* (Tuscon).

Finley, M. I. 1973 *The Ancient Economy* (Berkeley).

_____ 1982 "The Ancient City: From Fustel de Coulanges to Max Weber and Beyond," in B. D. Shaw and R. P. Saller eds., *Economy and Society in Ancient Greece* (New York) 3–23.

Foster, S. M. 1989 "Analysis of Spatial Patterns in Buildings (Access Analysis) as an Insight into Social Structure; Examples from the Scottish Atlantic Iron Age," *Antiquity* 63 40–50.

Frank, T. 1940 *An Economic Survey of Ancient Rome, Vol. 5, Rome and Italy of the Empire* (Baltimore).

Fustel de Coulanges, N. D. 1956 *The Ancient City. A Study of the Religion, Laws, and Institutions of Greece and Rome* (Garden City, N.Y.).

Garnsey, P. and Saller, R. 1987 *The Roman Empire, Economy, Society and Culture* (Berkeley).

George, M. 1997 *The Roman Domestic Architecture of Northern Italy*, BAR International Series 670 (Oxford).

Gilchrist, R. 1994 *Gender and Material Culture. The Archaeology of Religious Women* (London).

Gillings, M. and G. T. Goodrick 1996 "Sensuous and Reflexive GIS: Exploring Visualization and VRML," *Internet Archaeology* 1, http://intarch. ac.uk/journal/issue1/gillings_index. html.

Glick, T. 1995 *From Muslim Fortress to Christian Castle. Social and Cultural Change in Medieval Spain* (Manchester).

Golvin, J. C. 1988 *L'Amphithéâtre romain* (Paris).

Gonzázlez Fernández, J., 1990 *Bronces jurídicos romanos de Andalucía* (Sevilla).

Gorges, J. G. 1979 *Les Villas Hispano-Romaines. Inventaire et Problématique Archéologiques* (Paris).

Granger, F. 1955 *Vitruvius. On Architecture* (Cambridge, Mass.)

Greene, K. 1986 *The Archaeology of the Roman Economy* (Berkeley).

Grimal, F. 1983 *Roman Cities* (Madison).

Gros, P. 1990 "Nouveau Paysage urbain et cultes dynastiques: remarques sur l'idéologie de la ville augustéene à partir des centres monumentaux d'Athènes, Thasos, Arles et Nîmes", in C. Goudineau and A. Rebourg eds., *Les Villes Augustéennes de Gaule. Colloque d'Autun* (Autun) 127-140.

Guitart Duran, J. 1976 *Baetulo. Topografía arqueologica urbanismo e historia* (Barcelona).

Gummere, R. M. 1953 *Seneca. Ad Lucilium Epistulae Morales* (Cambridge, Mass.)

Gwynn, A. O. 1926 *Roman Education from Cicero to Quintilian* (Oxford).

Hanson, J. A. 1989 *Apuleius Metamorphoses* (Cambridge, Mass.).

Harrison, R. J. 1988 *Spain at the Dawn of History. Iberians, Phoenicians and Greeks* (London).

Hermansen, G. 1982 *Ostia. Aspects of Roman City Life* (Edmonton).

Hillier, B., 1996 *Space is the Machine. A Configurational Theory of Architecture* (Cambridge).

Hillier, B. and Hanson, J. 1984 *The Social Logic of Space* (Cambridge).

Hopkins, K. 1983 "Introduction" in P. Garnsey, K. Hopkins and C. R. Whittaker eds., *Trade in the Ancient Economy* (Berkeley) ix–xv.

Jacobs, J. 1962 *The Death and Life of Great American Cites* (New York).

Jaeger, W. 1943–1945 *Paideia. The Ideals of Greek Culture*, (London).

Jashemski, W. 1979 *The Gardens of Pompeii, Herculaneum and the Villas Destroyed by Vesuvius* (New York).

Jobst, W. 1983 *Provinzhaupstadt Carnuntum* (Vienna).

Jones, A. H. M. 1974 "The Cities of the Roman Empire. Political Administrative and Judicial Functions," P. A. Brunt ed., *The Roman Economy: Studies in Ancient Economic and Administrative History* (Oxford) 1–34.

_____ 1974 "The Economic Life of the Towns of the Roman Empire," in P. A. Brunt ed., *The Roman Economy: Studies in Ancient Economic and Administrative History* (Oxford) 37–38.

Jones, H. L., 1960 *The Geography of Strabo* (Cambridge, Mass.).

Jones, R. F. J., 1984 "The Roman Cemeteries of Ampurias Reconsidered," in T. F. C. Blagg, R. F. J. Jones and S. J. Keay eds., *Papers in Iberian Archaeology*, B.A.R. International Series 193 (Oxford) 237–260.

Jongman, W. 1988 *The Economy and Society of Pompeii* (Amsterdam).

Keay, S. J. 1983–1984 "The Coins from the Parking Excavations at Empúries," *Empúries* 45–46 151.

_____ 1984 *Late Roman Amphorae in the Western Mediterranean. A Typology and Economic Study: the Catalan Evidence.* B.A.R. Series 196 (Oxford).

_____ 1995 "Innovation and Adaptation: The Contribution of Rome to Urbanism in Iberia," in B. Cunliffe and S. J. Keay, eds., *Social Complexity and the Development of Towns in Iberia From the Copper Age to the Second Century A.D.* (Oxford) 291–337.

_____ 1997. "Urban Transformation and Cultural Change," in M. Díaz-Andreu and S. Keay, eds. *The Archaeology of Iberia. The Dynamics of Change* (New York and London): 192-210.

Kerényi, C. 1959 *Asklepios. Archetypal Image of the Phisian's Existance* (New York).

Knapp, R. 1983 *Roman Córdoba* (Berkeley).

Kriesis, A. 1965 *Greek Town Building* (Athens).

Kvamme, K. L. 1992 "Geographic Information Systems and Archaeology," in G. Lock and J. Moffett, eds., *Computer Applications and Quantitative Methods in Archaeology 1991* (Oxford) 77–84.

_____ 1993 "Appendix B. Computer Methods: Geographic Information Systems," in J. Haas ed., *Stress and Warfare Among the Kayenta Anasazi of the 13th Century A.D.* (Chicago).

_____ 1998 *Empuries Magnetometry* http://www.bu.edu/archaeology/www/db/geop/empr_m.gif.

La Torre, G. F. 1988 "Gli impianti commerciali ed artigianali nel tessato urbano di Pompei," in *Pompei. L'informatica al servizio di una città antica* analisi *delle funzioni urbane* (Rome) 75–102.

Lamboglia, N. 1955 "Scavi italo-spagnoli ad Ampurias," *Rivista de Studi Liguri* 21, 3–4 195–212.

Laurence, R. 1994a "Urban Renewal in Roman Italy: The Limits to Change," in M. Locock ed. *Meaningful Architecture: Social Interpretations of Buildings* (Brookfield, Vermont) 66–85.

_____ 1994b *Roman Pompeii. Space and Society* (New York).

126

_____ 1997 "Writing the Roman metropolis," in H. Parkins, ed., *Roman Urbanism. Beyond the Consumer City* (New York) 1-20.

Lewis, N. and Reinhold, M., eds. 1955 *Roman Civilization Sourcebook II: The Empire* (New York).

Llecha i Salvadó, M. T. 1985 "Nou plantejament d'una escultura Grega provinent d'Empúries," *Empúries* 47 276–281.

Llobera, M. 1996 "Exploring the Topography of Mind: GIS, Social Space and Archaeology," *Antiquity* 70 612–622.

Lock, G. R., and Harris, T. M. 1996 "Danebury Revisited: An English Iron Age Hillfort in a Digital Landscape," in M. Aldenderfer and H. D. G. Maschner eds., *Anthropology, Space and Geographic Information Systems* (New York) 214–240.

Locock, M. 1994 "Spatial Analysis of an Eighteenth-Century Formal Garden," in M. Locock, ed., *Meaningful Architecture: Social Interpretations of Buildings* (Brookfield, Vermont) 231–270.

Lomas, K. 1995 "Urban Elites and Cultural Definition: Romanization in Southern Italy," in T. Cornell and K. Lomas eds., *Urban Society in Roman Italy* (New York) 107–120.

López Mullor, A. 1977 "Cronología de unas taza de paredes finas de Ampurias," *Cronica del XVI Congreso arqueológico nacional* (Zaragoza) 943–956.

_____ 1979–1980 "Cronología de un tipo de cubiletes de paredes finas de Ampurias," *Ampurias* 41–42 453–462.

MacDonald, W. L. 1986a *The Architecture of the Roman Empire II*: An Urban Appraisal (New Haven).

_____ 1986b "Connection and Passage in North African Architecture" in C. McClendon ed., *Rome and the Provinces. Studies in the Transformation of Art and Architecture in the Mediterranean World* (New Haven) 29–36.

Mackie, N. 1990 "Urban Munificence and the Growth of Urban Consciousness in Roman Spain," in T. Blagg and M. Millett eds., *The Early Roman Empire in the West* (Oxford) 179–192.

Madry, S. L. H. and Rakos, L. 1996 "Line-of-Sight and Cost-Surface Techniques for Regional Research in Arroux River Valley, " in H. D. G. Maschner ed., *New Methods, Old Problems: Geographic Information Systems in Modern Archaeological Research* (Carbondale) 104–126.

Maiuri, A. 1956 *Pompeii* (Novara).

Maluquer de Motes, J. 1975 "Rodis i foceus a Catalunya," *In memoriam Carles Riba* (Barcelona) 221–239.

Mar Medina, R. and Ruiz de Arbulo y Bayona, J. 1986 "El foro republicano de Empúries. Metrología y composición," *Protohistoria catalana: 6é Col.loqui Internacional d'Arqueología de Puigcerdà (Puigcerdà, 1984)* (Puigcerdà) 367–374.

_____ 1988 "Sobre el ágora de Emporion," *AEA* 61 39–60.

_____ 1993 *Ampurias romana: historia, arquitectura y arqueología* (Sabadell).

Markus, T. A. 1993 *Buildings and Power. Freedom and Control in the Origin of Modern Building Types* (New York).

Maschner, H. D. G. 1996 "The Politics of Settlement Choice on the Northwest Coast: Cognition, GIS, and Coastal Landscapes," in M. Aldenderfer and H. D. G. Maschner eds., *Anthropology, Space and Geographic Information Systems* (New York) 175–189.

Mattingly, D. 1997 "Drawing a Line Beneath the Consumer City," in H. Parkins, ed., *Roman Urbanism. Beyond the Consumer City* (New York) 210–218.

McKay, A. G. 1975 *Houses, Villas, and Palaces in the Roman World* (London and New York).

Meiggs, R. 1960 *Roman Ostia* (Oxford).

Mierse, W. E. 1999 *Temples and Towns in Roman Iberia* (Berkeley and Los Angeles).

Millett, M. 1993 "Samian from the Sea: Cala Culip Shipwreck IV," *Journal of Roman Archaeology* 6 415–419.

Moeller, W. O. 1976 *The Wool Trade of Ancient Pompeii* (Leiden).

Morel, J. P. 1981 "Emporion en el marc de la colonització focea," *L'Avenç* 38 30–35.

Morris, M. 1994 "The Contrasting Social Environments of a Vernacular Building Tradition: A Study of the Inter-War Weekend Cabins in Cheshire," in M. Locock ed., *Meaningful Architecture: Social Interpretations of Buildings* (Brookfield, Vermont) 271–307.

Nevett, L. 1999 *House and Society in the Ancient Greek World* (Cambridge).

Nichols, R., and McLeish, K. 1976 *Through Roman Eyes* (London).

Nicolet, C. 1980 *The World of the Citizen in Republican Rome* (Berkeley).

Nieto Prieto, F. J.   1971–1972   "Una ara pintada de Ampurias dedicada a Esclapio," *Ampurias* 33–34 385–390.

_____ 1977 "Los esquemos compositivos de la pintura mural romana de Ampurias," *Cronica del XVI Congreso arqueológico nacional* (Zaragoza) 851–868.

_____ 1979–1980 "Repertorio de la pintura mural romana de Ampurias," *Ampurias* 41–42 279–342.

_____ 1981 "Acerca del progresivo des poblamento de Ampurias," *Revue d'études ligures* 47 34–51.

Nieto Prieto, F. J., Jover Armengol, A., Izquierdo Tugas, P., Puig Griessenberger, A. M., Alaminos Exposito, A., Martin Menendez, A., Pujol Hamelink, M., Palou Miguel, H., and Colomer Marti, S.   1989 *Excavacions arqueològiques subaquàtique a Cala Culip* I (Girona).

Nieto Prieto, F. J. and Nolla i Brufau, J. M.   1985   "El yacimiento arqueológico submarino de Riells-La Clota y su relación con Ampurias," *VI Congreso Internacional de Arqueología Submarina, Cartagena 1982* (Madrid) 265–283.

Nolla i Brufau, J. M.   1974   "Dos fragmentos de vasocolador hallados en Ampurias," *Miscelánea arqueológica* 2 75–79.

_____ 1974–1975 "Las ánforas romanas de Ampurias," *Ampurias* 36–37 147–197.

_____ 1977 "Los 'tituli picti' de Ampurias," *Cronica del XVI Congreso arqueológico nacional* (Zaragoza) 877–888.

_____ 1993 "Ampurias en la antigüedad tardía. Una nueava perspectiva," *AEA* 66 207–224.

Nolla, J. M. and Aquilué, X.   1984 "Notes sobre una cassola de cuina de ceràmica africana procedent d'Empúries," *Informació Arqueològica* 42 51–57.

Nolla i Brufau, J. M., Burch, J., Sagrera, J., Vivó, D., Aquilué i Abadías, X., Castanyer i Masoliver, P., Tremoleda i Trilla, J. and Santos Retolaza, M.   1996 "Les eglésies de Santa Margarida i Santa Magdalena d'Empúries (l'Escala, Alt Empordà)," *III Jornades d'arqueologia de les comarques de Girona, Santa Coloma de Farners* (Santa Coloma de Farners) 225–241.

Nolla i Brufau, J. M. and Casas i Genover, J.   1984 *Carta arqueològica de les comarques de Girona. El poblament d'època romana al norde-est de Catalunya* (Girona).

Nolla, J. M. and Nieto, F. J.   1982 "Una factoria de salaó de peix a Roses," *Fonaments* 3 187–200.

O'Callaghan, J. F.   1975   *A History of Medieval Spain* (Ithaca).

Oliva Prat, M.   1974 "Presencia de la Diputación de Gerona en Ampurias. Excavaciones en la basilica paleocristiana en el siglo XIX. Hallazagos arqueológicos y descubrimientos en el foro romano," *Miscelánea arqueológica* 2 87–100.

Osborne, R.   1991   "Pride and Prejudice, Sense and Subsistance: Exchange and Society in the Greek City," in J. Rich and A. Wallace-Hadrill eds., *City and Country in the Ancient World* (New York) 119–146.

Owns, E. J.   1991   *The City in the Greek and Roman World* (New York).

_____ 1996 "Residential Districts," in I. M. Barton ed., *Roman Domestic Buildings* (Exeter) 7–32

Pardo, J.   1996 "The Development of Empúries, Spain, as a Visitor Friendly Archaeological Site," in P. M. McManus ed., *Archaeological Displays and the Public. Museology and Interpretation* (London) 1–15.

Palauí, L. and Vivó, D.   1993   "Termes de la 'Basílica' d'Empúries," in R. Mar Medina, J. López and L. Piñol eds., *Utilització de l'aigua a les ciutats romanes* (Tarragona) 103–110.

Parkins, H.   1997 "The 'Consumer City' Domesticated?" in H. Parkins ed., *Roman Urbanism. Beyond the Consumer City* (New York) 83–111.

Pascual, R.   1974   "Sobre una estampilla anfórica de Ampurias," *Miscelánea arqueológica* 2 139–144.

Pearson, M. P. and Richards, C.   1994 "Order the World: Perceptions of Architecture, Space and Time," in M. P. Pearson and C. Richards eds., *Architecture and Order. Approaches to Social Space* (New York) 1–37.

Pena Jimeno, M. J.   1981 *Epigrafía ampuritana, 1953–1980* (Barcelona).

_____ 1992 "Emporiae," in F. Coarelli, M. Torelli and J. Uroz Sáez eds., *Conquista romana y modos de intervencion en la organizacion urbana y territorial. Primer congreso historico-arqueologico Hispano-Italiano. Dialoghi di archeologia* 10 (Rome) 65–77.

Pérez Obiol, R. and Julià, R.   1994 "Climatic Change on the Iberian Peninsula Recorded in a 30,000 Year Pollen Record from Lake Banyoles," *Quaternary Research* 41 91–98.

Perring, D.   1991 "Spatial Organization and Social Change in Roman Towns," in J. Rich and A. Wallace-

Bibliography

Hadrill eds., *City and Country in the Ancient World* (New York) 273–293.

Peterman, G. L. 1992 "Geographic Information Systems: Archaeology's Latest Tool," *Biblical Archaeologist* 55 162–167.

Plana Mallart, R. 1994 *La chora d'Emporion: Paysage et structures agraires dans le nord-est Catalan à la période pre-romaine* (Paris).

Ponsich, M. and Tarradell, M. 1965 *Garum et industries de salaison dans la Mediterranee occidentale* (Paris).

Puertas, R. 1982 "Lacipo (Casares, Málaga)," *EAE* 120.

Puig i Cadafalch, J. 1907 "Excavacions a Empuries," *AIEC* 1 467.

_____ 1908 "Les excavacions d'Empúries. Estudi de la topografía," *AIEC* 2 150–194.

_____ 1908 "Crònica de les excavacions d'Empuries," *AIEC* 2 558–560.

_____ 1909–1910 "Crònica de les excavacions d'Empuries," *AIEC* 3 706–710.

_____ 1911–1912a "Els temples d'Empúries," *AIEC* 4 303–322

_____ 1911–1912b Crònica de les excavacions d'Empúries, *AIEC* 4 671–678.

_____ 1911–1912c Adquisicions del Museu de Barcelona, *AIEC* 4 885–927.

_____ 1913–1914 "Excavacions d'Empúries," *AIEC* 5 102–103.

_____ 1920 "La colònia grega d'Empúries," *AIEC* 6 694–712.

_____ 1931a "Les excavacions d'Empúries," *AIEC* 8 56–59.

_____ 1931b "Sivella visigòtica d'Empúries," *AIEC* 8 150–151.

_____ 1934 *L'arquitectura romànica a Catalunya* (Barcelona).

Puig i Caldafalch, J., de Falguera, A., and Goday y Casals, J. 1909 *L'arquitectura romànica a Catalunya*, Vol. I (Barcelona).

Radt, W. 1988 *Pergamon: Geschichte und Bauten, Funde und Erforschung einer antiken Metropole* (Köln).

Raper, R. A. 1977 "The Analysis of the Urban Structure of Pompeii: A Sociological Analysis of Land Use (Semi-micro)," in D. L. Clarke ed., *Spatial Archaeology* 189–221.

_____ 1979 "Pompeii—Planning and Social Implications," in B. C. Burnham and J. Kingsbury eds., *Space, Hierarchy and Society. Interdisciplinary Studies in Social Area Analysis*, B.A.R. International Series 59 (Oxford) 137–148.

Revilla Clavo, V. 1995 "Los alfares: características y organización interna," in *Producción cerámica, viticultura y propiedad rural in Hispania Tarraconensis (siglos 1 a.C. – III d.C.)*. Cuadernos de arqueología 8 (Barcelona) 13–40.

Reynolds, J. 1988 "Cities," in D. Braund, ed., *Administration of the Roman Empire* (Exeter) 15–51.

Ripoll Perelló, E., 1972 *Ampurias. Description of the Ruins and Monographic Museum* (Barcelona).

Ripoll Perelló, E., and Martí Jusmet, F. 1968 "Materiales cerámicos de una cistérna romana de Ampurias," *Ampurias* 30 275–292.

Robinson, D. 1997 "The Social Texture of Pompeii," in S. E. Bon and R. Jones eds., *Sequence and Space in Pompeii* (Oxford) 35–144.

Rodà i de Llanza, I. 1985 "Á propos de la sculpture greque d'Emporion," *Actes du XII Congre International d'Archeologie Classique* (Athens) 256–261.

Romano, D. G. 1996 "Roman Centuriation and Land Division in the Corinthia," *AJA* 100 346.

_____ 1999 *The Corinth Computer Project* http://ccat.sas.upenn.edu /~dromano/corinth.html.

Romano, D. G. and Schoenbrun, B. C. 1993 "A Computerized Architectural and Topographical Survey of Ancient Corinth," *JFA* 20 177–190.

Romano, D. G. and Tolba, O. 1995 "Remote Sensing, GIS and Electronic Surveying: Reconstructing the City Plan and Landscape of Ancient Corinth," in J. Huggert and N. Ryan eds., *Computer Applications and Quantitative Methods in Archaeology 1994*. B. A. R. International Series 600 (Oxford) 163–174.

Rostovtzeff, M. I. 1926 *The Social and Economic History of the Roman Empire* (Oxford).

Ruggles, C. L. N. and Medyckyj-Scott, D. J. 1996 "Site Location, Landscape Visibility and Symbolic Astronomy: A Scottish Case Study," in H. D. G. Maschner, ed., *New Methods, Old Problems: Geographic Information Systems in Modern Archaeological Research* (Carbondale) 127–146.

Ruiz de Arbulo Bayona, J. 1984 "Emporion y Rhode. Dos asentamientos portuarios en el golfo de Roses," *Arqueologia Espacial* 4 115–140.

_____ 1993 "Contextos cerámicos de la primera midad del siglo II a.C. en la Neápolis emporitana," *Homenaje al Dr. M. Tarradell.* Estudis Universitaris Catalans 29 (Barcelona) 629–646.

Rykwert, J. 1964 *The Idea of the Town* (Hilversum, the Netherlands).

Saller, R. P. 1991 "Review of Engels 1990," *Classical Philology* 86 351–357.

Sanmartí i Grego, E. 1974–1975 "Nota acerca de una imitación de la sigillata aretina detectada en Emporion," *Ampurias* 36–37 251–261.

_____ 1978 *La cerámica campaniense de Emporion y Rhode*, Monograph Emporitanes 6 (Barcelona).

_____ 1988 "Datación de la muralla griega meridional de Ampurias y caracterización de la facies cerámica de la ciudad en la primera mitad del siglo IV a. de. J.C.," *Revue des Études Anciennes* 90 99–137.

_____ 1993a "Grecs et Ibères à Emporion. Notes sur la population indigène de l'Empordà et des territoires limitrophes," *Documents d'Archéologie Méridionale* 16 19–25.

_____ 1993b "Els íbers a Emporion (segles VI III a.C.)," *El poblament ibèric a Catalunya. Actes.* Laietania 8 (Barcelona) 85–102.

_____ 1994 "Una primera aproximació al coneixement de les pedreres de l'antiga Empúries (L'Escala, Alt Emporda)," *Annals de l'Insitut Gironins* 33 139–155.

_____ 1995 "Recent Discoveries at the Habour of the Greek City of Emporion (L'Escala, Catalonia, Spain) and its Surrounding Area (Quarries and Iron Workshops)," in B. Cunliffe and S. Keay eds., *Social Complexity and the Development of Towns in Iberia From the Copper Age to the Second Century AD*, Proceedings of the British Academy 86 (Oxford) 157–174.

_____ 1996–1997 "La transformació conjunt de la muralla romana d'Empúries en pedrera, observacions sobre els sistemes emprats en l'explotació del llenç meridional i assaig de cronologia," *Annals de l'Institut d'Estutdis Gironins* 36 449–467.

Sanmartí i Grego, E., Aquilué i Abadías, X., Castanyer i Masoliver, P., Santos Retolaza, M., and Tremoleda i Trilla, J. 1994 "El anfiteatro de Emporiae," *El Anfiteatro en la Hispania romana: bimilenario del anfiteatro romano de Mérida. Coloquio International, Mérida, 26–28 de Noviembre 1992* (Badajoz) 119–138.

Sanmartí i Grego, E., Castanyer i Masoliver, P., and Tremoleda i Trilla, J. 1986 "Las estructuras

griegas de los siglos V y IV à. de J.C., hallados en el sector sur de la Neápolis de Ampurias. Campaña de excavaciones del año 1986," *Cuadernos de Prehistoria y Arqueología Castellonenses* 12 141–184.

_____ 1989 "Darreres excavcions a Empúries. El sector de la Neàpolis," *Tribuna d'Arqueologia 1988–1989,* (Barcelona) 79–88.

_____ 1990 "Emporion. Un ejemplo de monumentalización precoz en la hispania republicana. Los santuarios helenísticos de su sector meridional," in *Stadtbild und Ideologie die Monumentalisierung hispanischer Stadte zwischen Republik und Kaiserzeit : Kolloquium in Madrid vom 19. bis 23. Oktober 1987* (München) 117–143.

_____ 1992 "Nuevos datos sobre le historia y la topagrafía de las murallas de Emporion," *Mitteilungen des Deutschen Archèologischen Instituts, Abteilung Madrid* 33 102–112.

Sanmartí i Grego, E. and Nolla J. M. 1986 "Informació preliminar sobre l'excavació d'una torre situada a ponent de la ciutat grega d'Empúries," *6è Col.loqui Internacioal d'Arqueologia de Puigcerdà, (Puigcerdà, 1984)* (Puigcerdà) 159–191.

_____ 1993 *Empúries' Itineraries* (Barcelona).

Sanmartí i Grego, E., Nolla, J. M., and Aquilué, J. 1983–1984 "Les excavacions a l'àrea del pàrking al sud de la Neàpolis d'Empúries (informe preliminar)," *Empúries* 45–46 110–153.

Sanmartí i Grego, E., Nolla i Brufau, J. M. and Mar, R. 1986 "La datation de la partie centrale du rempart méridional d'Emporion (L'Escala, Alt Empordà, Catalogne)," *Documents d'Archéologie Méridionale* 9 81–110.

Sanmartí i Grego, E. and Santiago, R. A. "Une lettre grecque sur plomb trouvée à Emporion (Fouilles 1985)," *Zeitschrift für Papyrologie und Epigraphik* 68 (1987) 119–127.

Sanmartí i Grego, E. and Santos Retolaza, M. 1986–1989 "Algunes observacions entorn dels nivells tardo-republicans d'Empúries," *Empúries* 48–50, 2 292–309.

Santiago, R. A. 1990 "Notes additionnelles au plomb d'Emporion 1987," *Zeitschrift für Papyrologie und Epigraphik* 82 176.

Santos Retolaza, M. 1991 "Distribución y evolución de las vivienda urbana tardorrepublicana y altoimperial en Ampurias," *La Casa Urbana Hispanorromana.* (Zaragoza) 19–34.

Shackleton Bailey, D. R. 1993 *Martial. Epigrammata* (Cambridge, Mass.).

Bibliography

Sillières, P. 1995 *Baelo Claudia. Une cité romaine de Bétique* (Madrid).

Smith, A. T. 1999 "The Making of an Urartian Landscape in Southern Transcaucasia: A Study of Political Architectonics," *AJA* 103 45–71.

Smith, J. T. 1997 *Roman Villas. A Study in Social Structure* (London and New York).

Smith, N. 1995 "Towards a Study of Ancient Greek Landscapes: The Perseus G.I.S.," in G. Lock and Z. Stancic eds., *Archaeology and Geographical Information Systems: A European Perspective* (London) 239–248.

Snively, C. S. 1979 *The Early Christian Basilicas of Stobi: A Study of Form, Function, and Location*, Doctoral Dissertation (Ann Arbor).

Sorrell, A. 1976 *Roman Towns in Britain* (London).

Spivey, N. 1997 *Etruscan Art* (New York).

Stambaugh, J. E. 1988 *The Ancient Roman City* (Baltimore).

Takács, S. A. 1995 *Isis and Sarapis in the Roman World* (Leiden).

Todd, M. 1993 "The Cities of Roman Britain after Wheeler," in S. J. Green ed., *Roman Towns: The Wheeler Inheritance. A Review of 50 Years' Research* (York).

Trocoli, I. G. 1993 "The Contribution of the Harris Matrix to the Development of Catalan Archaeology," in E. C. Harris, M. R. Brown III, and G. J. Brown eds., *Practices of Archaeological Stratigraphy* (London) 47–56.

Tsujimura, S. 1990 "Ruts in Pompeii: The Traffic System in the Roman City," *Opuscula Pompeiana* 1 58–86.

Unwin, D. 1981 *Introductory Spatial Analysis* (New York).

Upton, D. 1992 "The City as Artifact," in A. E. Yentsch and M. C. Beaudry eds, *The Art and Mystery of Historical Archaeology: Essays in Honor of James Deetz* (Boca Raton).

Vallet, G. 1967 "La cité et son territoire dans les colonies grecques d'occident," *Atti del VII Convegno di Studi sulla Magna Grecia* (Taranto) 67–142.

Vallois, R. 1953 *Les constructions antiques de Delos: documents* (Paris).

Van West, C. and Kohler, T. A. 1996 "A Time to Rend, A Time to Sew: New Perspectives on Northern Anasazi Sociopolitical Development in Late Prehistory," in M. Aldenderfer and H. D. G. Maschner eds., *Anthropology, Space and Geographic Information Systems* (New York) 107–131.

Vidman, L. 1969 *Sylloge inscriptionum religionis Isiacae et Sarapicae* (Berlin).

Villaronga, L. 1977 *The Aes Coinage of Emporion*, B.A.R. Supplementary Series 23 (Oxford).

Wacher, J. 1997 *The Towns of Roman Britain*, 2nd ed. (New York).

Wagner, C. G. and Alvar, J. 1980 "El culto de Serapis en Hispania," in J. Arce ed., *La religion romana en Hispania. Symposio organizado por el Instituto de Arqueología "Rodrigo Caro" de L.C.S.I.C del 17 al 19 de diciembre de 1979* (Madrid) 323–333.

Wallace-Hadrill, A. 1991 "Elites and Trade in the Roman Town," in J. Rich and A. Wallace-Hadrill eds., *City and Country in the Ancient World* (New York) 241–272.

_____ 1994 *Houses and Society in Pompeii and Herculaneum* (Princeton).

_____ 1995 "Public Honor and Private Shame: the Urban Texture of Pompeii," in T. Cornell and K. Lomas eds., *Urban Society in Roman Italy* (New York) 9–26.

Walton, A. 1979 *Asklepios. The Cult of the Greek God of Medicine* (Chicago).

Wansleeben, M. 1988 "Geographic Information Systems in Archaeological Research," in S. P. Q. Rahtz ed., *Computer Applications in Archaeology 1988* (Oxford) 435–452.

Ward-Perkins, J. B. 1974 *Cities of Ancient Greece and Italy: Planning in Classical Antiquity* (York).

Warmington, E. H. 1957 *Remains of Old Latin* (Cambridge, Mass.).

Weber, M. 1958 *The City* (Glenco).

_____ 1988 *The Agrarian Sociology of Ancient Civilizations* (London).

Wheatley, D. 1995 "Cumulative Viewshed Analysis: A GIS-Based Method for Investigating Intervisibility, and its Archaeological Application," in G. Lock and Z. Stancic eds., *Archaeology and Geographical Information Systems: A European Perspective* (London) 171–185.

_____ 1996 "The Use of GIS to Understand Regional Variation in Earlier Neolithic Wessex," in H. D. G. Maschner ed., *New Methods, Old Problems: Geographic Information Systems in Modern Archaeological Research* (Carbondale) 75–103.

Bibliography

Whittaker, C.R. 1995 "Do Theories of the Ancient City Matter?," in T. Cornell and K. Lomas eds., *Urban Society in Roman Italy* (New York) 9–26.

Wiseman, J. 1996 "Window on Ancient Maritime Trade," *Archaeology* (Nov.–Dec.) 10–13.

Wycherley, R. E. 1949 *How the Greeks Built Cities* (London).

Zanker, P. 1987 *Augustus und die Macht der Bilder* (München).

Zubrow, E. B. W. 1994 "Knowledge and Representation and Archaeology: a Cognitive Example Using GIS," in C. Renfrew and E. Zubrow eds., *The Ancient Mind: Elements of Cognitive Archaeology* (Cambridge) 107–118.

www.ingramcontent.com/pod-product-compliance
Lightning Source LLC
Chambersburg PA
CBHW061000030426
42334CB00033B/3302